Conservatism in Crisis?

Conservatism in Crisis?

Anglo-American Conservative Ideology
after the Cold War

Bruce Pilbeam

First published 2003 by
PALGRAVE MACMILLAN
Houndmills, Basingstoke, Hampshire RG21 6XS and
175 Fifth Avenue, New York, N.Y. 10010
Companies and representatives throughout the world

PALGRAVE MACMILLAN is the global academic imprint of the Palgrave Macmillan division of St. Martin's Press, LLC and of Palgrave Macmillan Ltd. Macmillan® is a registered trademark in the United States, United Kingdom and other countries. Palgrave is a registered trademark in the European Union and other countries.

ISBN 0–333–99765–4

This book is printed on paper suitable for recycling and made from fully managed and sustained forest sources.

A catalogue record for this book is available from the British Library.

Library of Congress Cataloging-in-Publication Data
Pilbeam, Bruce, 1974–
    Conservatism in crisis? : Anglo-American conservative ideology after the Cold War / Bruce Pilbeam.
        p. cm.
    Includes bibliographical references and index.
    ISBN 0–333–99765–4
    1. Conservatism – United States. 2. United States – Politics and government – 1989– 3. United States – Politics and government – Philosophy. 4. Conservatism – Great Britain. 5. Great Britain – Politics and government – 1979–1997. 6. Great Britain – Politics and government – 1997– 7. Great Britain – Politics and government – Philosophy. I. Title.

JC573.2.U6P55 2003
320.52′0973–dc21   2002193094

10 9 8 7 6 5 4 3 2 1
12 11 10 09 08 07 06 05 04 03

Printed and bound in Great Britain by
Antony Rowe Ltd, Chippenham and Eastbourne

Contents

Acknowledgements

Most of all, I wish to thank Gaynor for all her support, patience and understanding, without whom this book would not have been completed.

I would also like to acknowledge the support of the Economic and Social Research Council for funding the research for this book. For comments on earlier drafts, I am grateful to Andrew Gamble, Mike Kenny, Noël O'Sullivan and Matthew Festenstein. All opinions expressed within are, of course, my own.

Material included in Chapter 3 has previously appeared in C. Pierson and S. Tormey (eds) *Politics at the Edge* (Palgrave Macmillan, 2000). Material from Chapter 6 has appeared in *Journal of Political Ideologies*, Vol. 6, No. 1 (2001). Material from Chapter 7 has appeared in *Political Studies*, Vol. 51, No. 1 (2003).

1
Introduction: Understanding Conservatism after the Cold War

At the beginning of the 1990s, a propitious set of circumstances appeared to exist for the flourishing of a confident and assertive conservative ideology. Indeed, history appeared to be on conservatives' side, with their major enemies – both within and without – decisively defeated. The collapse of the Soviet Union brought to a close nearly half a century of Cold War conflict, while the long-term retreat of labour movements and left-wing ideologies throughout the West was all but concluded. With the discrediting of many of the Left's most cherished ideals, including the state management of industry and centralized planning, it seemed that the 1990s would be a decade in which conservatism would be at its most triumphant. As argued most notably by Francis Fukuyama, the disappearance of the only seeming alternative to Western capitalism could be read as signifying 'the end of history' itself, at least in terms of fundamental ideological conflict (Fukuyama, 1989, 1992).

It was hardly unexpected, therefore, that in marking their Cold War victory many conservatives would loudly trumpet triumphalist notes. American conservative Norman Podhoretz asserted that 'unreconstructed hard-line anti-communist cold warriors' like himself were proven by communism's demise to have been 'right about everything, wrong about nothing' (Podhoretz, 1990, p. 9). Magnifying conservatives' sense of self-satisfaction has been the belief that they have also been responsible for setting the domestic political and intellectual agendas of recent decades. Upon this basis, Edwin Feulner, president of leading conservative think-tank the Heritage Foundation, claims that 'Nowadays Conservatism is not only the dominant but even the sole intellectual tradition in America' (Feulner, 1998, p. ix).

The argument of this book is somewhat different. While the difficulties of the Left in coming to terms with the post-Cold War world have been amply explored, much less attention has been paid to the problems the Cold War's ending has produced for the Right. In fact, despite conservatism's victory over socialism, what will be shown is that it too has been disoriented by the Cold War's conclusion, is often not as confident or assertive as initially it may appear, and is possibly even exhausted as an ideology of contemporary relevance.

On the surface, these suggestions may seem curious. Yet while the self-assuredness noted above is undeniably evident among post-Cold War conservatives, a sense of disillusionment and uncertainty has proved at least as common. For example, British conservative Kenneth Minogue detected a distinct mood of pessimism at a conference of British and American anti-communist intellectuals meeting in Berlin in 1992 (the latter including Podhoretz, Irving Kristol and Gertrude Himmelfarb, the former including Peregrine Worsthorne and Ferdinand Mount). Although the meeting's purpose was celebratory – the aim being to 'enjoy some of the pleasures of triumph' – Minogue testifies that 'a sense of gloom [was] more real among the participants than any sense of triumph' (Minogue, 1992/3, pp. 81, 83). The reality was that speaker after speaker simply identified new threats to Western society to replace the one just vanquished, ranging from anti-Western hatred to political correctness.

In other words, conservatives may not be wholly comfortable with the world they have won. Within conservatism, Minogue is far from alone in perceiving disquiet and dissatisfaction among conservatives (see Kesler, 1998; Scully, 1997; Steyn, 1997). What is interesting is how little enthusiasm has been mustered for the belief that history has reached a harmonious end-state, with Fukuyama's thesis in particular seeming to have found few friends (though even it was not the unqualified celebration of liberal capitalism's triumph it is often taken to be). That is, few appear to have embraced the optimistic conviction that humanity's greatest struggles have been consigned to the past. While this might have been expected among Fukuyama's radical opponents, it is more surprising to find widespread scepticism equally apparent among supposedly victorious conservatives. In common with his left-wing critics, conservative reviewers of Fukuyama also stressed that there are many problems still besetting Western societies, such as crime and social disorder (Crowther, 1990; Johnson, 1992; Minogue, 1991/2). Irving Kristol – one of the most prominent American conservative intellectuals – went as far as to argue against Fukuyama's thesis that 'I don't believe a word of it' (Kristol, 1989, p. 27).

Moreover, it is by no means certain that conservatives have achieved any form of intellectual supremacy. Even conservatives may not believe that their triumphs over the Left have granted them ideological pre-eminence. For example, British conservative David Willetts is dismayed that 'Despite all the advances we have made since 1979, the collapse of the socialist left has not given Conservatives the intellectual dominance which we deserve' (Willetts, 1996b, p. 82). Similarly, Alfred Sherman, co-founder of the Centre for Policy Studies, believes that 'The lot of Conservatives, in the philosophical sense... in our time is not a happy one' (Sherman, 2000, p. 20).

What, then, accounts for this mood? The possibility to be considered is that, if socialism is an anachronism in the post-Cold War world, so is conservatism. Although concurrence with Fukuyama's thesis is rare, a view more widely assented to is that all traditional ideologies have been rendered obsolete by the conclusion of the conflict between capitalism and socialism. In fact, a number of reasons are given by critics for believing in this obsolescence: for example, the inability of conventional ideologies to deal with environmental concerns, or cope with developments such as increasing social diversity or globalization. Many of these will be looked at critically in later chapters.

According to Christopher Lasch, both left- and right-wing ideologies 'have exhausted their capacity either to explain events or to inspire men and women to constructive action' (Lasch, 1991, p. 21). Indeed, the very labels of Left and Right may be regarded as having lost their significance (Giddens, 1994). Even if history has not come to an end, the question remains to be answered: have we witnessed the end of conservatism?

The nature of this book

In addressing the issue of conservatism's status, the method will be to set out and examine the most distinctive features of Anglo-American conservative ideology since the Cold War's conclusion, in terms of its continuities with and differences from conservative doctrines of the past. An issue to clarify at the outset is what more precisely constitutes this book's subject matter. Perhaps most important to emphasize is what it is not about: it is not, except tangentially, about the fortunes of the Conservative or Republican parties, or of those campaigning organizations (like the Christian Coalition) commonly associated with conservatism. The principal concern is with intellectual conservatism, not conservative politics.

Nonetheless, conservative ideology is not merely, or even largely, an academic construct: politicians have always played a significant part in the development of conservative thought, as have writers and thinkers operating outside of academia. In relation to the present context specifically, while the influence of intellectual figures – such as Michael Oakeshott, Friedrich Hayek and Leo Strauss – upon conservative thinking remains strong, the actual role of intellectuals in defining conservative ideology today is much less so. As one writer surveying the condition of American conservatism at the close of the 1990s rightly observes: 'The characteristic figures of conservative intellectual culture are no longer professors and intellectuals. The characteristic figures are lawyers and journalists' (Lindberg, 1999, p. 4). 'Non-intellectual' figures are similarly central in defining contemporary British conservative ideology.

Acknowledging this truth, the net is to be cast widely in terms of the writings to be examined, to include those not only of intellectuals but also of the broader conservative ideological penumbra of politicians, journalists and think-tank pamphleteers. Of course, a problem with this casting is that determining how far it is legitimate to apply the conservative label becomes itself a significant challenge – as another observer notes, it 'is often very difficult to say whether or not a person is conservative' (Kekes, 1997, p. 351). For reasons to be discussed below, self-descriptions are not always adequate. This being the case, it will be unavoidable to apply some amount of judgement as to what constitutes the boundaries of conservative ideology.

A related issue is a terminological one. Discussion is to include consideration of not only 'traditionalist' forms of conservatism but also free-market varieties. Yet this immediately raises the question of whether 'conservative' is the correct umbrella label. One way to avoid difficulties or contrived circumlocutions, popular among British writers, is to use the term 'the New Right'. However, this is problematic for two main reasons.

First, because it has different meanings within British and American politics: whereas in the former it refers to the broad spectrum of right-wing ideologies that enjoyed a resurgence in the 1970s and 1980s (Gamble, 1994, pp. 34–68), within the latter it is employed in two ways, yet both different to the British. Among American commentators, it refers either to the post-war conservatism of the 1940s and 1950s that rejected the anti-modernism and isolationism of the pre-war 'Old Right' (Nash, 1996, p. 100) or, in relation to post-1960s conservatism, to activist organizations like the Conservative Caucus and the Moral Majority (Gottfried, 1993, pp. 97–117). Second, because employing the specific New Right label would seem implicitly to emphasize the continuities between conservative ideology of the Cold War and post-Cold War era, when it is a crucial aim of this book also to stress discontinuities.

(Where analyses of the New Right are mentioned subsequently, unless otherwise indicated it is the British sense of the term that is being discussed.)

Other alternatives are the more general labels of 'Right' or 'right-wing'. However, although these can be useful shorthands, again the contemporary context militates against their complete appropriateness, since it is also to be argued that Left and Right are far from unproblematic designators of ideological positions today. Although no single term is wholly satisfactory, 'conservative' will therefore suffice. This may at least be justified by reference to common American usage, in which the conservative movement is typically taken to include libertarians alongside traditionalists (see Gottfried, 1993; Nash, 1996). A more principled justification for considering the two perspectives together will be set out below.

It is also important to highlight that the approach taken in this book is different to that of most texts on conservative ideology, which fall broadly into two categories: defences by conservatives and critiques by their opponents. While the present work is certainly not an example of the former, nor is it straightforwardly an example of the latter. Put briefly, rather than being a discussion of the problems *with* conservatism, it is more a study of the problems *of* conservatism. In part, this is simply because there exists already a more than sufficient number of texts dealing with conservatism's failings. Yet more than this, precisely because the issue to be examined is conservatism's intellectual exhaustion, the need to mount a vigorous assault upon its tenets is largely redundant.

Indeed, on the whole today it is more imperative to critique conservatism's critics than conservatism itself. Students of modern conservatism are in many ways not well served by the academic or critical literature. As will become apparent, conservatives frequently appear to have been more comfortable fighting their older socialist adversaries than present-day ones; yet it is equally true that many critics evidently prefer combating past forms of conservatism. In particular, much tilting at Thatcherite and Reaganite windmills has continued to take place long after the passing of the Thatcher–Reagan era. A sub-theme of this book will thus be a questioning of opponents' understandings of contemporary conservatism.

Also notable is that, although more critical attention has probably been paid to conservative ideology of the 1970s and 1980s than of any other period (a small sample: Blumenthal, 1986; Gamble, 1994; Levitas, 1986; Hoover and Plant, 1989), relatively little in-depth analysis of subsequent developments has been undertaken. In fact, the most illuminating studies of present-day conservatism are those penned by former conservatives: by John Gray on British conservatism (Gray, 1993a, 1995) and Michael Lind on American (M. Lind, 1996). Gray is an erstwhile champion of free-market liberalism and, later, traditionalist conservatism, while Lind is a one-time executive editor of the conservative foreign policy journal, the *National Interest*. However, although both present valuable insights, their arguments are very much coloured by overriding concerns to denounce former intellectual allies.

A final feature to highlight here is that, as well as textual analysis, research for this book involved the use of in-depth interviewing of a range of contemporary conservative thinkers and writers. This, it is felt, adds an extra level of nuanced understanding to the discussion. However, before it is possible to turn to the substantive concerns of the inquiry, a number of preliminary questions regarding the framework within which it is to be conducted need to be considered. Specifically, two sets of issues must be examined: first, concerning the meaning and nature of conservatism; and, second, regarding the contextual historical background.

What is conservatism?

The first question to address is why conservatism is being discussed as an ideology, rather than a philosophy or doctrine. The point is that although this book is not about party politics nor is it merely concerned with abstract theory. As Michael Freeden argues, a key feature of ideologies that distinguishes them from political philosophies is that they 'straddle' the worlds of political thought and political action (Freeden, 1996, p. 76). Discussion in terms of ideology locates theoretical debates within the concrete disputes and contests of the societies in which they occur.

A useful understanding of ideology in terms of its rootedness within social reality is provided by István Mészáros, who argues that ideologies are 'concerned with the articulation of rival sets of values and strategies that aim at controlling the social metabolism' (Mészáros, 1989, p. 10). A guiding principle of this book, therefore, is that ideologies are not constituted merely as sets of free-floating ideas about the world, but are centrally concerned with offering differing views as to how society should be organized. Indeed, as will be argued, it is through its rivalries with other ideologies that conservatism can best be understood.

A further principle emphasized by Mészáros is the importance of understanding ideologies in terms of the specific historical context in which they function. The problem with ahistorical interpretations – focusing solely upon the internal characteristics of sets of ideas – is that they are unable to grasp the dynamics of ideologies in the context of societies in motion. That is, a historical approach is necessary to account for the way in which changes in ideologies are intimately related to wider social changes. It is for this reason that the post-Cold War setting is to be central to understanding contemporary conservatism. Another implication of adopting a dynamic, historical approach is that a purely abstract definition of conservatism must be rejected.

In terms of these principles, the study of conservatism that comes closest to the ambitions of this book is George Nash's comprehensive account of post-war American conservative thought. Nash argues that the effort to determine an a priori definition of conservatism 'is misdirected. I doubt that there is any single, satisfactory, all-encompassing definition of the complex phenomenon called conservatism, the content of which varies enormously with time and place' (Nash, 1996, p. xiii). His own method he presents as being simply to examine 'conservatism as an intellectual movement *in America, in a particular period*' (p. xiv).

The impatience Nash displays towards the attempt to establish a simple, all-inclusive definition of conservatism – in his words, a 'dubious enterprise' – is an attitude for which sympathy is easy to express. Following Nash would suggest that all that needs to be stated about the present work is that it aims to examine conservatism as an ideology in Britain and America, in the post-Cold War period. Nonetheless, attractive as Nash's stance is, the dismissal of all attempt at definition leaves no satisfactory basis for resolving many issues, such as the positioning of free-market writers. As will be seen, this issue cannot be resolved only by considering their own contentions, because a variety of standpoints is in evidence.

This being the case, it is unfortunately not possible to follow Nash in sidestepping the issue of conservatism's characterization. Even so, it must be stressed that the conclusions drawn at this stage possess only a tentative and conditional quality. It is to be maintained that a more definite account can only be offered a posteriori.

Bearing this caveat in mind, what is conservatism? Many conservatives prefer to distance themselves from the label of ideology, because they disdain the abstract theorizing they believe characterizes ideological thinking (which, clearly, contrasts with the view of ideology outlined above). The most notable adherent to this perspective is Oakeshott, for whom being conservative simply reflects the natural disposition of human beings 'to prefer the familiar to the unknown, to prefer the tried to the untried' (Oakeshott, 1962, p. 169). The dependence of the ideologue upon abstract reason leads him to attempt to condense reality into a limited number of set principles, which thereby distorts the subtleties of actual experience. What the conservative appreciates is that it is necessary to defer to insights derived from a practical or empirical basis, understanding reality via the accumulated wisdom of past experience, as embodied in custom and tradition.

The problem with this 'dispositional' argument is that, without admitting the need for appeal to any abstract principles, conservatives are left with scant basis for discriminating between customs and practices, not all of which – such as the traditions of the decried ideologue – are likely to find conservative favour. Furthermore, since the distinction relied upon, between abstract and practical styles of reasoning, is itself a conceptual distinction not derived from a tradition-based understanding, the very basis for distinguishing a disposition from an ideology may be considered 'ideological' (Vincent, 1994, pp. 224–5).

The denial that conservatism is an ideology is also ideological in the sense in which it is understood in this book, in that it is deployed by conservatives as much to assert conservatism's superiority over competing doctrines as purely to describe what being conservative means. However, the most significant problem with the dispositional argument is that, in depending upon an ahistorical psychological proposition about human nature, it is of little value in explaining conservatism in any historically specific manner.

Considering attempts to offer more definite accounts, undoubtedly the most common type of definition of conservative ideology is in terms of the desire to conserve. This is the basis, for example, of Samuel Huntington's argument for a 'positional' understanding of conservatism (Huntington, 1957). According to Huntington, although conservatives do not offer blueprints for how society should be organized, they nonetheless possess a definite positional commitment: to oppose any fundamental challenge to the existing social order, whatever that order may be and in whatever context.

However, defining conservatism simply in terms of the desire to conserve is notoriously problematic; as conservative philosopher Roger Scruton scornfully writes, in itself it is a decidedly 'limp' definition (Scruton, 2001b, p. 10). It is flawed because it leaves too vague the circumstances requiring conservatives' defensive efforts: for example, how long must an institution have been in existence before it is considered established? Equally, in that few conservatives have ever opposed all change, without further principled appeal the line between unacceptable 'radical' and acceptable gradual change is similarly unclear. Taking a bare attitude towards change as defining of conservatism leads, on the one hand, to denying the label to the very many avowed conservatives who have actively sought change (such as advocates of dismantling the welfare state), and, on the other, to the inclusion within the ideology's boundaries of many who would not ordinarily be considered conservatives (such as Soviet communists who defended their regime during the Cold War).

A further way to define conservatism is as a set of substantive shared beliefs, ones that are adhered to by all conservatives in whatever time or place. Typical suggestions for eternal conservative verities are: the importance of order and authority; respect for history and tradition; and belief in a divine order. A modern exemplar of this approach is Russell Kirk, who identifies 6 essential 'canons' of conservative thought (Kirk, 1953, pp. 7–8). A major difficulty, though, is that little agreement exists even as to how many principles should be enumerated. Although Kirk believes it should be 6 Dunn and Woodard suggest 10 (Dunn and Woodard, 1996, p. 48) and Clinton Rossiter no less than 21 (Rossiter, 1962, pp. 64–6). Yet however many tenets are chosen, the most serious problem is that no single set of unchanging beliefs encompasses the concerns of conservatives in every time and place. Whatever list is drawn up, examples of conservatives who do not hold to any number of its items can always be found. As W. H. Greenleaf concludes from his examination, conservatism's history has contained a wide range of differing ideas and commitments, from individualist to collectivist and from libertarian to authoritarian (Greenleaf, 1973, pp. 177–9).

Ultimately, the most profitable approaches to understanding conservatism are those that emphasize the reactive side of conservative ideology. There is much truth, therefore, in Karl Mannheim's description of conservatism as essentially a 'counter-movement' (Mannheim, 1986, p. 84), with its doctrines having developed largely in reaction to those of its ideological adversaries. One means of conceiving conservatism in this way is suggested by Lincoln Allison, who describes conservatism's basic orientation as anti-humanism, opposing the 'overweening' pretensions of humanist ideologies (Allison, 1984, p. 19). With similar intent, Noël O'Sullivan describes the common foundation of conservatism as a commitment to limits, derived from a belief in the inherent imperfectability of the human condition (N. O'Sullivan, 1976, pp. 9–14). An American conservative who stresses respect for limits is Bruce Frohnen (Frohnen, 1993, pp. 144–75).

Thus, what all conservatives share is belief in an objective limit to humanity's capacity either to comprehend or shape society. This conviction has influenced the range of conservative thought, from respect for custom and tradition over the new and unknown to the rejection of planning and commitment to unconscious market rule. Of course, belief in limits is not unique to conservatives, and can seem a broad and vague idea. However, what both Allison and O'Sullivan also highlight is a historically specific dimension: conservatism's distinctiveness resides in its emergence as reaction to the 'hubristic' ideas of the French Revolution and the Enlightenment. In this way, the 'conservatism' of the caveman clinging to stone-age traditions can be distinguished from that of a modern thinker like Burke (N. O'Sullivan, 1976, p. 9). By locating conservatism within the matrix of ideological conflicts of the modern era, it is therefore possible to avoid the pitfalls of an ahistorical understanding.

This is as far as definitional inquiry can be taken; to repeat the point, no final word on understanding conservative ideology should be given in an introduction. Most important, the nature of conservatives' reactive stances will be seen to have been in many respects transformed by the circumstances of the post-Cold War context. What will be shown is that the best way to understand conservatives' present-day attitudes towards limits and hubristic rationalism is by comparing them with those of other contemporary writers – such as postmodernists and environmentalists – who also today articulate 'anti-humanist' beliefs.

Varieties of conservatism

Regardless of what may unite conservatives, conservatism does not constitute a homogenous ideology. It is, therefore, necessary to differentiate varieties of conservative doctrine. However, before examining the main strands of which conservatism is composed, a prior issue to consider is the relationship between British and American perspectives. In that a key argument of this book is that the contemporary orientations of both can be understood within the same framework, it is necessary to offer justification for analysing them together.

The most significant challenge to the legitimacy of talking of Anglo-American conservative ideology is the notion of American exceptionalism, the idea that America's history has led it to develop an ideological spectrum qualitatively different from those of European societies. This is the argument, for example, of Louis Hartz, who argues that America has not developed the polarized ideologies of socialism and conservatism because it does not possess the legacy of class relations that European societies inherited from their feudal pasts (Hartz, 1955). Instead, the universal American ideology is a form of Lockean liberalism, based upon the values of individual liberty, progress and democracy. To attempt to be a conservative in the European mould – implying a commitment to such lingering feudal notions as hierarchy and order – is to fail to be true to the American experience; the only tradition Americans can authentically 'conserve' is a liberal one.

This understanding is also accepted by some American conservatives. For example, Rossiter avers that 'the one glorious thing to be conservative about has been the Liberal tradition of the world's most liberal society' (Rossiter, 1962, p. 207). However, although it may be agreed that the specifics of context are necessary to understand any ideology, the idea that conservatism is in some sense alien to American society, or at least possesses an identity wholly different from that of its European relatives, ought to be rejected. As Michael Lind observes, exceptionalist arguments rely upon caricatures, of the natures of both American and European societies (M. Lind, 1995, pp. 224–33). Several aspects of American history, such as the practice of slavery, clearly do not accord with a liberal spirit. Moreover, when a less parochial perspective is adopted and comparison is made with non-European societies – especially those of Africa and Asia – the United States can be seen to possess a much more similar cultural identity to Europe than is at times recognized.

In any case, a considerable number of American conservatives have sought to forge a conservatism analogous to European varieties. For example, Kirk attempts to graft a 'Burkean' conservatism on to American conditions by arguing that the American way of life is essentially an import of traditions from seventeenth-century Britain (Kirk, 1953, 1993). Similarly, Thomas Fleming disputes the conventional view of the republic's origins by contending that 'the Founding Fathers of the United States were not particularly liberal', many being staunchly British and basically 'reactionary' (T. Fleming, interview by author, 2 October 1998).

Although these are not universal beliefs among American conservatives, few do not place some emphasis upon non-liberal values and traditions. Yet the assumption that America cannot possess a true conservative philosophy also implies believing in a highly distorted ideal-type of 'Old World' conservatism as anti-modern, anti-liberal and pre-capitalist in orientation. While such characteristics are to be found within British conservatism, it hardly exhausts its range. In fact, the incorporation of 'modern', 'liberal' and 'non-feudal' elements within British conservatism occurred in parallel to the decline of feudal-aristocratic forms of conservatism, some long while ago.

Further historical justification for considering British and American conservative ideologies side-by-side can also be given. As Noël O'Sullivan points out, the dissimilarities between national schools of conservative thought were much more striking before the First World War than after (N. O'Sullivan, 1976, p. 29). This change was brought about by the challenges posed by the twin enemies of Soviet communism and the rise of collectivism, which presented conservatives across Western societies with a set of common preoccupations that previously they had lacked.

It is especially easy to draw parallels between the concerns of British and American conservatives since the 1970s; as John O'Sullivan argued from the perspective of the 1990s, conservative (and liberal) trends in Britain and America 'have tracked each other closely in the last two decades' (J. O'Sullivan, 1997b, p. 8). During the Thatcher–Reagan era, clear links were forged between British and American conservatives, as a result of their shared desire to undo the consensus settlement of the post-war period. Similar issues were raised, together with similar responses. As is to be argued, the context of the post-Cold War world is very different, yet a continuity that will be demonstrated is that a significant cross-fertilization of ideas remains apparent. For example, many American conservatives contribute to British publications and think-tanks (Lanz, 2001; Murray, 1990) and vice versa (Minogue, 1996; Scruton, 2000c).

Critical differences do exist, of course, between British and American conservatives, which will need to be noted during discussion. However, as important as this is, equally important is to avoid merely presenting a bland checklist of similarities and differences: the contention of this book is that the same basic paradigm can be utilized to understand both. Still, it is also worth highlighting that, in terms of the most distinctively contemporary debates, many are primarily American led. Madsen Pirie, President of the Adam Smith Institute in Britain, believes that whereas in the 1980s free-market ideas 'flowed almost entirely from Britain to America', in the 1990s this trend 'to some extent reversed', citing the strong influence of free-market think-tank the Cato Institute and libertarian journal *Reason* upon the Adam Smith Institute (M. Pirie, interview by author, 19 June 1998). Yet, as will be seen, this flow is of more than just free-market ideas: contemporary arguments around such issues as the degraded state of modern culture and the weakened fabric of civil society also frequently originate in America.

It is time to turn to the question of conservatism's composition. A major difficulty in constructing any ideological typology is that whatever categories are identified rarely possess discrete boundaries; furthermore, the concerns and arguments of strands within an ideology change over time. For these reasons, no definitive categorization is to be attempted. Instead, what will be offered is an account of the broad orientations of types of conservative, without claiming category boundaries to be either fixed or permanent.

Within the secondary literature, various classifications are suggested, yet no clear consensus exists as to where, or how many, divisions should be drawn (see, for example, Dunn and Woodard, 1996; Greenleaf, 1973; Peele, 1984; Norton and Aughey, 1981). Still, the place to start is with traditionalist forms of conservatism. The perspective of traditionalists, who are also labelled 'organic' or 'Burkean' conservatives, is characterized by ambivalence towards the modern world and the rationalist legacy of the Enlightenment; they are also frequently pessimistic in outlook. Traditionalists usually reject individualism and emphasize instead the priority of organic communities. As much as they share other conservatives' distaste for socialism, they therefore also possess a strong aversion towards liberalism, often including economic liberalism.

Key ideological touchstones are the notions of continuity, order and authority, as well as beliefs in natural inequality and hierarchy. Within British conservatism, exponents include Worsthorne, Scruton and writers for the *Salisbury Review*. Among American conservatives, traditionalist conservatism is to be found within the writings of the likes of Kirk and Richard Weaver and, more contemporarily, Frohnen. A principal American traditionalist journal is *Modern Age*.

A particular strand of American traditionalism that can be distinguished is that which is commonly dubbed 'paleoconservatism'. Main proponents of this perspective are centred around the Rockford Institute and its journal *Chronicles*, including Fleming (*Chronicles*'s editor) and Samuel Francis. Holding to traditionalist viewpoints, paleoconservatives adopt particularly antagonistic stances towards other conservatives. Most notable, paleoconservatives are suspicious of what they regard as the globalizing zeal of mainstream conservatives (supporting the isolationist and protectionist standpoint of Pat Buchanan) as well as their supposed acquiescence to 'big government'. Paleoconservatives also emphasize specifically Southern conservative traditions – whereas many present-day conservatives appear to miss the certainties of the Cold War, paleoconservatives seem to be as interested in refighting the Civil War, with issues such as states' rights and appeals to the antifederalist tradition figuring heavily within their writings.

However, a problem with using the traditionalist label simply to differentiate conservatives concerned with social issues from free-market conservatives is that many who focus upon cultural and moral questions do not share the anti-modernism of arch-traditionalists. This is especially apparent among American conservatives, with the mainstream of post-war American conservatism never having sought any form of rolling back of modernity; in this sense, a positively reactionary component has always been much weaker than within the British tradition. In fact, mainstream American conservatives have typically sought to marry traditionalism in the social spheres with the defence of market capitalism in the economic. This is true across journals from the *National Review* to *Policy Review*.

One of the more difficult strands of American conservatism to place within the conservative spectrum is neoconservatism. Notable figures include Podhoretz, Irving Kristol, Michael Novak and Daniel Bell (even if Bell has always been uneasy with the label), while an array of journals can be identified with a neoconservative viewpoint: *Commentary*, the *Public Interest* (dealing with public policy issues), the *National Interest* (foreign affairs) and the *New Criterion* (culture and the arts). A younger generation to have inherited the neoconservative label is typified by William Kristol and writers for the conservative magazine he edits, the *Weekly Standard*.

The historical difficulty in placing neoconservatism derives from the fact that most originally regarded themselves as liberals, who became disaffected by the 'leftward' turn liberalism took in the 1960s. Liberalism's association with radical political movements and the spread of alternative lifestyles led neoconservatives to believe in the need to reassert traditional moral values and a democratic capitalist vision. They also reacted to what they saw as the overextension of the state's role by the Great Society programmes of the era.

Even so, neoconservatives continued to see themselves as defenders of the New Deal settlement of the 1930s, and thus qualified supporters of the welfare state. Nor have neoconservatives ever been advocates of laissez-faire economics. Indeed, excessive liberalism in the economic sphere is seen as a threat to custom and tradition, identified by Bell as capitalism's 'cultural contradictions' (Bell, 1978) and responsible for Irving Kristol's giving only two rather than three cheers for capitalism (Kristol, 1978). For these reasons, neoconservatism might be considered a relatively 'moderate' strand. Yet on the issues of opposing the counter-culture and fighting communism, neoconservatives were far more combative during the Cold War era. Indeed, in both areas they were at the forefront of ideological battle.

However, the failure of fixed definitions to capture the essence of historically evolving ideologies is well illustrated by the case of neoconservatism, in that the distinction between neoconservatism and mainstream conservatism no longer holds much meaning. As will be demonstrated in subsequent chapters, there is little remaining attachment either to the welfare state or political liberalism among neoconservatives to continue to warrant the 'neo-' prefix. Politically, most had by the 1980s already migrated from the Democratic Party to the Republicans. Yet the demise of communism and the attention now paid by all types of conservative to cultural conflict also make neoconservatism a far less distinctive perspective. This is recognized by many neoconservatives themselves. According to Podhoretz, neoconservatism has now 'merged into the general conservative movement' (N. Podhoretz, interview by author, 11 September 1998). This belief is shared by Irving Kristol (Kristol, 1995, pp. 37–8).

Within British conservatism, a strand to distinguish is that of 'one-nation' or so-called 'progressive' conservatism, which derives its views from the tradition of Disraeli and Harold Macmillan; a modern exponent is Ian Gilmour (Gilmour, 1978, 1992). Like other traditionalist conservatives, they are typically more concerned with the social fabric than with economics, though in that they are much less anti-modern, accepting such developments as the growth of the welfare state, may seem closer in spirit to American neoconservatives (at least in relation to the latter's more 'liberal' period). However, they differ from neoconservatives in adopting less belligerent ideological stances, being most noted in the 1970s and 1980s for opposing the New Right's aggressiveness. In part, one-nation conservatism's concern with meliorating rather than exacerbating social divisions derives from its incorporation of a paternalistic aristocratic component, which finds only meagre parallel in the American context.

Compounding the problems of classification further is the fact that a number of streams of conservative thought are based upon highly particular positions. This is the case with British Oakeshottians and American Straussians. Although Oakeshott was a firm believer in tradition and prime critic of rationalism, the affinity of his arguments with liberal principles – in terms of his preference for a non-instrumental conception of civil association – distinguishes them from those of more illiberal traditionalist conservatives (see Gray, 1993b, pp. 40–6). Indeed, Oakeshott's philosophy may even be described as libertarian. The influence of Oakeshott has been strong upon British conservatives, like Minogue and Shirley Letwin, yet their arguments do not fit easily into a simple libertarian/traditionalist system of categorization.

Equally, Strauss, like many traditionalist conservatives, exhibits a manifestly anti-modern outlook, yet his emphasis upon the value of reason, the universality of natural law, and his preference for specifically ancient conceptions of philosophy and society is more individual (Strauss, 1953). Furthermore, a commonality between Oakeshott and Strauss – even if there are not many – is that both were centrally concerned with the nature of philosophy, making the translations of their perspectives into political ideologies less than comfortable propositions. Nonetheless, Straussians like Allan Bloom, Harvey Mansfield and Thomas Pangle are significant voices within modern conservatism.

Turning to the free market's proponents, opinion divides sharply over whether or not their doctrines should be considered a part of, or at least reconcilable with, conservatism. The cornucopia of labels alone suggests the difficulty in placing free-market beliefs, with 'neo-', 'classical', 'market', 'free-market' and 'economic' liberalism, as well as simply libertarianism, all being options. However, it is also possible to substitute conservatism for liberalism to give 'free-market' or 'economic' conservatism; or even for 'libertarian conservatism' to be used as a designation. Of course, different labels may imply different shades of commitment, even if it is rarely clear where lines are supposed to be drawn.

One who unmistakably rejects the conservative label is Hayek, preferring his philosophy to be seen as that of an 'Old Whig' (Hayek, 1960, p. 409). To him, conservatism is no more than a form of unprincipled pragmatism, which cannot be trusted to follow consistently a definite course, such as opposing collectivism (though, it may be noted, the 'pragmatic' characterization of conservatism suffers from many of the same deficiencies as the dispositional and positional arguments). Many others disavow any connection with conservatism. For example, Edward Crane and David Boaz, President and executive Vice-President of the Cato Institute, argue that conservatism is a doctrine too resistant towards change to fit with their 'market liberal' agenda (Boaz and Crane, 1993, p. 8). Pirie also argues that he is not a conservative, describing himself simply as a supporter of free markets (M. Pirie, interview by author, 19 June 1998).

The belief that economic liberalism should be kept separate from conservatism is also often shared by critics. For example, Gray has come to believe that economic liberalism is alien to 'real' conservatism, since support for free markets is incompatible with concern for the values of community and continuity (Gray, 1995, pp. 87–119). Many traditionalist conservatives agree. Thus, American conservative John Vinson wishes to deny libertarians the conservative label on the basis that they are 'more concerned with cash than character, possessions more than posterity' (Vinson, 1996, p. 30). Particularly noteworthy is Oakeshott's dismissal of the rationalism he saw as inherent in Hayek's anti-collectivism: 'A plan to resist all planning may be better than its opposite, but it belongs to the same style of politics' (Oakeshott, 1962, p. 21).

However, some supporters of free markets argue that a commitment to liberalism in the economic sphere is compatible with social conservatism. For example, Willetts believes that the needs of free markets and communities exist in harmony (Willetts, 1992a, pp. 92–108). One problem with excluding conservative exponents of free-market ideas is that it would require a substantial reassessment of the place of numerous figures – including, in Britain alone, Lord Hugh Cecil, Enoch Powell and Keith Joseph – within conservatism's history. Indeed, a strong affinity with free-market liberalism may be apparent from conservatism's origins: Robert Nisbet argues that there was no serious difference between Burke and Adam Smith in their assessment of the correct role of government and laissez-faire economics (Nisbet, 1986, p. 37).

It would be especially difficult to consider American conservatism distinct from the free-market tradition. Indeed, one writer claims that Hayek's version of classical liberalism was 'the bedrock on which the generation of American conservatives who came of age after 1945 built a political movement' (Glasner, 1992, p. 49). If this may be an exaggeration, it does testify to the significance of free-market ideas to American conservatives. Many also argue that free-market economics depend upon social conservatism. For example, Charles Murray argues that 'My brand of libertarianism is very respectful of Edmund Burke and I think that a libertarian society is only going to function if in fact there are a great many very strong conservative institutions in place' (C. Murray, interview by author, 22 September 1998).

In fact, Hayek believed much the same, even if he did not wish to be branded a conservative: 'a successful free society will always in a large measure be a tradition-bound society', in which 'reverence for grown institutions, for customs and habits' is necessary (Hayek, 1960, p. 61). He also shared many of Oakeshott's misgivings about rationalists' beliefs in the powers of reason and the possibility of consciously controlling society (pp. 54–70).

Ironically, given Gray's subsequent intellectual trajectory, probably the most persuasive argument for believing there to be a particular affinity between market liberalism and conservatism is provided by Gray's reading of Hayek. As Gray argues, Hayek's standpoint was premised upon a similar view of human beings' limited capacities as that of sceptical conservatives. In particular, it is his belief that the majority of human knowledge is tacit in nature – of which the subject is not explicitly aware – that underpins Hayek's commitment to a spontaneous market order as preferable to a planned one (Gray, 1984, pp. 14–15). Indeed, Gray's recognition of the importance in Hayek's philosophy of custom and tradition leads him to side Hayek with Oakeshott in appreciating the compatibility of libertarian individualism and cultural traditionalism (pp. 129–30).

Furthermore, and in contrast to Gray's later interpretations, what will be documented in the following chapters is that beliefs in the social constitution of individuality and the value of tradition and community are widespread among contemporary free-market thinkers. Thus, 'conservative' concerns clearly inform their arguments. None of this is to suggest that tensions do not exist between free marketeers and (other) conservatives, as well as between shades of free-market thinking. Nor is it necessary, or fruitful, to force the conservative label upon those unwilling to accept it. Even so, it can be seen that there are not only conventional, but also principled reasons for including free-market doctrines within conservative ideology's bounds.

A historical excursus

Before examining the post-Cold War background against which contemporary conservatism operates, it will be worthwhile to provide a brief historical overview. In light of the issues to be explored, the place to begin is with how conservatives oriented themselves in the wake of the Russian Revolution of 1917.

As already suggested, after the First World War the threat of socialism governed the nature of conservatives' concerns across the Western world. Since the end of the nineteenth century, conservatives had had to come to terms with the emergence of mass democratic politics, together with growing labour movements and the spread of left-wing ideas. Yet the Bolshevik Revolution meant that conservative fears of socialist catastrophe took on an even greater urgency. Moreover, the onset of a worldwide capitalist slump at the close of the 1920s made the intellectual defence of an unqualified free-market doctrine increasingly untenable. In the context of mass unemployment and widespread industrial bankruptcy (Hobsbawm, 1994, pp. 87–92), many of the assumptions of neo-classical economics – for example, that markets are spontaneously self-equilibriating – appeared patently erroneous. Thus, the gradual extension of state activity into more and more areas became widely accepted alongside the progress of collectivism. By the end of the 1930s, an intellectual consensus had evolved practically across the ideological spectrum that free-market capitalism was unsustainable (Furedi, 1992, p. 172).

In Britain, conservatives of the inter-war period did continue to articulate free-market ideas, with proponents of laissez-faire like Ernest Benn remaining vocal (Greenleaf, 1983, pp. 295–308). However, the need to accommodate to the threat of socialism and to acknowledge the reality of capitalism's condition meant that many conservatives accepted the greater regulatory and welfare roles the state had taken on. Intellectual legitimation for this acceptance came in the form of the 'Middle Way' – as propounded by Macmillan in a 1938 book of the same name – implying that it was possible to chart a course between full-blooded socialism and free-market capitalism, presented as in the interests not of a single class but of the whole of society.

In America, the traditionalist conservatism of the 'Old Right' that existed between the wars was anti-statist, yet often also anti-modern and isolationist in spirit (which explains its discrediting by the time of America's entry into the Second World War). Yet in the inter-war period, the term conservative almost wholly signified those who were unqualified defenders of business (Gottfried, 1993, p. 3). As such, the particular target of their resentment was the assumption by federal government of increased responsibility for welfare and the economy that occurred with Roosevelt's New Deal. The politics of this era partly explain the common identification in America of free-market beliefs with conservatism, and statist doctrines that in Europe would be described as social democratic with liberalism.

Yet capitalism's evident failings explain Gillian Peele's conclusion that rather than there being any significant intellectual conflict between Left and Right, 'the primary divisions in American intellectual life in the 1930s were *within* the far left' (Peele, 1984, p. 23). Most of those who would later become neoconservatives partook in or inherited their outlook from this intellectual climate, with many indeed describing themselves as one-time Trotskyists. As Irving Kristol argues, as a child of the Depression he 'could not take seriously the seemingly blind faith in "free enterprise" ' that characterized much of the conservatism of the 1930s (Kristol, 1995, p. 82).

The Second World War, in both Britain and America, entailed a further extension of the state's power. Furthermore, the economic restructuring necessitated by war solved, for the time, the capitalist crisis of the 1930s. As a result, by the 1940s the view had gained widespread intellectual credence that capitalism had entered a distinctly new phase, of organized or managed capitalism, which stood in contrast to the crisis-ridden free-market version of the past. This was announced by, among others, James Burnham in his 1941 *The Managerial Revolution*, who saw the New Deal settlement as part of a worldwide trend towards planned societies. After the war, belief in this view – together with assertions of the 'end of ideology' (by, for example, Bell) and the continuing advances made by the doctrines of welfare liberalism and Keynesian demand management – meant that the ideological pillars of a consensus-based philosophy came into place in the 1940s and 1950s.

Resistance to the onward march of collectivism was given impetus by the publication of Hayek's *The Road to Serfdom* in 1944 and Karl Popper's *The Open Society and Its Enemies* in 1945. These writers warned against the threat to liberal societies posed by collectivist ideologies and of the need for principled resistance. However, in Britain post-war conservatism was dominated by the views of Macmillan and other 'progressives', such as Rab Butler, who accepted much of the consensus settlement. The influence of libertarian arguments among conservatives was therefore largely marginalized by the dominance of pragmatic accommodationism, which partially accounts for Hayek's attitude towards conservatism.

Although conservatives largely followed the intellectual pace set by the Left, the immediate post-war decades did see a number of works theorizing conservative principles, by conservatives like Quintin Hogg, and the establishment of ideas-producing bodies mirroring those of the Left, including the Conservative Political Centre and the Bow Group. By stressing the conservative tradition of pragmatism and adaptability, it was possible for Middle Way conservatives not only to justify accommodation to collectivism and the welfare state, but also to retain some form of intellectual counter to 'ideological' socialism.

By contrast, the immediate post-war years in America saw the emergence of ideologically assertive forms of conservatism in the shape of the (first) 'New Right'. Hayek's work was a particular inspiration, though anti-consensus conservatism found its focus with the establishment by William Buckley of the *National Review* in 1955. A principal aim of *National Review* conservatives was to revive the anti-New Deal conservatism of the 1930s.

The experiences of fascism and Stalinism also had a major impact throughout intellectual circles in the post-war era, in generating scepticism towards Enlightenment values like progress and rationality. Among conservatives, crucial to many of their understandings of the events of the 1930s and 1940s was that there is a definite association between modernity and what they perceived to be 'totalitarian' ideologies.

This belief informed, though in different ways, the anti-modernism of conservatives as diverse as Strauss and Oakeshott. In America, the questioning of modernity was responsible for the rise, in parallel to that of libertarianism, of traditionalist conservatism as expounded by writers such as Kirk and Weaver. Though such conservatives shared with libertarians distaste for the New Deal legacy, they were also concerned about the assumptions of all modern beliefs, including free-market liberalism, together with the moral implications of the new mass consumer culture.

However, for many American conservatives libertarianism and traditionalism were not seen as opposed (Nash, 1996, pp. 141–71). Buckley and the *National Review* were as much concerned with preserving American culture as promoting economic liberty. Offering a theoretical justification for this synthesis of ideas was Frank Meyer, who theorized a 'fusion' between the need for individual liberty and the need for moral community, as representing the true American tradition. A prime reason for believing this synthesis necessary was the desire to create a unified doctrine to pursue a common goal: fighting communism. America's inheriting of the pre-eminent global position after the Second World War meant that it fell to American conservatives to take the lead in the ideological war against communism. Despite tensions between libertarians and traditionalists – which certainly existed – anti-communism became the 'glue' that bonded together the various strands of American conservatism during the Cold War.

For many conservatives, the 1960s have become distinguished as the decade in which the seeds were sown for all that has latterly gone wrong with Western society. Yet if the decade is best remembered for its radicalism and the counterculture, it was also an era of conservative discontent. One of the most important developments within American conservatism was the emergence of neoconservatism. Although neoconservatives disagreed with *National Review* conservatives' hostility to the New Deal, tensions between them were meliorated by a common antagonism towards the developing 'adversary culture' and the socialist menace.

However, conservative discontent was also the result of a growing dissatisfaction with accommodation to the post-war consensus. In Britain, the affluence of the past decades had begun to falter by the mid-1960s, with falling industrial output and rising inflation. The reappraisal of the economic orthodoxies of the consensus was given momentum by the establishment in 1957 of the free-market think-tank the Institute of Economic Affairs and by Enoch Powell, both challenging the consensus in the late 1950s and 1960s. In many respects, 'Powellism' prefigured

'Thatcherism', by attempting to combine nationalistic with economically liberal doctrines.

In America, the culmination of the political efforts of activist conservatives was the nomination of Barry Goldwater as the Republican can-
didate for the 1964 presidential election. If Powell prefigured Thatcher,
Goldwater prefigured Reagan. Goldwater's ideological reference points
were the dual aims of a scaling down of the New Deal welfare state and
a scaling up of the war against communism. Yet Goldwater's landslide
defeat was significant, in revealing the weakness of the conservative
forces behind his nomination. Similarly, the authority of the arguments
of the Institute of Economic Affairs and Powell in Britain was undermined by the fact that, despite problems, managed capitalism was not in
the 1960s in crisis.

However, during the 1970s the conservatism that would give the
Thatcher and Reagan governments of the 1980s their intellectual under-
pinnings gathered new force, as an invigorated anti-consensus ideology.
A sign of this was the proliferation of new think-tanks, such as the
Heritage Foundation (established in 1973) in America and the Centre for
Policy Studies (1974) in Britain. Yet, as before, there was not a unified set
of perspectives or prescriptions.

One aspect of the conservative revival of the 1970s and 1980s was the
resurgence of free-market ideas. These were given new energy especially
by economists like Milton Friedman. Of course, different strategies were
embraced – by, for example, monetarists and disciples of the Austrian
School – such as over whether macro- or micro-economic remedies were
the order of the day. Nonetheless, there was a unity in the belief that
freeing the market was the necessary antidote to the poison of collectivism. Moreover, whether or not free-market ideas are compatible with
conservatism, many conservatives embraced them.

Alongside the reassertion of free-market beliefs, traditionalists
sought to reinvigorate the priorities of nation, tradition and authority.
Certainly for British conservatives, a change from the past was the readi-
ness with which conservatives adopted explicitly principled stances.
With many seeking to furnish conservatism with a clearer intellectual
basis, the idea of pragmatically following a consensus-based course was
abandoned. Thus, in the introduction to a volume of conservative writings of the late 1970s, Maurice Cowling asserted – contra Oakeshott –
the importance of conservatives theorizing a definite public doctrine
(Cowling, 1978, pp. 20–4). Many, like Scruton, also became more willing
to describe their own beliefs in ideological terms (Scruton, 1984, p. 7).

Few of the ideas articulated were particularly new; as the discussion of earlier historical periods shows, anti-consensus voices had existed long before. The significant change in the 1970s was the change of circumstances. If the slump of the 1930s seemed to legitimate the arrival of the Keynesian or managed state, recession and economic instability in the 1970s appeared by contrast to discredit it, as falling industrial production, rising unemployment and inflation made their return (Hobsbawm, 1994, pp. 403–18). Furthermore, perceptions of a revived danger from Soviet communism also suggested the need for a conservative ideological counter-offensive.

As seen previously, for some, such as neoconservatives, the conditions of the 1970s provoked doubts about liberalism in the economic sphere, though not any fundamental doubt about capitalism as such. Yet if one fear united conservatives in Britain and American, it was the fear of decline, both economic and moral, the belief that their societies were on a downward spiral. Thus, even if the marriage of the various strands of conservatism may have been one more of convenience than total compatibility, the belief that the only way to reverse decline was to develop an intellectual alternative to consensus provided some unity. The core of this unity was combating the enemies within, the labour movement and the Left, and communism without, meaning that an offensive on all fronts – economic, political and cultural – was believed necessary.

In many respects, this revived conservatism failed to achieve its goals; as will be seen in later chapters, even many conservatives recognize conservative governments' failures either to roll back the state or to restore traditional moral values. One issue on which conservatives do tend to lay claim to unambiguous success is that of burying socialism, in all its forms, though largely by downplaying the internal weaknesses of the Soviet Union and the domestic Left responsible for their respective disintegrations. Part of what is to be looked at in the final section of this introduction is what the end of the conflict with socialism means for conservatives.

The post-Cold War context

To provide a framework for examining conservatism in the post-Cold War era, it will be useful to consider five propositions relating to the idea of conservative disorientation. While the aim of this book is not simply to prove or disprove these, they will be valuable for understanding the discussions of subsequent chapters.

Conservatives no longer possess any significant defining purpose, either enemies to fight or 'big ideas' to promote

When Fukuyama declared history's end, he saw this as meaning that fundamental class conflict was over and that 'all of the really big questions had been settled' (Fukuyama, 1992, p. xii). If conservatism is understood as a reactive ideology, then a major argument for regarding it as obsolete is that the ending of the Cold War means that it no longer possesses any significant defining purpose.

It is necessary to examine in more detail what the Cold War signified. In its narrowest sense, the conflict was about the military struggle between the Soviet Union and the West. Yet it also had a much broader and deeper meaning. As Minogue puts it, the Cold War referred 'to something over and above the hostility between the post-1945 victors' (Minogue, 1992/3, p. 81). In fact, the 'real location of the Cold War ... was in the mind', because it was a war about values and ideas.

Moreover, for conservatives, the Cold War conflict was bound up with their longer-term historical rivalries. This is implicit in Novak's argument that the end of the Cold War marked the conclusion of the 'war of 1848–1989' (Novak, 1997, p. 23). That is, the battle with Soviet communism was part of the greater war against socialism. However, the Cold War was not solely about the socialist threat; rather, it was intimately connected to the conflict with all left-wing ideologies. As leading American anti-communist Whittaker Chambers asserted in the 1950s, 'when I took up my little sling and aimed at Communism, I also hit something else' (Chambers, 1952, p. 741), that something else being New Deal liberalism. In other words, all varieties of left-wing doctrine, including beliefs in collectivism and state planning even of relatively modest varieties, were part of the ideological struggle. Therefore, the defeats suffered by conservatives' internal opponents during the 1980s can be seen as related to the conclusion of the external conflict.

For these reasons, the notion of the 'post-Cold War era' may be used to refer to the demise of all of conservatives' historic foes. Of course, it is possible to regard a lack of substantial conflicts or issues in a positive light, whether or not history is believed to have reached its end. For example, Tod Lindberg argues that, with conservatives' adversaries no longer opposing them on fundamental matters, the fact that the era of 'intellectual ferment' is over should be viewed as a tribute to conservatism's success (Lindberg, 1999, p. 3). Similarly, Douglas Hurd welcomed at the end of the 1990s the fact that we are 'left with humdrum politics' in the absence of mortal threats to society (D. Hurd, interview by author, 25 June 1998).

Yet others are less positive. Scruton thinks that, if Fukuyama's end-of-history thesis were true, we would live in a world 'in which nothing is really worth dying for ... [and] in which human aspiration will dwindle to such a point that all life can be organized by a team of managers' (Scruton, 1996b, p. 430). Furthermore, many are uneasy that an absence of dragons to slay and 'big ideas' to promote may mean that there is a vacuum at the heart of conservative ideology (see J. Patten, 1995, pp. 1–9; S. Letwin, 1996, p. 173; J. O'Sullivan, 1997a).

In fact, subsequent chapters will show that many threats to the integrity of Western society are still identified by conservatives (some of which were noted at the start of this one) and that 'new' ideas are forwarded. The questions to be explored, therefore, are how significant or convincing contemporary menaces are in comparison to those of the past, and whether new agendas can provide conservatives with a distinctive purpose comparable to those of defeating socialism or undoing the post-war consensus.

Despite the absence of viable alternatives to capitalism, free-market conservatism is bankrupt

Although many conservatives recognize that it may have produced a vacuum within conservatism, there are further implications of the Cold War's ending that far fewer consider. Most fundamental, Gray argues that it is not solely left-wing ideologies that stand discredited in the light of communism's failure, but all those imbued with Enlightenment values and commitments (Gray, 1993b, pp. 245–50). This, in his mind, means that the 'rationalist' liberalism of free marketeers must also accept the damning judgement of history. While many of the specifics of Gray's arguments are to be contested in this book, that the collapse of communism has implications for the constitutions of all contemporary ideologies is a suggestion very much to be endorsed. These deeper implications, therefore, are also part of the 'post-Cold War' paradigm to be employed.

On the status of free-market beliefs specifically, Gray argues that, outside conservatism, 'neo-liberalism is a dead ideology' (Gray, 1997, p. 76). Yet he is not alone in detecting a waning in its strength. In fact, it is not only critics who may believe that neo-liberalism is, if not dead, at least severely enervated. Willetts, for example, argued in 1994 that 'One of the most significant intellectual events of the past five years, which has passed largely unnoticed is the collapse of Neo-Liberalism as a significant intellectual force within this country' (Willetts, 1994, p. 26). What may be surprising to those who read his end-of-history thesis simplistically is that Fukuyama believes that the limitations of libertarianism became increasingly apparent during the 1990s and that, since our entering the new millennium, the libertarian wave has crested: 'The great free-market revolution that began with the coming to power of Margaret Thatcher and Ronald Reagan at the close of the 1970s has finally reached its Thermidor, or point of reversal' (Fukuyama, 2002).

Gray offers a number of reasons for believing market liberalism to be bankrupt, including its lack of concern for the destruction wrought by unfettered market forces upon the common environment, natural and social, and its pursuit of progress and economic growth at the expense of moral concerns such as social justice (Gray, 1997, pp. 76–8). As later chapters will show, these types of criticism are common among critics such as communitarians and environmentalists. Yet while the questioning of free-market beliefs is hardly a new phenomenon, what may be difficult to understand today is its widespread nature. Whereas, for example, in the 1930s and 1940s the realities of slump and the seeming success of economic management made free-market doctrines appear less than credible over the course of the 1990s the American and British economies performed relatively well, if unevenly, as Fukuyama for one acknowledges (Fukuyama, 2002). The point about present-day attacks on capitalism, and what makes them especially hard for free marketeers to refute, is that critics focus less upon capitalism's lack of dynamism than on the problems caused by too much growth and progress.

The problem for conservatives is that the demise of socialism has not translated into any widespread enthusiasm for a free-market philosophy. As Norman Barry argues, 'despite the collapse of communism, and the diminishing appeal of even a less repressive socialism, economic liberalism holds little allure' (Barry, 1996, p. 56). Of particular interest in Gray's analysis is his argument that it is the specific conditions of the present context that make free-market liberalism redundant. Thus, during the 1970s and (early) 1980s 'neo-liberalism was a compelling response to otherwise intractable dilemmas' (Gray, 1995, p. 87). However, now that the argument against socialism and state planning has been won, a 'new' debate within society has emerged, concerning the limitations of market institutions and the cultural underpinnings necessary to sustain them. In this debate, 'neo-liberal thought has little to contribute' (p. 88). In other words, now that it has defeated its antagonists, it is necessary for capitalism to display a less harsh, more socially aware face. Whether or not market liberalism ever was a compelling ideology, many critics suggest that its prescriptions are particularly inappropriate in the post-Cold War context. As Gray's notion of a 'new' debate implies, a free-market model is not the only one on offer to Western societies, even in the absence of socialist ones. Instead, it is possible to argue that a new conflict has replaced the one between socialism and capitalism, which Michel Albert has dubbed 'capitalism against capitalism' (Albert, 1993), that is, between a model of capitalism of free, unfettered markets and a more regulated, socially concerned one. Free marketeers' beliefs do not, therefore, possess an uncontested dominance. The issue to be considered in the following chapters is how vital free-market ideology remains in the light of the many challenges it continues to face.

The main focus of conservatives' concerns has shifted away from economics and politics to issues concerning the social and cultural fabric

Whether or not free-market ideology is marginalized more widely, a separate question relates to its strength within conservatism. On this, it is valuable to contrast two different interpretations. According to Gray, conservatism since the ascendancy of the New Right has fallen all but entirely into free-market liberalism's grip. Indeed, 'the hegemony within conservative thought and policy of neo-liberal ideology is so complete that there is now no historical possibility – political or intellectual – of a return to traditional conservatism' (Gray, 1995, pp. vii–viii).

Yet, alternatively, it is possible to argue that since its 1980s heyday, a retreat from a full-blooded free-market ideology has occurred. For example, in support of his contention that neo-liberalism has collapsed, Willetts observes how 'Its fountainhead, the Institute of Economic Affairs, is now producing works by ethical Socialists in praise of the family and by anguished Catholic capitalists' (Willetts, 1994, p. 26), rather than bold free-market programmes. (Willetts's reference is to works like Dennis and Erdos, 1992, and Novak, 1990.)

Writing on American conservatism, Andrew Sullivan also perceives such a change:

> the dominant ideas that have emerged in the last few years bear only the faintest resemblance to the major themes of the 1980s: economic freedom, smaller government and personal choice. Although libertarians are certainly numbered among the intellectuals of the right of the late 1990s, they are clearly on the defensive. What is galvanizing the right-wing intelligentsia at century's end is a different kind of conservatism altogether: much less liberal, far less economic and only

nominally skeptical of government power. It is inherently pessimistic –
a return to older, conservative themes of cultural decline, moralism
and the need for greater social control. (Sullivan, 1998, p. 48)

Objections to this depiction may be obvious, given that the revived
conservatism of the Thatcher–Reagan era was not just free market based.
As William Kristol argues, against Sullivan's portrayal, 'it's a rewriting of
history to claim that in the good old days [of the 1980s] conservatives
were tolerant libertarians', unconcerned with cultural and moral issues
(W. Kristol, interview by author, 20 October 1998). However, if the
moral and cultural themes Sullivan identifies are not new within conservatism, it is still arguable that they have acquired a much greater
prominence. At the very least, it is difficult not to detect a shift in the
focus of conservative writings. Digby Anderson, Director of the Social
Affairs Unit, also perceives a general 'move away from the grand old
themes of politics, the economy, defence ... to what you might call cultural issues' (D. Anderson, interview by author, 22 June 1998). This is
certainly borne out by the Social Affairs Unit's output, which has come
to include, for example, studies of the images to be found in women's
magazines (Anderson and Mosbacher, 1997) and the content of the
modern news media (Minogue, 1997). In that these areas are more usually investigated by left-wing academics in cultural studies departments,
one way to understand this change might be that, if conservatism is
essentially a reactive ideology, conservatives have followed the shift of
their opponents on to the terrain of culture.

However, the pessimism Sullivan argues characterizes conservatives'
engagements with cultural themes may also be suggestive of their lack of
affinity with the cultural climate of the post-Cold War world.
Equally, linking their desire to rearticulate more traditional, less liberal,
social doctrines to libertarians having been put on the defensive may
indicate a sense of disillusionment with conservatives' past economic
and political agendas. Both of these possibilities will need to be
explored.

Despite a social and intellectual climate hostile to radicalism, traditionalist conservative doctrines lack purchase

If free-market conservatives face difficulties in relating to the post-Cold
War world, there are reasons for supposing that traditionalist conservatives might fare better and their doctrines find greater intellectual

resonance. In order to check unfettered market processes, many of the free market's critics argue for the need to conserve. For example, Anthony Giddens assumes what appears to be a Burkean guise in arguing that 'surely there comes a point at which endless change is not only unsettling but positively destructive' (Giddens, 1994, p. 2). Similarly, Lasch argues for the need to check unfettered progress and revive a belief in limits (Lasch, 1991, pp. 21–81). Many ambitions favoured by critics, such as the preservation of communities and the protection of the natural environment, might be thought to be ones with which traditionalist conservatives can readily concur.

Yet if scepticism about radical change has become widespread, it is not necessarily the case that conservatives benefit from this climate, or that others wish to associate themselves with conservatism. In particular, traditionalist conservatives are perceived as being unable to adapt to such realities of the contemporary world as the increased diversity of lifestyles and ethical beliefs.

A way to understand this is by considering Giddens's defence of tradition. According to Giddens, we live in a 'post-traditional social order' (Giddens, 1994, pp. 5–9, 83–7). This is not one in which tradition has disappeared, but in which tradition has changed in character. Whereas in the past traditions were essentially closed – not open to question and imposed upon society to consolidate hierarchy and inequality – today's global, cosmopolitan world makes such closure far less tenable, because social knowledge is greater and more diffused; in Giddens's terms, society has become more reflexive. Consequently, traditions must now be able to command the support of those who live within them and be open to dialogical revision. It is for these reasons that Giddens feels able to urge progressives to embrace the conservation of traditions. The problem for Giddens with many traditionalist conservatives is that, because their defences of tradition rely upon the unreflective preservation of the past implied in the closed conception, their ideology remains an outdated form of dogmatic 'fundamentalism' (pp. 45–50).

In other words, even to the extent that notions like tradition and conservation are no longer solely the preserve of conservatives, the particular nature of conservatives' conceptions may still make them appear obsolete. A further issue to consider, therefore, is how well traditionalist conservatives can adapt to a 'conservative' climate that is nonetheless frequently hostile to their doctrines. A particular aim will be to distinguish the 'conservatism' of conservatives from that of more contemporary 'conserving' philosophies.

Contemporary conservatism is characterized by increased factiousness and disunity

A final indicator of conservatives' difficulties is increased tension between strands of conservatism. Although conservatives have always had differences between them, in the past relative unity and cohesion was provided by the existence of shared enemies. The Cold War's conclusion may be responsible, therefore, for exposing and exacerbating stresses within conservative alliances. As Podhoretz argues, the 'end of the Cold War has opened up various splits that were papered over' by the existence of a common foe (N. Podhoretz, interview by author, 11 September 1998).

This is undoubtedly apparent among American conservatives. Indeed, a number of writers refer to a 'conservative crack-up' in relation to the American conservative movement, as possibly having dissolved into its constituent factions (see Judis, 1990; Starobin, 1995; Tyrrell, 1992; *Weekly Standard*, 1997). Most obviously, the familiar tension between free-market and traditionalist conservatives may have increased in intensity. For example, David Frum believes that 'The relationship between libertarians and conservatives, never easy, has deteriorated markedly over the past few years' (Frum, 1997b, p. 20). Yet many other tensions are identified, for example, between paleoconservatives and neoconservatives, and between neoconservatives and a more stridently religious faction – centred around the journal *First Things* – that one observer labels 'theoconservatives' (Heilbrunn, 1996). With the increase in stresses and strains within conservatism comes the proliferation of new labels.

As will be seen, there are also bases for hostilities within British conservatism to have increased. An important issue to address throughout this book, therefore, is whether newer sources of unity can be found. Yet finding these may prove more difficult in the present context, because whereas all conservatives could agree on how socialism should be regarded, it is much less obvious how conservatives should view many other ideologies. Although many treat doctrines such as communitarianism and environmentalism with revulsion, other conservatives are keener to recognize the affinities these ideologies may have with conservatism. Consequently, the potential for 'papering over' tensions may be much less.

The following chapters will explore the major themes of contemporary conservatism in relation to these five propositions. What will become clear is that few of present-day conservatives' ideas are fundamentally new; rather, it will again be the context in which they are developed that is significant. In terms of the issues to be discussed, a degree of selectivity is inevitably employed. For reasons of space, no attention is to be paid to conservatives' search for new external enemies. Furthermore, only passing consideration will be given to a number of issues traditionally considered in relation to conservatism. For example, conservatives' views of race and immigration are only touched upon in the terms in which they are conventionally addressed, to allow discussion to focus upon such issues as multiculturalism and identity politics. The primary basis for selection, therefore, is the objective of identifying the most distinctive features of post-Cold War conservatism.

2
Rolling Back or Rolling Forward? The Role of the State in an Uncertain Age

The purpose of this chapter is to explore conservatives' attitudes towards the state and how they mediate the competing claims of liberty and authority. Central to this exploration is the question of whether the state should be viewed as enemy or ally; and, consequently, whether the ambition should be to diminish or bolster its authority. Of course, examining the tension between these standpoints is a common undertaking of analyses of conservatism. In particular, it is one of the most salient themes within writings on the 1970s and 1980s, seen as arising from the conflicting demands for a 'free economy' and a 'strong state' (Gamble, 1994). Since the intention here is not to re-rehearse familiar debates, the focus is to be upon those issues that are most distinctive to the post-Cold War era.

The specific background to conservatives' contemporary understandings is fourfold: first, the seeming triumph of a global free-market ideology following the defeat of communism; second, the legacy of conservative governments' attempts to pursue avowedly anti-statist agendas; third, the emergence of new 'post-socialist' regulatory politics and policies of the Left; and fourth, a perceived growth of moral and cultural malaise. The argument of this chapter is that the perspectives of present-day conservatives can only be understood by reference to this context, not merely inferred from general principles. What will also be shown is that the tensions that exist within conservatism regarding the state's legitimate roles cannot simply be reduced to differences between 'types' of conservative, but reflect strains within conservative agendas as a whole.

Even so, as a starting point, it is worth beginning with a general overview of conservative attitudes towards the state.

Background and perspectives

According to Tobias Lanz, 'One of the themes that has unified conservative thought over the last two hundred years is the antipathy towards the modern state' (Lanz, 2001, p. 15). However, since conservatism does not constitute a homogenous ideology, there is not a single conservative perspective on the state.

One way of distinguishing between conservative theories is in terms of a split between individualist and collectivist varieties (Greenleaf, 1973; Hoover and Plant, 1989, pp. 76–90). The former, in placing a premium on the role of free-choosing individuals within society, prioritize liberty as a core value. Consequently, they believe in the strict circumscription of state activity. The influence of this viewpoint within modern conservatism grew especially with the ascendance of economically liberal doctrines since the 1970s (Gamble, 1994, pp. 45–61).

Proponents of economic liberalism proffer a range of arguments as to why the state should be rolled back. For example, that state planning is less responsive than the discovery mechanisms of the market to ever-changing demand; that the state protects outmoded industries and practices which the market subjects to discipline; and that the state distorts prices and the labour market through regulation and subsidy. Theirs being a 'negative' view of liberty, economic liberals believe that only when individuals are allowed to make decisions free from external interference will both freedom and wealth creation be maximized.

By contrast, collectivists are more concerned with the preservation of communal values and institutions. This perspective is most common within traditionalist conservative writings. For example, Nisbet and Scruton both emphasize the promotion of authority as a central component of conservative philosophy (Nisbet, 1986, pp. 34–41; Scruton, 2001b, pp. 17–37), with any concern for freedom very much subordinate to the priority of preserving order. If individualists take relatively optimistic views of individuals' reasoning capacities, such conservatives possess more sceptical attitudes towards human nature, with strong sources of authority deemed necessary to rein in man's destructive passions. Indeed, according to Scruton, 'The state has the authority, the responsibility, and the despotism of parenthood' (Scruton, 2001b, p. 105).

For these reasons, traditionalist conservatives forward very different prescriptions to those of the free market's devotees. Worsthorne – writing on the cusp of the Thatcher era – offers a diametrically opposite diagnosis of the ills of corporatism, viewing the problems of contemporary society as resulting not from too little but from 'too much freedom'

(Worsthorne, 1978). What is required is 'not so much a splendid libertarian crusade as an ugly battle to restore some minimum of public
order' (p. 150). Pessimism regarding the intellectual and moral capacities of ordinary people often leads such conservatives to distrust democracy, favouring the vesting of authority within an elite. Worsthorne, for
example, argues for the preservation of a natural ruling class to maintain
a well-ordered society.

However, qualifications to the above picture need to be noted. First,
conservative opinion is not so neatly divisible into two camps. Both
American neoconservatives (Bell, 1978; Kristol, 1978) and British one-
nation conservatives (Gilmour, 1978) have presented more benevolent
views of the modern state than individualists, yet not simply because
they believe in constraining liberty. Such conservatives have also valued the
state's roles as provider of welfare and regulator of the economy. Their
acceptance of the welfare state is motivated by either a paternalistic
concern for the condition of the working class or fears that too much
social inequality produces instability. Equally, although they are by no
means hostile to capitalism, they worry about the dynamism of the economic sphere overflowing into the moral and social realms and thereby
undermining settled values and customs.

Furthermore, there are significant differences between the 'anarcho-
capitalism' of the most dedicated libertarians and the more modest aspirations for a limited state of mainstream free-market advocates. The
state is typically accepted by the latter as necessary to provide the framework within which the market functions, such as the rule of law and
defence against external enemies. It may also have some role in dealing
with 'market failure' in the areas of monopolies and public goods, and
offer at least minimal welfare support.

At the same time, commitment to limited government is derivable
not only from economic precepts. As much as it may be founded upon
a positive belief in individuals' reasoning capacities, it may also be
grounded in contrary anti-rationalist principles. Of most relevance here
is the argument presented by Oakeshott, who argues that human falli-
bility makes believing that the state is capable of consciously shaping
and determining collective social ends a prime example of rationalist
folly (Oakeshott, 1962). In other words, misgivings of a very different
sort to those of economic liberals may nonetheless produce similar
distrust of an extended state. Moreover, even the most authority-centred
conservatives often avow anti-statist sentiments. For example, Nisbet
worries that the enervation of traditional values may be caused not only
by the decline of authority but also by the rise of the interventionist

state (Nisbet, 1986, p. 41). As will be discussed in the next chapter, traditionalist conservatives hold the modern state culpable for weakening the institutions of civil society, such as the family, leaving them incapable of fulfilling their function of transmitting values between generations. Nor do traditionalist conservatives regard all forms of freedom dimly. In fact, it is not impossible for such conservatives to defend specific liberties, if they are conceived of as tradition-bound rather than the product of abstract reason. Burke believed that, from the Magna Carta onwards, 'it has been the uniform policy of our constitution to claim and assert our liberties, as an *entailed inheritance* derived to us from our forefathers' (Burke, 1968, p. 119). In other words, liberties that survive the test of the passage of time embody the wisdom of the ages, becoming as much a part of our historical inheritance as other values passed down by tradition.

Even American conservatives may argue that, in defending the liberties enshrined in the Constitution, they do not need to appeal to abstract principles. Following Burke, Kirk distinguishes between the aims of the French Revolutionaries – to impose untested, abstract ideals upon society – and those of their American counterparts, who sought, he argues, simply to preserve in the new world the historically accumulated liberties of the old (Kirk, 1993). Furthermore, Fleming emphasizes that the target of American conservatives' anti-statist ire 'is not the constitutional republic that took shape in the late 18th century, but the Jacobin state knocked together by Wilson and Roosevelt' (Fleming, 1997, p. 11). In other words, since the original republic was one that 'took shape' in evolutionary fashion its legacy may be defended; it is because the modern state is a very different entity – 'knocked together' with rationalist hubris – that it ought to be reviled.

Nonetheless, it is worth considering another possible division between theories of the state, between British and American perspectives. This is suggested by Robert Devigne, who argues that whereas American conservatives believe in the devolution of power – from the federal to state level – and prioritize the mediating structures of society, British conservative theory 'prescribes limiting the delegation of social policies to institutions outside the central state' (Devigne, 1994, p. 164). Citing Scruton's dismissal of those who argue for devolving power from central to local government (Scruton, 2001b, pp. 149–52), Devigne concludes that for British conservatives 'devolution is a sign of weakness rather than strength' (Devigne, 1994, p. 98).

There is certainly an element of truth in Devigne's distinction: the federal character of the American republic is responsible for a widespread attachment to the value of decentralization, and is certainly highly prized by conservatives. However, while American conservatives' preference for state instead of federal government may contrast with many British conservatives' hostility towards local authorities, this antipathy need not imply any whole-hearted attachment to the central state. In fact, it is typically less that British conservative theory demands centralization as an end in itself than that the authority of the central state is viewed as the means by which the more 'hostile' elements of civil society (such as local authorities and trade unions) may be neutralized, in the hope that this will allow the ones conservatives prefer to flourish.

British conservatives' disdain for local authorities arises principally from their suspicion, especially strong in the 1970s and 1980s, that they operate under the malignant influence of the Left. Even though he may be a critic of devolving power to local government, Scruton also argues that conservative social policy ought to focus upon institutions such as the family and schools, rather than central government (Scruton, 1996a, pp. 24–7). In fact, as will be illustrated in Chapter 3, both British and American conservatives usually profess a preference for the institutions of civil society over any level of state activity.

Lanz's contention is therefore correct to an extent, in that there are a number of bases for unity between different shades of conservative. Almost all find at least some role for the state, as custodian of law and provider of defence, while similarly sharing a distrust of its use to pursue 'utopian' or 'rationalistic' ends. Nonetheless, as will become evident, modern conservatism embodies a number of tensions as regards the proprietary roles of the state and civil society. What needs to be examined next is how the different threads of conservative argument relate, interweave and conflict in the post-Cold War period.

The onward march of freedom

There are a number of reasons for imagining the post-Cold War world to be highly favourable towards anti-statist agendas. Foremost among these, the demise of Soviet communism appeared to vindicate beyond question the superiority of free-market economics worldwide. At the same time, the final death throes of socialist and working-class parties and movements throughout the West itself added further weight to this vindication. Consequently, all varieties of statist agendas – from nationalization programmes to Keynesian demand management – appeared discredited. Feulner's contention that history has borne witness to 'the intellectual triumph of the philosophy of freedom over the various utopias of central planning' (Feulner, 1998, pp. ix–x) is one with which many conservatives concur.

Also of significance following the Cold War's conclusion is that much of the rationale that led even many conservatives to accept an extended role for the state disappeared. Since many conservatives regarded the fight against communism to be the chief priority of the post-war period, this meant accepting the political means by which it was to be waged. Writing in 1952, Buckley – a prime architect of the conservative anti-communist coalition in America – argued that conservatives would have 'to accept Big Government for the duration', including expansive military and intelligence sectors, high levels of taxation and the centralization of power in Washington; put candidly, the only way to combat the external threat of communism was 'through the instrument of a totalitarian bureaucracy within our shores' (quoted in Gottfried, 1993, p. 16). Although some libertarians rejected any such compromise, the argument for temporary acquiescence to big government was accepted by many shades of conservative opinion throughout the period of conflict. Yet as Newt Gingrich argues, 'With the end of the Cold War, the case for a strong central government has been dramatically weakened' (Gingrich, 1995, p. 102).

Of course, conservatives' acceptance of an extended state was in the past premised upon more than just the need to enlist it in the fight against communism. Throughout the twentieth century, conservatives were also motivated by pressure to accede to – along with the desire to contain – left-wing and working-class demands. With the defeat of socialism and the disaggregation of the working class, the consequent revision of the relationship between capital and labour severely eroded conservatives' need to make such compromises. With a less accommodating stance already initiated during the Thatcher–Reagan period, the further unravelling of the Left and the working class during the 1990s might be assumed to have presented the perfect opportunity for ever more radical assaults – political and intellectual – upon the state sector.

Perhaps the clearest indicator that anti-statist and free-market ideas have triumphed is their seeming acceptance by conservatives' opponents: few left-wing intellectuals any longer write of abolishing capitalism in favour of a planned economy. Furthermore, many conservatives take comfort in the fact that, even if conservative parties suffer electorally, their ideas appear to be accepted across the board. For example, Michael Barone argues that the reason left-wing politicians like Clinton and Blair enjoyed electoral successes in the 1990s was only because they embraced conservative programmes (Barone, 1997, p. 10).

Indeed, in response to Clinton's pronouncement during the 1996 presidential campaign that the era of big government was over, the *Weekly Standard* trumpeted on its front cover, 'WE WIN' (*Weekly Standard*, 1 October 1996). Similarly, Pirie argues that from a free-market standpoint, the electoral defeat of the Conservative Party in 1997 did not matter, since the victory of New Labour represented the triumph of a party equally committed to free-market beliefs (M. Pirie, interview by author, 19 June 1998).

In fact, *pace* Willetts's suggestion of a collapse of intellectual neo-liberalism, market liberal ideas have continued to be espoused strongly, especially by think-tanks such as the Adam Smith Institute and the Cato Institute. Indeed, during the 1990s a number of forceful articulations of libertarian programmes were presented – by American writers such as Gingrich (Gingrich, 1995), Murray (Murray, 1997) and David Boaz (Boaz, 1997), and British conservatives such as John Redwood (Redwood, 1993) and Alan Duncan (Duncan and Hobson, 1995).

Of note in these writings is the fact that all devote space to savouring the bankruptcy of state planning, and stress the confirmation communism's demise provides of the free market's superiority. The other most distinctive argument within contemporary free marketeers' armoury is the necessity of adapting to the realities of globalization, which will be discussed in detail in Chapter 5. However, another striking characteristic of these writings is the fact that, as much as they may emphasize the significance of contemporary developments, many take the form of a restatement of fundamental beliefs; as Gingrich argues, the Cold War's conclusion means that 'The time has come for a reversion to first principles' (Gingrich, 1995, p. 102). Seemingly in agreement with this idea, Duncan and Hobson provide a chapter-by-chapter reiteration of the basic libertarian case, bearing titles such as 'The Threat Taxation Poses to Liberty' and 'The Importance of Property Rights to Prosperity'.

Duncan and Hobson's goal is to 'liquidate' the state that has grown seemingly so inexorably, with their initial aim being no less than a halving of the state sector's present size, from approximately 40 to 20 per cent of GDP (Duncan and Hobson, 1995, pp. 395–439). The means by which this downsizing is to be achieved is via such familiar prescriptions as further privatizations, reducing taxation, deregulation and the greater use of market mechanisms in the public sector. One particularly notable element of their and other free marketeers' agendas is the argument for devolving the responsibilities of the state to the civil society sector, for example, welfare provision to voluntary organizations. The credibility of these proposals will be examined in the next chapter.

The most important target of anti-statist conservatives remains the welfare sector, especially because its growth proved one of the most intractable problems faced by conservative governments during the 1980s. Yet it is possible here to identify another difference between American and British conservatives, Barry arguing that the former focus more on the specifically moral consequences of state welfare provision (Barry, 1997, p. 339).

Certainly, this is a particular concern of American conservatives – for example, Gingrich argues that reducing welfare is a 'moral imperative' (Gingrich, 1995, p. 71; see also Himmelfarb, 1996c). One reason for this may be that the American welfare state is much smaller, in both size and scope; consequently, purely economic arguments, such as the tax burden it represents, carry less weight. Indeed, Himmelfarb is willing to admit that, since America is a rich country, 'We can afford to sustain a large population on welfare if we think it necessary and desirable' (Himmelfarb, 1995a, p. 17). However, her belief that welfare dependency has many 'de-moralizing' effects makes this, in her eyes, a far from desirable proposition. This is the reason why many neoconservatives, as noted in Chapter 1, are no longer as indulgent towards state welfare as once they claimed to be.

In fact, though, this is a key area in which harmony between moral conservative and 'rational' libertarian concerns can be identified. Undoubtedly the most influential writer to combine these elements is Murray. Arguing along utilitarian lines, Murray contends that the fundamental mistake of welfare liberals is their failure to recognize that individuals act as utility maximizers (Murray, 1984, 1990, 1996). Increasing welfare payments therefore simply increases welfare dependency, since many individuals make the rational determination that living on welfare is their most attractive life-option.

The main effect of 'over-generous' welfare programmes is, according to Murray, not the alleviation of poverty, but the underpinning of immoral lifestyles that would otherwise not be viable. In particular, it is the sustaining of single-parent families, fostering a culture of illegitimacy and family fragmentation, which is the major problem. The final result of these processes is the growth of an intransigent 'underclass' at the bottom of society. Only by severely scaling down welfare programmes will the combination of reduced incentives and resultant rejuvenation of personal morality lead to the regeneration of family and social cohesion.

Although different factors may be cited in explaining welfare dependency – other writers highlight the rise of non-working households rather than that of single-parent families – a belief in the imperative need to roll back the welfare state is common. Many have also enthusiastically adopted the underclass label to describe a feckless layer of society typified by antisocial and criminal behaviour (Himmelfarb, 1996a, p. 233). Furthermore – as Barry recognizes – it is by no means the case that British conservatives ignore the moral dimension of anti-welfare arguments. In fact, this area provides good illustration of the way in which modern British conservatives often follow American writers' lead, with many drawing upon Murray's analysis of the underclass 'problem' (Duncan and Hobson, 1995, pp. 383–4; Willetts, 1992b).

What may seem strange about the widespread adoption of the underclass label is that, historically, conservatives have often been scornful of left-wing analyses centred upon class. However, in a post-socialist context in which conventional class categories have lost much of their meaning it has become more acceptable, even to conservatives. Indeed, Himmelfarb argues that the emergence of the underclass suggests why we should be cautious about accepting Fukuyama's end of history thesis, as it reveals that the class issue has not been fully resolved by liberal democracy's triumph (Himmelfarb, 1989b, p. 26). In the light of her warning that the underclass may actually be 'subversive' of liberal democracy, again it can be seen that many conservatives did not believe, when Soviet communism disintegrated, that the end of traditional ideological conflicts heralded the arrival of an entirely conflict-free era.

The new Leviathan

Although many thinkers perceive the contemporary context to be one in which an anti-statist, individualist creed has decisively triumphed, contradictory trends may be discerned. As suggested in the previous chapter, conservatives' winning of the political battles of the past may not imply any straightforward victory for free-market beliefs.

For example, Minogue notes how railing against unrestrained individualism has become 'very much *à la mode*' (Minogue, 1994/5, p. 87). Rather than seeing themselves as unambiguous victors, even the most resolute supporters of free markets may on the contrary perceive that their arguments are not popular. Virginia Postrel, editor of *Reason*, identifies what she believes is a 'backlash' against free markets: although 'From the rhetoric, you'd think we were living in a laissez-faire country', at the same time 'intellectuals of all sorts are lining up to bash libertarians in general and markets in particular' (Postrel, 1997, p. 4). The very fact that, despite two decades of supposed hegemony for their ideas, free-market thinkers still feel the need to pen works setting out first principles is itself indicative of this sensitivity. In fact, Duncan believes that his own views are 'anti-cyclical' (Duncan, 1995, p. 21).

In other words, despite there being all but no question today that capitalism is the only viable economic system, there remains little positive support for market liberal doctrines. Consequently, although the Left's ambitions are no longer to transcend capitalism, a range of thinkers nonetheless contend that it needs to be restrained and regulated by mechanisms and values other than those of the market. For some this means a reinvigorated Keynesianism, for others the development of 'newer' frameworks and concepts, such as 'stakeholding' or a 'Third Way' between capitalism and socialism (Dionne, 1996; Giddens, 1998; Hutton, 1996). Yet common to all is the idea that allowing markets free rein is problematic, both for sustaining economic success and for achieving goals such as 'social justice'. Equally, it is far from the case that conservatives' political opponents unambiguously embrace anti-statist agendas. As E. J. Dionne notes, even when Clinton made his pronouncement of the end of the era of big government, this was followed by his 'promising a rather extensive list of things that the federal government could do' (Dionne, 1996, p. 329).

Such trends have not gone unnoticed by conservatives. For example, Jeane Kirkpatrick believes that the policies of the Clinton administration reveal that 'collectivist ideas are very strong today' (J. Kirkpatrick, interview by author, 16 September 1998). Similarly, Christopher DeMuth, President of the American Enterprise Institute, observes that, even though the intellectual underpinnings of state planning may have fallen into disrepute, the state itself continues to grow in size (DeMuth, 2000; see also McElwee and Tyrie, 2000). Furthermore, Oliver Letwin notes how although cynicism towards politicians may have become a prevalent feature of contemporary politics, a strong faith in the institution of government as solver of problems remains (O. Letwin, 1990, p. 246).

Indeed, David Henderson believes that anti-capitalist forces are as strong today as they ever were, citing a diverse array of groups and ideologies demanding capitalism's increased regulation, including anti-globalists, environmentalists and postmodernists. Upon this basis, we should recognize that 'There is no "neo-liberal hegemony"…Now as ever, liberalism, both as doctrine and as a programme of action, occupies ground that is strongly contested' (Henderson, 2000, p. 10).

What must be considered next are conservatives' responses to post-socialist arguments for extending the state's role. For example, many attack the notions of 'business ethics', 'stakeholding' and 'corporate governance', which demand businesses be made to take account of wider moral and social responsibilities, on the grounds that they create conflicts for firms with their responsibilities to shareholders and undermine their ability to operate freely within the marketplace (Johnston, 1998; Novak, 1997; Sternberg, 1998a, 1998b). As conservatives argue, these ideas require not just changes in business culture, but a growing role for the state in compelling firms to behave 'ethically'.

One difficulty conservatives have is determining whether their opponents' proposals are truly new, or simply disguised versions of older ones, with various 'old wine in new bottles' arguments much in evidence. An example of this latter mode of argument is offered by Elliott Abrams, who believes that the notion of a Third Way 'represents not a departure from outmoded and discredited ideas but at best a makeover, at worst a deception' (Abrams, 1999, p. 21). In particular, he believes that its proponents remain committed to 'big government'.

The problem with this argument is that it fails to take account of the very different context in which such ideas are today propounded, misled by the similarity of nomenclature to older notions of Third or Middle Ways. In fact, contemporary ones are very different to past doctrines that attempted to mediate between capitalist and socialist demands, since the latter are today exhausted. For example, rather than conventional economic grounds, it is more often upon moral ones that stakeholding and Third Way arguments are based.

Yet, as John O'Sullivan argues, this basis may provide even greater opportunities for the state to expand its activities:

> As the economic case for socialism evaporates moral arguments come to the fore. Intervention is urged not on grounds of greater economic efficiency, but to promote some concept of equity – race and gender quotas to remedy discrimination … or restraints on large retail stores that undermine 'community'. Unrestrained by any embarrassing test of economic success or failure, these moral interventions tend to multiply and grow vaguer. (J. O'Sullivan, 1997b, p. 9)

Indeed, he argues, a benefit for New Labour following the privatization programmes of the 1980s is that, with the state liberated from many of the responsibilities of ownership, it is much freer to impose its agendas on industry without directly bearing the consequences.

Demands for the increased regulation of morality provoke conservative reaction in relation to a variety of issues, such as calls for more stringent anti-harassment laws or to restrict 'offensive' speech. In response to these, conservatives of all types often position themselves as defenders of liberty. Columnist George Will, no radical anti-statist, condemns feminists who seek to prohibit pornography – despite agreeing that its existence leads to the coarsening of social life – on the basis that 'the First Amendment is a nullity if it protects only expression that is without consequences, or that has consequences universally considered benign' (Will, 1994, p. 30).

Unsurprisingly, libertarians argue strenuously that morality thrives best in spaces beyond the state's reach. For example, Tibor Machan claims that 'Generosity is a moral virtue that cannot flourish in a welfare state or in any sort of command economy', because it must be voluntary (Machan, 1998, p. ix). Similarly, Duncan and Hobson argue that the 'expansion of the State demoralises and poisons the life of the individual', by narrowing the opportunities for self-help and self-improvement (Duncan and Hobson, 1995, p. 363).

As noted at the outset, anti-statism may be founded upon a number of bases, with anti-rationalist conservatives equally finding much to criticize in the use of the state to promote virtue. According to Oakeshott, governing should not be 'concerned with moral right and wrong, it is not designed to make men good or even better' (Oakeshott, 1962, p. 189). This sentiment is articulated by a number of contemporary conservatives. For example, Minogue inveighs fiercely against 'hyperactive' regulationism as a response to moral decline. It is, he argues, an example of rationalist zealotry to imagine it possible 'to deal with moral collapse by the technical device of regulation' (Minogue, 1993b, p. 19). From the promotion of healthy eating to propaganda about AIDS, the mistake of rationalists is to believe that every identifiable problem can be solved by government intervention. Moreover, since there appears to be a never-ending supply of issues to be tackled, adopting this strategy means that the powers of government will simply expand indefinitely. In reality, Minogue argues, it is only through informal social mechanisms that moral behaviour is fostered.

History and tradition can also serve as bases for conservatives to resist the use of the law to regulate morality. For example, a *Spectator* editorial attacks the moralizing agenda of New Labour on the basis that 'the invocation of the law to make people fulfil their duties to themselves and to others is merely a reminder of how far removed we are from the private lives and public spiritedness of a century ago' (*Spectator*, 1995, p. 7). As will be argued in subsequent chapters, there is some romanticism in conservatives' historical conceptions of an independent and virtuous public sphere. Nonetheless, invoking the spirit of this – even if idealized – past, provides conservatives grounds for rejecting the notions that moral behaviour or good citizenship can be created by government dictat.

Another significant new argument for greater state regulation derives from theories of the 'risk society', implying that an ever-increasing and unpredictable array of social, environmental and economic dangers has come to confront society (Giddens, 1994). To cope with the more complex and unstable nature of the modern world requires not only greater caution but also the development of new regulatory mechanisms to curb the risks generated by science and business.

A number of conservatives challenge these arguments. For example, Mark Neal and Christie Davies critique a range of 'techno-moral panics' centred upon health and environmental scares – concerning subjects from nuclear power to genetically modified food – to expose the irrationality of the notion that the world has become a more unpredictable or hazardous place (Neal and Davies, 1998). The fact that in most parts of the world people live longer and healthier than ever before is held to demonstrate that 'Modern society is by any standard of comparison far less risky than any in the past' (p. 43). Health and environmental alarmism, they argue, not only is irrational but also does not justify expanding the state's regulatory role.

However, advocates of risk awareness typically found their arguments upon more than just empirical claims. Giddens, a key theorist of both risk and the Third Way, willingly concedes that life has not become more risky in an empirically measurable sense (Giddens, 1994, p. 4). Rather, what has occurred in our post-traditional age is that the sources and scope of risk have changed. That is, society has experienced a rise in manufactured risk, that which 'is a result *of* human intervention into the conditions of social life and into nature'. The significance of this is that human activity is believed to produce more far-reaching and uncertain effects than the risks of earlier ages.

By contrast, Neal and Davies argue that risks that exist today are in fact less dangerous than were those of the past. Whereas in earlier times risks commonly took the form of the invisible and mysterious – for example, bacteria and viruses – contemporary risks are more visible, and thus more amenable to human understanding (Neal and Davies, 1998, p. 43). Moreover, thanks to the advances of modern science, solutions to the problems created by contemporary risks, manufactured or otherwise, are far more likely and quickly to be found. Again, heightened risk awareness does not warrant an increase in state regulation.

Protecting society from health and environmental dangers is widely recognized by conservatives to underpin their opponents' arguments for increasing the power of the state. For example, John Patten – writing prior to the 1997 general election – describes what he imagines a New Labour Britain would be like as a result of the Left's preoccupation with safety:

> '[R]egulationism', with which Tories have to struggle hard enough when in government, would be unbound. The new Labour world would be perfectly harmonised, hygienic, safe, every element neatly labelled and run by a new-style burgeoning salariat, political correctness made flesh. It would also be perfectly dreadful, a 'Nurseryland' Britain. (J. Patten, 1995, p. 254)

Patten's mention of 'a new-style burgeoning salariat' highlights another significant concern of contemporary conservatives, which is with the nature of the elite that today control's society. In respect to this, John O'Sullivan's argument is again of interest, in his employment of the concept of a 'new class'.

Among conservatives, the idea of a new class was most notably adopted by neoconservatives in the 1960s, to explain the anti-capitalist sentiments they believed informed the reforming programmes of the era (Gerson, 1996, pp. 233–6). What they argued is that a left-wing intellectual elite had come to occupy the leading positions within society – in the media, academia, the economy and government – that sought to impose its agenda, despite its anti-capitalist antagonism holding little authority in the rest of society. O'Sullivan argues that today's 'new New Left' of intellectuals and regulators can similarly be characterized as constituting a new class, with politicians like Clinton and Blair its champions. In particular, he focuses on the anti-democratic quality of this elite:

> Everywhere this class seeks to extend its power through law, regulation and opinion management, and to emancipate itself from popular control by transferring powers from living democratic bodies to remote bureaucracies, the courts, quangos, new untested institutions and international bodies. (J. O'Sullivan, 1997b, p. 9)

Having power in not only public but also private bureaucracies, this class seeks to regulate 'not merely the economy but an ever-expanding area of social life'.

The idea of a new class holds widespread attraction for present-day conservatives, in allowing them to explain why society may be running counter to their preferred visions (for example, McElwee, 2000).

Himmelfarb's belief that the new class 'is the mirror image of the "underclass"' (Himmelfarb, 1996a, p. 244) reveals well conservatives' anxiety that their favoured middle-class values are being squeezed by antagonistic forces from both above and below.

Long-time advocate of new-class theory Irving Kristol also continues to employ the term, noting as well the use of health and environmental panics to justify increasing state regulation (Kristol, 1991). Its ideology is difficult to define, and therefore defeat, he claims, because 'it is both post-capitalist and post-socialist' (p. 151). Furthermore, the gravest of diagnoses may be forwarded. For example, Robert Bork argues that the baleful influence of those occupying the 'commanding heights' of the culture is today so pervasive, and possessing such authority in relation to society's morality, 'that it is not entirely accurate to call the United States a majoritarian democracy' (Bork, 1995, p. 141).

Whatever credibility new-class arguments may have in explaining the contemporary expansion of state regulation, it is nonetheless question- able whether the disparate array of adversary individuals conservatives cite constitute anything so coherent as a class. The notion of a new 'class' imputes too great a consciousness and unity to its purported members. As Kristol himself admits, the new class 'is a vague term' (Kristol, 1991, p. 148). Yet, he argues, 'no useful purpose is served by try- ing to give it too precise a meaning'; instead, 'one recognises its mem- bers when one sees them'. In fact, greater precision would serve useful purposes, not least to prevent such theories edging into the realms of conspiracy theory, with scheming liberals believed to be controlling and manipulating virtually every sector of society.

Further issues of contemporary moment are constitutional questions. In Britain, recent years have witnessed a surge of agitation around con- stitutional issues – including demands for the 'modernization' of the monarchy and the House of Lords, regional devolution and a written bill of rights – prompting in response a number of rejoinders by conserva- tives (Lansley and Wilson, 1997; Mawhinney, 1996; Mount, 1992). A fea- ture of current proposals that may be especially distinctive is the extent of change considered by conservatives' opponents. Digby Anderson sees the range of reforms placed on the political agenda by New Labour – from proportional representation to the break-up of the Union – as revealing an important difference with Labour programmes of the past (D. Anderson, interview by author, 22 June 1998). That is, because previ- ous Labour governments concentrated their attentions on economic issues, such as taxation and wealth redistribution, even though they were supposedly much more radical they never seriously contemplated the far-reaching constitutional changes considered by the present Labour administration. In other words, the changed focus of politics in the post-Cold War world may be what is responsible for giving agitation for constitutional reform its increased impetus.

In framing their critiques, many conservatives draw upon Burke, especially his belief that a society's real constitution resides in its culture and traditions, rather than explicitly stated principles (Burke, 1968, pp. 99–122). For example, John Patten argues against a written constitution and a bill of rights on the grounds that 'human affairs are too complex to be absolutely codified. Explicit principles are abridgements of practice' (J. Patten, 1995, p. 58). A culture of liberty, he argues, is something that either does or does not exist within a society; governments or constitutions cannot simply create it.

According to Minogue, the 'constitutional mania' of reformers represents an effort to embark upon a dangerous programme of social engineering (Minogue, 1993a). Charles Moore, editor of the *Daily Telegraph*, also articulates a widespread misgiving of conservatives, in arguing that the peril inherent in following the prescriptions of constitutional reformers is that they lead us into 'uncharted waters' (C. Moore, interview by author, 14 July 1998). Thus, even though conservatives may be sceptical about risk aversion in some spheres, they counsel its adoption in others.

Conservatives also emphasize the potentially anti-democratic character of current constitutional reforms. As O'Sullivan argues, although measures such as devolution for Wales and Scotland, and the ceding of powers to Europe, may be advanced in the name of strengthening democracy, their overall effect is to weaken Britain's central democratic institution, Parliament (J. O'Sullivan, 1997b, p. 9). Even the issue of a written constitution may be attacked on democratic grounds. For example, Patten worries that codifying rights in law means handing over the arbitration of disputes from society at large, as occurs with informally possessed liberties, to the courts (J. Patten, 1995, p. 58).

The question of who possesses jurisdiction over the exercise and interpretation of rights and liberties raises different issues in the American context by virtue of its written constitution. For this reason, American conservatives appeal less to an informal understanding of freedom to defend against the expansion of the state than to a strict adherence to the Constitution's original meaning. As Bork puts it, 'only the approach of original understanding meets the criteria that any theory of constitutional adjudication must meet in order to possess democratic legitimacy' (Bork, 1990, p. 143). Moreover, belief in 'original intent' appears to unite all varieties of conservative, from traditionalists (Bradford, 1994; Carey, 1995) to libertarians (Murray, 1997, p. xi).

A libertarian argument that may be derived from this doctrine is that, since the powers assigned by the Constitution to federal government for public expenditure are highly limited – specified purposes being those such as defence – the majority of federal spending, including health and education programmes, should be attacked by conservatives as unconstitutional (S. Moore, 1995).

However, while there are numerous aspects to the interpretative debates around the Constitution, the issue of most interest here is what conservatives identify as the problem of 'judicial activism', that is, their belief that rather than simply enforcing the law as a set of impartial, non-instrumental rules, the judiciary today takes an active 'political' role in actually creating law. According to Bork, judicial activism arises as a result of the new class's failure to achieve its goals through electoral means; consequently, it turns to the courts as an alternative avenue to accomplish them (R. Bork, interview by author, 10 September 1998).

The most theorized positions critical of this development are those of Strauss's disciples (Mansfield, 1991; Pangle, 1992). What contemporary Straussians reject is the postmodern assumption believed to undergird the malady of judicial activism: that the Constitution is simply a 'text', to be deconstructed according to whatever subjective interpretation the reader wishes to impose. The major danger with this approach is that it is believed to be a strategy of the Left to further the agendas of favoured interest groups, such as feminists. By contrast, Straussians argue for a definite, settled reading that rules out the subjective claims of particular interests.

Indicative of the sense in which many American conservatives perceive themselves to be lone voices in a world gone morally awry, the introduction to one symposium on judicial activism – suggesting with dismay that 'unconstitutional' rulings on issues such as abortion and euthanasia may imply a literal usurpation of politics by the judiciary – is moved to ask 'whether we have reached or are reaching the point where conscientious citizens can no longer give moral assent to the existing regime' (*First Things*, 1996, p. 18). That is, if the present regime is so thoroughly morally bankrupt, have the foundations of political obligation been dissolved? A similar sentiment is expressed by Fleming who is dismissive of the lack of 'backbone' of mainstream conservatives: 'For a real right to develop, it would require men and women willing to be viewed as virtual criminals ... To be genuinely radical, we have to accept the fact of being enemies of the regime, of being criminals, of being outlaws' (Fleming, 1997, p. 11).

Of course, most conservatives distance themselves from such extreme suggestions; as, for example, do William Bennett and Midge Decter in a follow-up symposium to the one cited above (*First Things*, 1997, pp. 19–24). Yet it is a measure of how antagonistic many American conservatives perceive the dominant political culture to be that they can be found debating such propositions at all.

'Big government Conservatism'

According to Fukuyama, a key reason for seeing libertarianism as bankrupt is that the terrorist attack of 11 September 2001 on the World Trade Center reminded 'Americans of why government exists, and why it has to tax citizens and spend money to promote collective interests' (Fukuyama, 2002). Prosecuting the 'war on terror', therefore, may again require suspending hostility to big government for the duration. However, what will be demonstrated in this section is that among many conservatives hostility had already been suspended long before this date.

For anti-statist conservatives, one of the hardest questions to answer is accounting for the state's growth. Especially difficult for them to explain are the records of conservative governments during the 1980s and 1990s. Simon Jenkins provides a detailed account of the Conservative Party's signal failure to diminish the British state sector during its time in power, despite repeated declarations that it intended to do so (Jenkins, 1995). Not only did the Conservatives fail to reduce its size in terms of share of GDP but also the extensive framework of regulation put in place to oversee the industries it privatized meant that changing ownership did not mean government relinquishing all control. Thus,

> the scope of the state that is left behind has remained persistently above 40 per cent, forced upwards by a roughly doubled level of real spending on the welfare state. Add this to the government-regulated but privately owned monopolies and what might be termed the 'state penumbra' has widened rather than contracted since 1979. (p. 243)

The centralization of power in spheres such as education, health, housing and the police meant that regulation of the remaining public sector also increased; furthermore, as the powers of elected local government were reduced, 'quangos' – unelected and unaccountable public bodies – proliferated under Conservative rule (pp. 264–5).

Many conservatives are well aware that the state did not shrink during the Conservatives' time in office. For example, Duncan and Hobson are candid in recognizing the Conservatives' failure to make major inroads into the size of the state (Duncan and Hobson, 1995, pp. 64–7, 83–8). Moreover, in spheres other than the economy, conservative politicians are also judged to have failed; Charles Moore argues that 'the attempt to get the state out of people's lives did not succeed except in the very strictly economic sphere' (C. Moore, interview by author, 14 July 1998).

A comparable story may be told about the American experience of conservative government during the 1980s. In fact, a significant increase in the share of the national product accounted for by the state sector occurred, rising from 31.7 to 36.1 per cent of GDP over the period of 1979 to 1989 (O'Shaughnessy, 1994, p. 94). Moreover, Reagan too was a great centralizer, garnering to federal government increased control over areas such as education, health and financial regulation (Frum, 1994, pp. 32–56).

Despite a seeming reinvigoration of free-market ideas occurring with the Gingrich-led Republican capture of Congress in 1994, the 'radical' agenda of Gingrich's Contract with America rapidly unravelled and dis-integrated (Frum, 1997a, pp. 29–35). Lastly, the acquiescence of George W. Bush to maintaining the welfare programmes of the past leads Will to believe that 'The conservatism that defined itself in reaction against the New Deal – minimal government conservatism – is dead' (Will, 2002).

Conservatives often argue that the changes made by conservative politicians nonetheless represent an improved state of affairs over that of previous eras. For example, Willets defends the regulation of Britain's privatized utilities as preferable to direct ministerial control on the grounds that decision-making is depoliticized (D. Willetts, interview by author, 22 June 1998). Of course, what is depoliticization to one person is to another a lack of accountability and democratic oversight. This argument also undermines conservatives' own criticisms of left-wing varieties of regulationism: the difference between conservative-approved forms and those of their opponents is far from clear. Moreover, the fact that Minogue's critique cited earlier was written during the Major era of government reveals that 'hyperactive regulationism' is not simply the preserve of the Left.

A number of explanations are typically advanced for conservative politicians' failures. For example, David Green – former Director of the Institute of Economic Affairs's Health and Welfare Unit – contends that, despite the rhetoric and apart from the privatization programmes, the Conservative Party simply made no concerted effort to reduce the state sector (D. G. Green, interview by author, 22 June 1998). In relation to the American context, DeMuth argues that although the Reagan administration made some headway in rolling back the state, the problem was that it had to share power with others in Congress who did not agree with its ambitions (C. DeMuth, interview by author, 16 October 1998).

However, the major flaw in conservative analyses lies in their attributing of responsibility for the growth of the state during the twentieth century all but solely to their opponents. For example, Willetts lays the blame squarely at the door of liberals and socialists, with culpable conservative politicians regarded simply as too weak, or otherwise unwilling, to resist the rise of collectivism (Willetts, 1992a, pp. 3–46). Conservatives' responsibilities for the state's expansion are seen as at best deviations from true principles, at worst forms of collaboration with the enemy.

The problem with such arguments is that they neglect the fact that using the state need not be an aberration from 'real' conservative principles; as seen at the beginning, not all strands of conservative ideology are hostile to an expanded role for the state. Moreover, the reasons behind even more ideologically committed conservative governments' lack of success in effecting a reduction in the state's size, can hardly be accounted for entirely in terms of the strength of their opponents. Instead, account must also be taken of the market's inability to fulfil such functions as the provision of welfare for large sections of society without the state's support; Willetts, for example, neglects in his attack on Macmillan and the Middle Way (Willetts, 1992a, pp. 30–1) that conservatives' acceptance of the welfare state at the time arose in the midst of an economic slump.

Furthermore, with the Thatcher and Reagan governments having implemented the most obvious privatizations and free-market reforms, and yet still failing to achieve a major rolling back of the state, it is difficult to see what realistic possibility there is for the severe reduction in its size radical free marketeers like Duncan and Hobson envisage. Contemporary libertarian agendas appear to amount to little more than calls for a redoubling of efforts, as if the question were merely one of political will.

However, a different response to the failure of conservative governments to reduce the size of the state is instead pragmatic acceptance. For example, at the start of the 1990s, Fred Barnes articulated a vision of 'big government conservatism' predicated on the belief that 'big government is a fact of life' (Barnes, 1991, p. 66). Since Reagan was the most ideologically conservative president for a half century, 'A good rule of thumb is that if Ronald Reagan couldn't get rid of a government program or agency, nobody can; it's here for life.' The aim of the big government conservative, he argues, is not to waste time trying to reduce the size of the state, but instead to make sure it fulfils conservative rather than liberal ends. In similar vein, William Kristol disagrees that 'big government per se' is at the root of contemporary problems, believing that it is rather the character of government policy that is important (W. Kristol, interview by author, 20 October 1998).

These stances create significant tensions within the conservative camp. For example, Frum is perturbed that 'quite a number of influential and visible conservatives have shown a dismaying willingness to throw in the towel on the Big Government issue', citing Bennett and Irving Kristol as other representatives of this trend (Frum, 1997a, p. 62). Charles Kesler is similarly disappointed at the apparent rise of big government conservatism since George W. Bush's accession to power, with conservatives seemingly all too willing to make compromises with welfare liberalism (Kesler, 2002).

Yet it is not only pragmatism that leads conservatives to accept big government. For conservatives who have always disdained economic liberalism, the statist orientation of the post-socialist Left may even be regarded in a positive light. Worsthorne, for example, argues that a regulated form of capitalism is far preferable to the 'capitalist triumphalism' of the Thatcher era. He thus commends the politics of New Labour, on the basis that it aims at 'stopping, or at any rate, regulating change, which is why I, and so many other small "c" conservatives, fearful of the erosions wrought by capitalism in everything we hold dear, are attracted to it' (Worsthorne, 1997, p. 34).

In fact, fears about these erosions are widespread among conservatives. For example, Lanz believes that the ideology of capitalism, with its commitment to materialism and neglect of tradition, is 'profoundly anti-conservative' (Lanz, 2001, p. 15). Indeed, a number agree with Worsthorne that it is necessary to repudiate past conservative orthodoxies. Thus, near the end of the 1990s, William Schambra wrote scathingly of the fact that 'conservatism wasted much of this century futilely extolling the virtues of rugged individualism and the untrammeled marketplace' (Schambra, 1998, p. 46).

The rejection, or at least qualification, of free-market liberalism is also prevalent among British conservatives. As one commentator suggests, 'One of the ironies of contemporary politics is that British Conservatives are almost as eager to denigrate the 1980s as US Democrats' (Prowse, 1994). For example, in arguing for a consensual doctrine of the social market, Chris Patten downgrades an emphasis upon assertive individualism (C. Patten, 1991), while David Hunt expresses concern about social atomization and dismisses outright laissez-faire (Hunt, 1994).

One explanation for conservatives' attempts to distance themselves from free-market liberalism may be found in the practical failings of free-market programmes, and not only in reducing the size of the state. Charles Leadbeater argued at the beginning of the 1990s – when the idea of the social market was the popular vehicle for anti-individualist thinking – that the social market's elevation to the high ground of British politics was 'the most important political consequence of the recession' (Leadbeater, 1991, p. 20). In other words, its failure to deliver on the promise of prosperity may be one reason why conservatives may not wish to associate themselves with economic liberalism.

However, while recession was certainly a feature of the early 1990s, this does not explain the continuing efforts of conservatives ever since to shift their focus away from the market. In fact, Barry's interpretation of the emergence of ideas such as the social market is most to the point, as representing attempts 'to soften the harsher edges of economic liberalism' (Barry, 1996, p. 69). That is, it is frequently a defensive manoeuvre. As will be detailed in the next chapter, various forms of communitarian and compassionate conservatism are central for many, regardless of changing economic fortunes.

By no means all conservatives see the qualification of a purely individualist ideology as necessarily implying a recourse to statism. Willetts, for example, although seeking to supplement a free-market philosophy with more social concerns, rejects the social market label precisely because the 'social' component often implies a turn to the state (Willetts, 1994, p. 24). Even so, Walter Olson – noting 'how tense' relations between libertarians and traditionalists have become – is correct in arguing that, 'In recent years a sizable phalanx of trad[itionalist] writers and thinkers has emerged who on principle, it seems, reject an appeal to such concepts as liberty, rights, individualism, and choice in resolving questions about the appropriate domestic scope of government' (Olson, 1997, p. 41).

The restoration of authority

It is not simply pragmatism or a reaction against free-market beliefs that may lead contemporary conservatives to take less enthusiastic stances towards liberalizing agendas. The desire to uphold authority – political and moral – is also grounds; indeed, conservatives may even be persuaded of the need to increase the state's power. In terms of conservatives who have always believed authority to be of central importance, Scruton is once more of interest. According to Scruton, the end of the Cold War means that conservatives actually have less reason to present themselves as defenders of freedom. During the era of Cold War conflict, when 'freedom meant "freedom from communist oppression"', it was a value conservatives needed to propound; however, 'with the collapse of the Soviet Empire and the emergence of a left-liberal consensus, the old battle-cry does nothing to distinguish conservatism from its rivals' (Scruton, 2001b, p. 6). In other words, conservatism should return to its older priorities, of defending order and authority.

Also again worth considering is Worsthorne. Worsthorne is dismayed at the fact that the authority of Britain's traditional ruling class has been severely eroded in recent decades, not only by the egalitarianism of post-war social democracy but also by the entrepreneurialism of the Thatcher years (P. Worsthorne, interview by author, 8 May 1998). As a result, he puts a very different interpretation on the emergence of a new class to John O' Sullivan, seeing in the rise of a New Labour intelligentsia the welcome possibility of reconstituting at least some form of authoritative elite:

> For just as Lord Salisbury took it for granted that a civilised society required people of a superior culture and education to do the governing and administering, so does Mr Blair, the main difference being that whereas the former entrusted the task to an old ruling class – which had been in situ for generations – the latter intends to entrust it to a new ruling class very much of his own making ... a new breed of highly educated Guardians (pun intended). (Worsthorne, 1997, p. 34)

Worsthorne is ambivalent about this development – after all, these 'Guardians' are not the traditional ruling class he has always known and believed in – but nonetheless Blairite managerialism is to be preferred to the pernicious meritocractic vision of Thatcherite ideology. (Although, after only a year of New Labour in office, Worsthorne had already become less sanguine regarding the potential of 'New Labour man' – P. Worsthorne, interview by author, 8 May 1998.)

However, other types of conservative also believe that a strengthening of authority is desirable. The pressing urgency accorded by many conservatives to combating cultural decay will be examined in Chapter 4, but a number of examples may be cited here of how this leads them to believe that the state is necessary to underwrite moral authority. For example, Bork argues that since 'government has withdrawn from the moral sphere ... we have a state of moral chaos' (R. Bork, interview by author, 10 September 1998). Although not wanting activist judges to pass moral judgements, Bork is not above asking government to do so – with society seemingly 'slouching towards Gomorrah', state censorship of films, television and the arts may be warranted to stop the cultural rot (Bork, 1996).

Similarly, Himmelfarb argues that the depth of society's 'de-moralization' today means that conservatives need to rethink their belief that rolling back the state and allowing markets free rein will automatically restore social and moral values (Himmelfarb, 1996a, pp. 246–8). Arguing against the claim that it is not possible to legislate morality, Himmelfarb prescribes just this. Leaving aside the truth or falsity of this proposition, it can be seen that far from all conservatives agree that the use of the law to enforce morality is misguided (see also Geisler and Turek, 1998).

As Dinesh D'Souza concludes, the anxieties of conservative writers on cultural malaise may be explained by the fact that they 'have lost their faith in the American people', seeing them as either foolish or depraved (D'Souza, 1997, p. 264). Yet a further question that may be put to statist cultural conservatives is that, as Irwin Stelzer argues, if they are willing to ask government to intervene in the moral sphere, why not also accept the need for economic regulation – to 'dull' the harsh edge of the knife of competition – to fulfil their moral goals? (Stelzer, 1997, pp. 85–97). Why, for example, not embrace notions such as stakeholding or business ethics? In other words, once support is given to state intervention in one sphere, it becomes far less tenable to reject it in others.

As will be seen in following chapters, pessimism regarding the current state of morality is most deeply felt by American conservatives. However, many British conservatives are far from unconcerned about its decline. For example, Margaret Thatcher also worries about too much freedom being responsible for a rising 'licentiousness' and 'coarsening' of the culture: 'liberty decays into licence in an atmosphere where all is permitted and nothing prohibited' (Thatcher, 1997b, p. 50). Order, authority and restraint, we are reminded, are the necessary complements to freedom. Moreover, Duncan and Hobson's decidedly non-liberal concerns at the relaxation of laws on abortion, divorce and censorship (Duncan and Hobson, 1995, pp. 314–26) attest to a highly qualified view of which aspects of state activity even libertarians may wish to include in any project of 'liquidation'.

Furthermore, a libertarian solution to the problem of welfare dependency is not the only one favoured. For example, Lawrence Mead rejects the claim of writers like Murray that the answer is to be found in the alteration of incentive structures (Mead, 1992, pp. 134–6). The supposition that individuals are basically rational utility maximizers ignores, he argues, the fact that welfare recipients are so corrupted by their experience of state welfare that their competence to function as normal, rational citizens is impaired. Hoping to effect change by eliminating the rational basis for remaining on welfare is therefore a mistake, since dependency is not a rational choice.

Although Mead opposes state welfare provision, his proposed solution is very different to that of libertarians, in that he wishes the state to adopt a more rather than less interventionist role. Specifically, what he advocates is 'workfare', with government obligating welfare recipients to partake in schemes designed to inculcate a work ethic. Like Bork and Himmelfarb, he desires a reduction in liberty – at least for the unemployed – and an increase in the state's authority. Unashamed to be espousing a form of authoritarian 'paternalism', he maintains that 'the solution to the work problem seems to lie, not in freedom, but in governance' (p. 181).

At least some conservatives have also come to recognize that antagonism towards the state may, in a climate of widespread social cynicism, undermine one of the key pillars of their own ideology, respect for the established order. For example, Will notes the 'contradiction' inherent in the fact that conservatives who advocate disrespect for government often neglect that conservatism itself 'depends on respect, even reverence, for our political regime' (Will, 1996, p. 44). This contradiction is equally relevant to understanding the dilemmas faced by British conservatives, in the light of the acute decline of respect experienced by established British institutions in recent times. As John Patten observes:

> The undermining of institutions in the United Kingdom seems in the mid-1990s to be endemic. Almost all the players in our constitutional arrangements are under attack, and their standing diminished, with the sole exception of the armed forces. It is an urgent task for the whole of the country, and not just a political party, to rekindle respect for our institutions. (J. Patten, 1995, p. 52)

Although Patten suggests that rekindling respect for traditional institutions is a task for the whole country, its extinguishing clearly has particular moment for conservatives. That is, since the constitutional arrangements he cites – including the Union and the monarchy – have always been the traditional bedrocks upon which British conservatism has grounded its appeals (Cannadine, 1994; Schwarz, 1997), any diminishing of respect for them poses an especially stark problem for conservatives. This being the case, while it may be one thing to attack the state in the abstract, many of the actual institutions of which it is composed are ones conservatives very much need to defend.

Finally, it should be understood that tensions within conservative ranks regarding attitudes towards the state do not simply correspond to a straightforward split between traditionalists and libertarians. For example, paleoconservative M. E. Bradford contends that most conservatives have become little more than collaborators with the Left in their willingness to use the state to achieve their goals; consequently, he feels more sympathy with libertarians than with other social conservatives (Bradford, 1991). Similarly, Fleming believes that is possible to forge 'a tactical alliance' with libertarians upon the basis of a common interest in rolling back government, which he argues is no longer shared by mainstream and neo-varieties of conservative (T. Fleming, interview by author, 2 October 1998). While it is questionable how stable such an alliance might be – as seen, conservatives like Fleming have very different reasons for disdaining the state to libertarians – these arguments confirm not only the suggestion of an increased factiousness among conservatives, but also that conventional divisions may be deficient.

Conclusion

One feature of contemporary debates worth highlighting at this stage is the perhaps surprising fact that many present-day conservatives appear to adopt highly 'humanistic' standpoints, defending liberty, rationality and the taking of risks, while their opponents, in counselling restraint, regulation and risk aversion, often appear to be much more sceptical towards human endeavour. Of course, this is not always the case: as also seen, many conservatives reject taking 'risks' with constitutional reform, or have lost faith in the moral character of individuals. Nonetheless, this is a theme that will be returned to in future chapters.

Overall, what has been shown is that the particular context of the post-Cold War world pulls conservatives in divergent directions: for some, it suggests the possibilities for ever-more radical market liberal programmes; for others, that an expanded state must simply be accepted as a unalterable reality; while for further writers, the need for restrictions on laissez-faire capitalism and individual freedom seems greater than ever. In other words, differences between conservatives over the role of the state and the priority that should be accorded liberty continue to provoke tensions, and often in more polarized form than in the past. However, one of the themes to be explored in the next chapter is conservatives' hopes that by focusing upon the sphere of civil society, a way out may be found from the hazards of either a pure individualism or an authoritarian statism.

3
Rediscovering the Little Platoons: Civil Society and Community

As indicated in the previous chapter, for many conservatives it is the realms existing beyond the state that are believed to play the most important roles in the formation and maintenance of a stable society of sound moral order. Indeed, Scruton believes that 'conservatism originates in an attitude to civil society' (Scruton, 2001b, p. 17), rather than to the state. The purpose of this chapter is to explore the roles played by the concepts of civil society and community in conservative thought, in particular to highlight the ways in which these have become especially central motifs for post-Cold War conservatism.

Of course, civil society and community are concepts that have become immensely fashionable throughout contemporary social and political discourses; moreover, interest in them has spread beyond purely academic discussions to find much wider favour. This can be seen across the political spectrum. As one commentator observes: 'civil society is hot. It is almost impossible to read an article on foreign or domestic politics without coming across some mention of the concept ... politicians of all stripes routinely sing its praises' (Zakaria, 1995, p. 1). A similar observation may be made regarding community: the 'word *community* has found a place, however fuzzy and imprecise, all over the ideological spectrum' (Ehrenhalt, 1995, p. 17).

This being so, much of what will be considered in this chapter will not pertain uniquely to conservatism. A further objective, therefore, is to distinguish what is distinctive in conservative uses: primarily, how the condition of the social fabric is believed to relate to all manner of issues concerning moral, cultural and economic malaise. What will again be seen is that the commitments of present-day conservatives do not always straightforwardly correspond to those suggested by conventional divisions. Finally, the problems that are raised for conservatives by their

usages of the concepts will be examined, problems which help illumi-
nate many of the wider difficulties faced by conservatives in the
post-Cold War era.

Reclaiming a tradition

Writers tracing the history of the concept of civil society usually note
that, although it is one with a long lineage, since Hegel – or at least since
Marx's critique of Hegel – interest in it fell into decline, only more
recently returning to the forefront of attention (Cohen and Arato, 1992,
pp. 1–26; Shils, 1991, pp. 5–8). One of the main impetuses behind this
resurgence of interest has been the efforts to determine the values and
institutions necessary for the transition of former Soviet societies into
Western-style capitalist ones. However, most significant for this chapter
is the subsequent reflection this has led to upon the condition of
Western societies themselves. For example, Green states in the introduction to his study of British civil society that:

> This book began as an attempt to consider the lessons the former
> communist countries of Eastern Europe might be able to learn from
> Western experience of voluntary welfare provision. But, as the study
> proceeded, it quickly became obvious that we in the West have done
> almost as much harm to our own voluntary associations as the
> communist countries. (Green, 1993, p. viii)

At the same time communitarianism, having originated within academic debates of the 1970s and 1980s, has also come to provide a more
widely adopted paradigm for understanding the condition of society,
communitarians' concerns in many respects mirroring those of writers
on civil society. Within this context, thinkers such as Robert Bellah,
Amitai Etzioni and Robert Putnam have sought to re-introduce a vocabulary of civil society and community into political and social discourses
(Bellah et al., 1985; Etzioni, 1995; Putnam, 1995, 2000).

Taking a critical stance on this development, Hobsbawm suggests that
'calls for an otherwise unidentified "civil society", for "community"'
represent 'the voice of lost and drifting generations' (Hobsbawm, 1994,
p. 11). Certainly, it is striking how many of these modern discussions are
framed around a notion of decline: that is, a perceived decline of communal sentiments, civic engagement and a sense of social and moral
obligations. In parallel to – and in large measure viewed as cause of – this
degeneration has been the supposed rise of an aggressive and socially

destabilizing individualism. Indeed, over many accounts hangs the spectre of a descent into Hobbesian anarchy; with the decay of the values of neighbourliness, trust and responsibility comes the ever-increasing prospect of individuals pitted against each other in bitter conflict (Walzer, 1991, p. 293).

The present popularity of communitarianism has not gone unnoticed by conservatives. For example, Joshua Abramowitz believes that it is 'a good time to be a communitarian ... the philosophy [is] *au courant* in the press and in academia' (Abramowitz, 1993, p. 119). Even libertarians may consider it 'the dominant political tendency of our times' (Duncan and Hobson, 1995, p. xiv). Similarly, many conservatives – such as Willetts and James Q. Wilson – have proved receptive to communitarian thinking, welcoming its ascendancy and drawing upon it for support (Willetts, 1992a, p. 189; J. Q. Wilson, 1993, p. 248). Conservative journals have also opened their pages to communitarians – for example, the *Public Interest* (Etzioni, 1994).

Equally, it is possible to argue that in fact 'communitarians are conservatives' (Abramowitz, 1993, p. 119). It is not difficult to see how a number might easily be assigned the 'conservative' label, with Etzioni owning to a highly conservative position on moral and social questions (Etzioni, 1994), and Alasdair MacIntyre seeking to recover pre-Enlightenment traditions of ethical discourse (MacIntyre, 1985). Among British communitarians, Henry Tam expresses sympathy for a conservative philosophy in the spirit of Hume and Burke (Tam, 1998, pp. 34–6).

With some justification, conservatives may lay claim to primogeniture in terms of many of the ideas to be found in modern communitarian and civil society discussions. For example, criticism of the atomizing effects of liberal individualism can be traced back to the conservative reaction to the French Revolution. Conservatives thus frequently display a distinct annoyance at the disregard shown to their contributions; for example, Novak takes academic communitarians to task for ignoring the long conservative tradition of upholding the idea of community (Novak, 1989, pp. 123–9).

In attempting to reclaim – as well as gain authority from – this tradition, conservative writings abound with references to Burke's belief that the first principle of social feeling is to be attached to the 'little platoon' (Lawlor, 1992, p. 27; Willetts, 1992a, p. 67; Zinmeister, 1996, p. 4). Equally common is to be reminded of Tocqueville's claim that small-scale 'associations' are essential to a democracy's survival (Eberly, 1998, p. 44; Gingrich, 1995, p. 103; Schambra, 1994, p. 35). What these thinkers are lauded for is the priority they gave to the local and particular, as against the universalism of their Enlightenment-inspired contemporaries.

Of modern interest, one of the most significant intellectual sources for contemporary conservatives is the work of Nisbet, a champion of the idea of community some decades before the emergence of academic communitarianism (Nisbet, 1953). Furthermore, many neoconservatives of the 1960s and 1970s also displayed degrees of unease about a purely individualist form of capitalism. Most significant for the present discussion is the work of Berger and Neuhaus, who argued that the massive expansion of the state has caused enormous social damage by eroding the buffers that exist between it and the individual, such as neighbourhood and voluntary organizations (Berger and Neuhaus, 1977). These they termed 'mediating institutions', with this conception proving particularly influential upon subsequent conservative understandings of civil society.

While conservative discussion of themes relating to civil society and community is hardly therefore a new development, what is notable today is the prominence given to the concepts. The widespread popularity of the notions may lead some conservatives to be cautious – as Murray argues, 'civil society has become such a trendy phrase that I'm almost embarrassed to be caught using it' (C. Murray, interview by author, 22 September 1998) – yet, nonetheless, they are ubiquitous within conservative arguments.

Probably the most obvious variety of conservative to be proponents of a communitarian philosophy is those most committed to a traditionalist perspective. Good examples of this type are Scruton (Scruton, 1996a) and Frohnen (Frohnen, 1996), both of whom present Burkean accounts of the nature of community. Yet stressing the link between conservatism and a valuing of community is prevalent among conservatives much more widely. This has become all but *de rigueur* for British conservatives setting out their visions (see Milne, 1994). Most notable, Willetts places a concern for community at the heart of his notion of 'civic conservatism' (Willetts, 1992a, 1994).

Civil society is, of course, of prime significance to free-market thinkers, with writers for think-tanks such as the Institute of Economic Affairs and the Cato Institute affirming its importance (Green, 1993, 1996; Machan, 1998). However, illustration of the centrality of civil society to all modern conservatives is shown by the case of the Heritage Foundation. In 1996 its principal periodical, *Policy Review*, was relaunched as *Policy Review: the Journal of American Citizenship*, with an editorial announcing the journal's key objective for the future as that of 'articulating and advancing the conservative vision of civil society' (Meyerson, 1996, p. 5). Much space has since been devoted to articles attending to this project.

Many other conservatives have oriented their thinking around the idea of civil society, such as Don Eberly, founder of the 'Civil Society Project' (Eberly, 1994, 1998), William Schambra (Schambra, 1994, 1998) and Michael Joyce (Joyce, 1994, 1998). Nor can it go unnoted how the concepts of civil society and community have been embraced by conservative politicians. For example, in 1995 William Bennett and Republican Senator Dan Coats co-crafted a 'Project for American Renewal', a package of legislative measures designed to re-energize the provision of welfare by private organizations (Coats, 1996; Coats and Santorum, 1998).

Even more significant, civil society themes figure highly on the agenda of George W. Bush, with advocates such as Eberly numbering among his advisers. Indeed, the use of terms such as 'civility', 'responsibility' and 'community' in Bush's inauguration speech – a speech for which Putnam was consulted – prompted Etzioni to describe it as a 'communitarian text' (*Washington Post*, 1 February 2001). Finally, one of William Hague's proposals as Conservative Party leader was to establish an Office of Civil Society, aimed at strengthening the role of voluntary organizations and 'faith communities' in dealing with social problems (Conservative Party, 2001).

Meanings and agendas

What then do conservatives mean by the terms civil society and community? In addressing this question, it is impossible not to observe one of the most conspicuous features of all modern writings, which is the general lack of clarity and consensus. Undoubtedly, this indeterminacy is a major factor in the terms' widespread attractiveness, explaining their appeal across the political continuum. Yet in this regard there is also some accuracy in Duncan and Hobson's dismissal of the term community as little more than 'a meaningless metaphysical abstraction' (Duncan and Hobson, 1995, p. 11). Moreover, Hobsbawm's suggestion that today civil society and community are 'vapid phrases' that have 'lost their traditional meanings' (Hobsbawm, 1994, p. 11) is a useful corrective to the idea that they can be understood simply in terms of historical definitions. In fact, the way in which the concepts are usually defined today is to meet specifically modern concerns.

One of the most important sources for an understanding of civil society is the liberal tradition. According to Gray, thinkers like Locke and Smith 'represented as an inherent and universal truth the connexion between individualist culture and a civil society encompassing market institutions' (Gray, 1993b, p. 279). Of particular relevance here, Gray believes that within New Right thought the same conflating of civil society and individualism is apparent, with neither 'neo-liberalism nor its conservative critics' truly recognizing the 'cultural foundations and historical limits of individualist civil society'. However, what will be demonstrated in this chapter is that, today at least, conservatives of all types appear more than willing to recognize these limits.

The basic sense in which most American conservatives understand civil society is, as suggested earlier, derived from the idea of mediating institutions originated by Berger and Neuhaus. Thus, the usual way in which it is defined is by the presentation of lists of such institutions. For example, Himmelfarb believes that civil society comprises 'the institutions that mediate between the individual and the state: family, community, churches, local authorities, private enterprises, voluntary associations' (Himmelfarb, 1995b, p. ix). Eberly also agrees that what constitutes civil society is 'mediating institutions', noting particularly Berger and Neuhaus's conception (Eberly, 1994, p. xxxi).

An issue immediately raised by Himmelfarb's account is how the concepts of civil society and community are supposed to relate. As implied by her definition, one way to understand the relationship is to treat communities as themselves institutions of civil society. Yet also common is for the terms to be employed essentially as synonyms. For example, as a means of explaining what is meant by community, Dunn and Woodard proffer a comparable list of institutions to Himmelfarb, including the family, churches and voluntary associations (Dunn and Woodard, 1996, p. 51). Similarly, in defining the conservative view of community, Brad Miner offers a quotation from Burke on civil society (Miner, 1996, p. 58).

Considering community in its own right, it is often easier to understand what the conservative conception is not than what it actually is. For example, Joyce argues that 'Community is not a nation... [it] is not a class, a gender, or an occupation' (quoted in Boyte and Kari, 1997, p. 41). Such a negative description does at least reveal a part of what is attractive about the concept for conservatives, in that it allows them to present social solidarities in a depoliticized form. That is, it enables them to forward a philosophy of social bonds free from the ideological entanglements of notions such as class or gender. In similar vein, Dunn and Woodard present the conservative stress upon community – which in their view embodies the values of variety and complexity – as being in contrast to the social vision of the ideologue, who prizes uniformity (Dunn and Woodard, 1996, p. 77).

In many respects, the clearest accounts of community are to be found among traditionalist conservatives like Scruton. Scruton defends many of the same philosophical principles as communitarians, including belief in the embeddedness of ethical values within historically determined communities; the social construction of the self; and the erroneousness of abstract conceptions of freedom and rights (Scruton, 1994, pp. 432–7, 493–5). However, Scruton argues more than just that community is the source of individual identity, but that the bonds that tie individuals together are pre-political in nature (Scruton, 2001b, pp. 19–26). In other words, membership of society is not – as suggested by liberal theory – contractual, but based upon deep-rooted and ineliminable instincts of belonging that exist prior to political arrangements. Being part of a community is therefore not a voluntary choice, but an unavoidable feature of social existence. Furthermore, a community is expected to share a substantially common set of cultural and moral norms.

The idea that sources more 'fundamental' than politics are essential in the constitution of societies is also common among writers on civil society. For example, Eberly writes that, 'Free societies must be replenished with things that classical philosophers would describe as "pre-political," those things that are more important than and prior to politics and economics' (Eberly, 1994, p. xxiii). Much of the appeal of this notion of the pre-political is not only that it fits in with traditional conservative principles but also that it ties in with the disillusionment that has been suggested is felt by conservatives towards conventional political and economic agendas. Thus, it is believed, the remedy for society's problems must be found in other spheres.

A further belief possessing broad agreement across the spectrum of conservatism is the independence of civil society from the state. According to many, the emergence of civil society was largely a spontaneous development: for example, Wilson believes that it 'was neither foreseen nor planned by anyone' (J. Q. Wilson, 1993, p. 246). Accompanying this view is the belief that the rise of the interventionist state is responsible for civil society's decline. Gingrich contends that 'De Tocqueville's description of voluntary organizations as the backbone of America would remain true today if these efforts were not completely overshadowed by a gigantic federal bureaucracy' (Gingrich, 1995, p. 103; see also Murray, 1997, pp. 57–8).

It is not only libertarians who share this conviction. Will also argues that there is an inverse relationship between the size of the state and the vitality of civil society: 'There is … a zero-sum transaction in society: As the state waxes, other institutions wane' (quoted in Skocpol, 1996, p. 292). A similar belief, expressed in more lyrical form, is articulated by Novak: 'When Leviathan falters, civil society stirs. When Leviathan relaxes, civil society expands' (Novak, 1994, p. 16).

For this reason, devolving responsibility from the state to the institutions of civil society is a key feature of many conservative agendas. One much preferred strategy is the re-energizing of the voluntary sector. For example, Green yearns for a return to the nineteenth-century heyday of the friendly societies (Green, 1993, 1996). Accordingly, his vision is one of groups of parents and teachers establishing private schools and the revival of voluntary hospitals. Similarly, Keith Joseph argues for the recovery of the role of friendly societies as a means of encouraging a sense of stakeholding in society (Joseph, 1996, pp. 43–4), revealing that not all conservatives are sceptical towards the latter concept.

Even conservatives most committed to the value of authority may wish to limit government in relation to civil society. For example, Scruton argues that the conservative vision of community 'must be founded first and foremost on the attempt to separate civil society and state' (Scruton, 1996a, p. 16). However, this belief derives not from a principled concern for increasing liberty, but because limiting government is deemed necessary to defend the traditional values of a common culture. His desire to see schools and universities privatized thus arises not from any devotion to the tenets of economic liberalism, but because he believes this will 'emancipate the institutions through which our inheritance is transmitted' (p. 24). In a similar vein, Fleming advocates the rolling back of big government 'not on the grounds of abstract individualism, but in defence of real human communities' such as families and church parishes (T. Fleming, interview by author, 2 October 1998).

Another important issue concerns to what level of social unit conservatives believe community refers. As Willetts observes, conservatives may argue that it is either the nation itself that embodies the spirit of community, or the plurality of institutions or networks that comprise the nation (Willetts, 1992a, p. 71). As a point of difference, it can be argued that the national rather than local level is a more common basis for British conservatives' understandings than those of their American counterparts, because of the latter's historical attachment to the principles of federalism. For example, while Scruton is unambiguous as to the importance of a national focus (Scruton, 1996a, pp. 27–8), it is plain from the statement cited above that Joyce believes that nation and community are not the same. Moreover, Nisbet contends that the spirit of nationalism has not been as creative a force as localism in American history (Nisbet, 1976, pp. 267–8; see also Schambra, 1998, pp. 44–9). However, it is also the case that British conservatives value sub-national social units; nor can it safely be argued that American conservatives do not value the national (see Chapter 5).

Regardless of any differences over how civil society or community should be defined, a clear aspect upon which most conservatives appear to agree is that in recent years a marked deterioration in civility and sociability has occurred. To this may be attributed almost any and every social disorder: 'The consequences of civil society's decline are evident throughout our daily life, in soaring rates of crime, divorce, illegitimacy, neighborhood deterioration, welfare dependency, chemical addiction, suicide, and virtually every other indicator of pathology' (Schambra, 1994, p. 33).

It is in particular the great moral harm supposed to have been caused by civil society's degeneration that most exercises conservatives' minds, notably the culture of dependency perceived to be the result of state rather than voluntary welfare provision (Eberly, 1998; Himmelfarb, 1995a). As observed in the previous chapter, as much as the growth of the welfare state may be an economic concern for conservatives, its displacing of alternative forms of welfare provision is believed to have at least as significant moral consequences.

Values supposed especially to have disappeared with the decline of civil society are those of responsibility and duty. Importantly, the elevation of these values frequently goes hand in hand with a denigration of the value of individual rights. For example, Will claims that

Our political discourse is so saturated with rights talk... that the tributaries of nonlegal rhetoric are drying up. There is excessive concentration on two polarities of social life – the individual and the state – and insufficient attention to civil society's intermediary institutions... Our hard-edged rights talk slights the grammar of cooperative living. (Will, 1992, pp. 174–5)

In fact, the lack of strong mediating institutions may be to blame for the widespread cultural crisis identified by many contemporary conservatives. As Coats argues, 'America's cultural decay can be traced directly to the breakdown of certain institutions – families, churches, neighborhoods, voluntary associations – that act as an immune system against cultural disease' (Coats, 1996, p. 24). By contrast, when civil society is strong 'it infuses a community with its warmth, trains its people to be good citizens, and transmits values between generations'. Indeed, the role of civil society in the recovery of virtue, character and civility features as a core theme throughout contemporary writings (see Chapter 4).

A final characteristic of conservative invocations worth noting is that they are often imbued with a sense of loss and nostalgia. Conservatives appear to believe that at some (frequently unspecified) time in the past, society truly was comprised of the virtuous and independent institutions they so highly prize. Their writings are thus filled with exhortations constituted by 're-' prefixed terms, enjoining us to 'rebuild', 'reinvigorate' or 'revitalize' our social values and institutions. However modish the concepts of civil society and community may be, for conservatives at least the issues at stake are nonetheless most definitely rooted in the past.

Individualism, pluralism and the market

What has been shown so far is that conservatives' present-day moral concerns tend to lead them away from any purely individualist conception of civil society, in which the status of individual rights has to be qualified to facilitate the training of citizens to be good. The mechanisms needed to promote this vision will be discussed below. Yet what of the belief in pluralism and diversity, which supposedly separates conservative conceptions from those of the ideologue?

Among British conservatives, those influenced by Oakeshott's theory of civil association show some scepticism towards the demands of communitarian prescriptions. As noted in the last chapter, for Oakeshott it is a mistake to believe that the state should be used to pursue common goals. Underlying this denunciation is the distinction he draws between forms of social organization (Oakeshott, 1975b, pp. 116–29). On the one hand, there are enterprise associations, in which members are united in the pursuit of shared ends, while on the other there are associations of practice, governed by sets of general rules but within which individuals pursue their own chosen objectives. While the former model may be appropriate for organizations such as companies, it is the mistake of the rationalist to believe in attempting to impose this conception on society as a whole. By contrast, Oakeshott's preference is for a civil association characterized by a framework of non-instrumental rules, in which the state does not seek to impose substantive goals or beliefs.

Adopting a similar outlook, Noël O'Sullivan expresses suspicion towards the communitarian zeal perceived to have infected parts of the conservative school (N. O'Sullivan, 1989, pp. 167–91). He is also disquieted at the notion that the bonds of community should be viewed as resting upon pre-political sources, arguing that this idea downgrades the real essence of civil order – the impersonal, abstract bond of law – and therefore has disturbing implications for individual freedom. Moreover, he suggests, were substantive bonds of pre-political commonality truly the requirement of civil association neither British nor American society could have been created from the disparate peoples which first constituted them.

It is possible here, therefore, to suggest another distinction between British and American conservatism, also highlighted by Devigne. Thus, Devigne argues, there is a difference between the fundamental belief of modern British conservative theory that humanity 'is incapable of either generating or sustaining a substantive political unity' and the contrasting fears of American conservatives of 'an American polity that does not believe in substantive truths' (Devigne, 1994, p. 193). Equally, O'Sullivan suggests not only that Scruton, in arguing for the necessity of a shared common culture, is guilty of 'the greatest of political errors', but also that this is 'the one to which the British conservative tradition stands most deeply opposed' (N. O'Sullivan, 1989, p. 180). In other words, like Devigne, he believes that British conservative theory rejects the ambition to create a substantive social unity.

As discussed in the previous chapter, Devigne's understanding does possess merit. However, as will be explored later, many British conservatives evidently do desire a strong sense of moral and cultural unity. Moreover, it is not only arch-traditionalists like Scruton who criticize the tenets of liberal theory in formulating a vision of civil society. So does Willetts, despite being a far greater enthusiast for free markets. Willetts also denounces the liberal contractarian tradition for its failure to account adequately for the role played by society in the constitution of individual identity (D. Willetts, interview by author, 22 June 1998; see also Willetts, 1992a, pp. 65–9). Furthermore, and emphasizing his agreement with Hegel's critique of Kant on this point, he rejects prioritizing the role of autonomous individuals in moral reasoning. Indeed, Willetts argues, one of the strongest attractions of a community centred philosophy is its provision of an answer to the 'is/ought' ethical dilemma, by treating moral obligations as embodied in the social relations of particular communities. The labels of 'father', 'son' or 'neighbour' not only describe an individual's social identity, but also imply the duties and obligations to which he should adhere.

In fact, while it was shown in Chapter 1 that thinkers like Hayek were not wholly unaware of the need for non-market institutions and customs to underpin the market, these relatively rare allowances stand in contrast to the widespread commitment of present-day libertarians to a broader conception of civil society. Many do not define it in purely individualistic terms, appearing at great pains to stress that civil society is a sphere in which much more occurs than simply market exchanges between autonomous individuals and firms. For example, Walter

Block – explaining that libertarianism is not to be confused with libertinism – prescribes a strengthening of non-state institutions such as the family to inculcate moral and spiritual values within individuals (Block, 1994, p. 124). J. A. Dorn, former Director of the Cato Institute's 'Project on Civil Society', similarly believes in re-energizing civil society as a means of reinvigorating moral virtue (Dorn, 1996, p. 140). Furthermore, Daniel Klein makes a bid for the inclusion of libertarianism within the communitarian fold, by arguing that only a libertarian economic agenda can provide the resources to fulfil the social goals of communitarianism (D. Klein, 1994).

In other words, some distance seems to have been travelled by economic liberals since the time when Adam Smith could contend that society functions not because of anyone's benevolence, but as the unconscious result of individuals pursuing their own self-interest. Yet it is also common today to find the argument forwarded that it is a mistake to view Smith merely as a champion of selfish laissez-faire. Rather, it is claimed, he should be recognized as being as much concerned with other-regarding moral injunctions, essential for the maintenance of a just society. For example, Brian Griffiths, former head of Margaret Thatcher's Policy Unit, seeks to remind us that Smith was author of not only *The Wealth of Nations* but also *The Theory of Moral Sentiments* (Griffiths, 2001, p. 23; see also Green, 1993, p. 2; J. Q. Wilson, 1991, pp. 139–48). Such efforts to modify the widespread perception of Smith, whatever their intellectual validity, reveal very clearly the problem with Gray's view of market liberals as unconcerned with the limits of an individualist conception of civil society.

Conservatives also often maintain, as does Kirkpatrick, that there is in any case no necessary contradiction between a vigorously individualistic culture and one in which associational activity is strong (J. Kirkpatrick, interview by author, 16 September 1998). However, one of the most developed attempts to reconcile free-market and community-based philosophies is to be found in Willetts's civic conservatism (Willetts, 1992a, 1994). Market forces should not, Willetts contends, be seen as the dire threat to the stability of traditional institutions critics claim, since history confirms that these latter can and have flourished during periods of rapid economic advance; as, for example, in the nineteenth century. The present-day fragility of community institutions cannot, therefore, be attributed to the operation of the market, since the two share a long history of peaceful co-existence.

At the same time, he acknowledges that a commitment to the market is not itself sufficient for a truly satisfactory conservative creed. Instead, the fostering of virtues such as honesty and fairness, and the preservation of non-market institutions, are also vital to provide the cultural and moral environment required by a just capitalist society. Accordingly, what Willetts seeks is a balance between the two elements of the market and the community, 'to avoid the twin perils of crude neo-Liberalism and a retreat into the cosy embrace of big government' (Willetts, 1994, p. 27). The point, therefore, is that even among those who do not blame the market for communities' enervated condition, the need to supplement a free-market ideology with communitarian considerations is apparent.

In fact, it is worth examining in more detail the treatment of the market in conservatives' conceptions. As Krishan Kumar observes, among all writers on civil society, the clear tendency today is to emphasize its non-economic dimensions (Kumar, 1993, pp. 383–4). This appears the case as much in conservative writings as in others. For example, many do not even mention economic bodies in their lists of institutions supposed to constitute civil society: Coats mentions families, churches, neighbourhoods and voluntary associations (Coats, 1996, p. 24); Joyce presents the same list (Joyce, 1998, p. 41); and so do Novak and Schambra, though both adding schools (Novak, 1994, p. 22; Schambra, 1994, p. 32).

Even when economic organizations are cited, it is frequently not for their economic roles. For example, Adam Meyerson includes 'business enterprises' as part of civil society, yet it is their ability to generate 'creative answers to social problems' (Meyerson, 1996, p. 6) that is emphasized above their activities in the sphere of production. Most significantly, the market may not just be ignored or marginalized but treated as a sphere actually separate from civil society. Eberly implies just this, in expressing the hope that the rediscovery of civil society marks a departure from 'reliance on either the state or the market as mechanisms for social improvement' (Eberly, 1998, p. 47). Likewise, Feulner – in describing what he believes to be the major pillars of present-day conservatism – distinguishes economic issues from those that are 'broadly cultural or civil society' ones (E. Feulner, interview by author, 22 October 1998). In fact, a cultural conception of civil society is probably the dominant among all varieties of conservative today.

Why civil society? Why now?

In his introduction to a volume of writings on civil society, Dionne poses two of the most fundamental questions relating to the issues under discussion: 'Why Civil Society? Why Now?' (Dionne, 1998, p. 1). Explaining why civil society and community have become such significant concepts for conservatives is the next important task to undertake.

While their attachment to these notions is, of course, explicable in terms of familiar ambitions – such as rolling back the state – reasons specific to the post-Cold War era may be adduced. It has already been noted how the collapse of communism was a key factor in returning civil society to the centre-stage of discussion. Green argues that many free marketeers 'changed their tune' from believing that markets alone are sufficient for capitalism to function, in response to their own experiences of attempting to rebuild the economies of the former Soviet bloc (D. G. Green, interview by author, 22 June 1998). The economic and social problems that remained even when the old bureaucratic structures had been dismantled reopened their eyes to the importance of a strong culture of civil society.

However, even if true, in itself this does not explain why re-examining civil society should also be felt necessary in relation to the West. One reason may be that the Cold War conflict provided Western societies with sufficient identity and purpose not to require any further inquiry into their own constitutions. This idea is suggested by Eberly, who argues that 'during the cold war, the need for a well-defined identity and moral purpose was reinforced as America led a unified democratic front against Communism. Her core principles needed little further articulation' (Eberly, 1994, p. xix). In the absence of the Cold War conflict, the explicit articulation of these principles becomes necessary.

Nonetheless, even without Soviet communism to provide a sense of purpose – together with ready proof of capitalism's superiority – societies confident in their identities might be felt to have little need for such self-reflection. It is precisely because such confidence is frequently lacking, including among conservatives, that concerns over the condition of civil society have reappeared. For conservatives in particular the problem faced is that it is often the free-market doctrines with which they are associated that are held responsible for civil society's enfeebled condition. In other words, one reason conservatives have sought to revive community-centred discourses is to answer the charge that they are simply committed to a destructive free-market ideology, responsible for the atomization of society and the disintegration of social bonds.

It is, therefore, as a corollary to the distancings from an unfettered individualism discussed in the last chapter that the search for more social doctrines has taken place, with recognition evident among many conservatives that they have been damaged by losing the language of community and solidarity to their opponents. Most notable, this is apparent in the various attempts to promote a 'compassionate conservatism', by conservatives like Marvin Olasky, intended to present a more socially aware side of the ideology by showing concern for problems such as poverty (Olasky, 2000).

In this connection, it is significant to note the numerous efforts by British conservatives to re-interpret Thatcher's famous dictum that 'there is no such thing as society'. For example, Michael Howard heroically attempts to argue that 'far from extolling the virtues of a selfish and irresponsible individualism, she was in fact advocating the duties of neighbourliness' (*Observer*, 16 October 1994). According to David Howell, what Thatcher meant was that 'there's no such thing as a state conception of society', rejecting the view that the state is responsible for social welfare in favour of delegating this to individuals, families and communities (D. Howell, interview by author, 14 July 1998). Michael Portillo, also seeking to develop a more compassionate brand of conservatism, argues that Thatcher simply meant that there are no unalterable social structures that excuse antisocial behaviour (Portillo, 1997, p. 12). Conservatives nonetheless believe that 'We are social animals and society is what we make it ... None of us would wish to live in a grabbing and inhumane society made up of greedy and selfish people.'

One strategy open to conservatives is to claim that it is not they but their opponents who are responsible for the rising tide of antisocial individualism. For example, Karl Zinmeister blames a liberal 'generation of American thinkers ... disdainful toward any but the most cosmopolitan and individualistic ways of living' for associating small-town community life with the image of being narrow and claustrophobic (Zinmeister, 1996, p. 4). Equally, Howell argues that it was the permissive generation of the 1960s who were responsible for creating a 'selfish society' in which 'everyone did their own thing' (D. Howell, interview by author, 14 July 1998).

Yet some conservatives are willing to stress the role of capitalism itself in civil society's deterioration. Thus, according to Bennett, 'Unbridled capitalism is a problem. It may not be a problem for production, but it's a problem for human beings. It's a problem for that whole dimension of things we call the realm of values and human relationships' (quoted in Starobin, 1997, p. 106). If conservatives are now able to make such admissions, it can be understood why they may treat the market as existing outside the sphere of civil society.

In fact, for many writers it is very much a case of rejecting conservatism's own past sins. For example, Green elaborates his vision of 'civic capitalism' – in which the need for communal solidarities alongside the operations of the market is emphasized – by contrasting it with the 'hard-boiled economic rationalism' of the Thatcher years (Green, 1993, pp. 1–4). At the very least, the focus upon economics to the neglect of social issues is often called into question. For example, Eberly writes, 'how sufficient is economic advancement, many are asking, if our schools do not function, if crime defies control, and if children have lost their innocence' (Eberly, 1994, p. xix).

In response to the anti-market rhetoric of many American conservatives, Starobin suggests that 'community-oriented conservatives... sound a lot like, well, Karl Marx' (Starobin, 1997, p. 106). However, as Dionne notes, it would be a mistake to view these conservatives as anti-capitalist per se (Dionne, 1998, p. 6). Rather, what they have come to accept, along with their critics, is that capitalism needs to be constrained if it is not to generate untoward effects outside the sphere of production. While this is not an entirely new insight among conservatives, it has become a much more widely accepted proposition. Although conservatives may not yet have adopted the banner of classical Marxism, many do not appear confident in avowing an undiluted classical liberalism.

A further problem for conservatives to which programmes centred upon the notion of civil society may provide an answer is the question of what unifying goal is able to fill the vacuum left by communism's demise. Thus, the search for a new shared purpose has also been a motivating force behind the conservative embracing of civil society themes. For example, Meyerson argues that 'the restoration of American citizenship... is the most important unifying principle of conservatism in the post-Cold-War era', able to unite libertarian, religious, 'growth-and-opportunity' and nationalist conservatives in common cause (Meyerson, 1996, p. 6). If all varieties of conservative can agree that strengthening civil society is a crucial objective, rifts within the conservative camp exposed by socialism's defeat might be repaired.

Tensions and dilemmas

Emphasizing the value of civil society and community by no means confers upon conservatives unambiguous benefits. In fact, a number of tensions and dilemmas may be highlighted. One possible problem is that by adopting a rhetoric of communal bonds, conservatives lose the distinctiveness that a more stridently individualistic philosophy can afford them. That is, with all parts of the political spectrum using this language, conservatives may surrender the basis upon which to offer any alternative. For example, as Leadbeater notes, the conclusions drawn by Willetts in formulating his idea of civic conservatism 'sound very like those of the left intellectuals he recently criticised in his pamphlet *Blair's Gurus*' (Leadbeater, 1996, p. 30; see Willetts, 1996a). Although the aim of reviving civil society may give conservatives a new purpose in the post-Cold War world, this may be at the expense of abandoning any strong foundations for a distinctive ideology.

Nor may promoting civil society straightforwardly provide conservatives with clear common goals. The mere fact that all types of conservative may believe sustaining civil society to be a valuable aspiration does not mean that there are not serious differences over how it is conceived or its condition accounted for. For example, there remain libertarians who reject outright the diagnosis that individualism is responsible for civil society's parlous condition. Duncan and Hobson argue that it is 'one of our principal contentions that it is the State and not the possessive individualism of the last fifteen years which has corrupted ordinary men and women' (Duncan and Hobson, 1995, p. xvi). Of particular interest is their distaste for the embracing of communitarian themes by other conservatives. To them, the invocation of community is little more than a mask for coercion: whether the form is that of 'High Toryism', 'One Nation Toryism' or 'Civic Conservatism', all such doctrines share the same disreputable intellectual roots as fascism and communism, in making the interests of the individual subordinate to those of the community (pp. 5–11, 239–42, 298–302).

Similarly, Boaz forcefully rejects the communitarian attack upon individual rights (Boaz, 1997, pp. 59–93). Moreover, he worries about the paternalism of many conservatives: 'Conservatives want to be your daddy, telling you what to do and what not to do' (p. 104). Such antagonism may be reciprocated, with Bork concerned about the common equation of libertarianism with conservatism for exactly the reason that libertarians – whom he deems only 'quasi or semiconservatives' – do not recognize the pressing need for restraints upon individual autonomy (Bork, 1996, p. 150). What such disagreements reveal is that a renewed concern for civil society and community may actually bring the tensions between the individualist and authority-centred elements within conservatism further to the fore. Raising civil society as the banner under which to rally the conservative movement may not produce the easy unity some may expect.

Consideration of the libertarian position also highlights another important issue, which is the illiberalism implicit in much communitarian discourse. Although the renewed attendance to social questions implied by the adoption of civil society themes may seem intended to

soften the harsh face of a free-market-centred ideology, the actual measures necessary to recover a more civilized way of life may be far from
'soft'. For example, one collection of essays by British and American
writers arguing for the restoration of civic virtue is bluntly entitled *This
Will Hurt*, its contributors' suggestions ranging from the stigmatizing of
illegitimate children to a return to the painful and public punishment
of criminals (D. Anderson, 1995a). Coats also believes that it will require
'tough love' to rejuvenate civil society (Coats, 1996, p. 26).

Equally, Himmelfarb – whose arguments are drawn upon by Olasky –
makes clear exactly what a conservative means by compassion. It does
not imply 'a soft-hearted ... approach to social problems, in which sentiment prevails over reason' (Himmelfarb, 2001, p. 3). Instead, it should
mean today what it meant to the Victorians: Victorian philanthropists
understood that being compassionate might require them to 'restrain
their benevolent impulses', since the primary objective of their compassion was to impart the values and discipline necessary for 'the moral
improvement of the poor' (Himmelfarb, 1991, p. 6).

This is also the concern of Mead, in whose hands the needs of community are made to justify workfare. As discussed in Chapter 2, Mead
differs from libertarians in believing that the solution to the problem of
welfare dependency is a bolstering of authority. Yet he also couches his
argument in the language of community and citizenship, like communitarians displaying scepticism towards the liberal notion of individual
autonomy (Mead, 1992, pp. 19–23, 181–4, 237–9). Mead's preference for
workfare is thus defended on the grounds that it will reawaken a sense
of communal responsibility within the non-working poor.

However, the ambiguity as to how free or open civil society should be
cannot be understood purely in terms of a simple libertarian/authoritar-
ian divide. In fact, a tension between avowals that civil society is valued
for its openness and freedom and claims that it must be conceived in
relatively closed terms is to be found throughout conservative writings.
It is quite possible to find the language of both conceptions side-by-side.
According to Eberly, 'The realm of civil society is free and largely
autonomous, but it nevertheless imposes constraints and obligations on
the individual and limits his choices. In other words, talk of civil society
implies a return to authority and order' (Eberly, 1996, p. 31).

How then is this co-mingling of terms such as 'free' and 'autonomous'
with talk of 'constraints' and 'authority' to be understood? The overall
implication of most conservative accounts is that whatever freedom is to
be allowed must be within the limits prescribed by the requirements of
order, since – in this demoralized age – the needs of the latter must be

prioritized over those of the former. That is, the service into which conservatives wish to press the concept of civil society, as part of their programmes of moral and cultural regeneration, very much militates against any ostensible liberalism.

Even when consideration is given to many of those who style themselves as libertarians, there is frequently little that is liberal in spirit in their recommendations. For example, Murray – in a book setting out to define what it means to be a libertarian – argues that a major reason we should be opposed to the state's displacing of civil society's institutions is its usurpation of 'the web of parental pressures and social stigma that kept illegitimacy rare' (Murray, 1997, p. 58). In other words, even libertarians look to civil society not only for the possibilities it offers as a realm of freedom but also because it is seen as more effective at enforcing a strict morality than is a too 'liberal' state (see also Boaz, 1997, pp. 239–41).

Important to note here as well is the frequent disregard for any public/private distinction in contemporary conceptions of civil society. Civil society may not only refer to the public sphere but also, as indicated in Himmelfarb's definition, include institutions such as the family (see also W. J. Bennett, 1994b). Thus, the rediscovery of civil society not only provides justification for the increased moral regulation of public spaces but also may countenance intrusion into almost every corner of individuals' lives. As one critic warns, the blurring of the distinction between the realms of the social and the personal has many illiberal implications (H. N. Hirsch, 1986, p. 425).

The conflict between the stated conception of civil society and the agenda its revival is intended to fulfil also creates tensions within conservative accounts in other ways. Another of great significance is between civil society's supposed independence from the state and the means necessary for its regeneration. This can be seen from an examination of Coats and Bennett's 'Project for American Renewal', the declared aim of which was to turn over federal responsibility for aspects of welfare provision to private voluntary organizations. Yet, as Boaz observes, even if overstating the case, the means by which this was to take place 'shows a faith in government almost as breathtaking as that of the architects of the Great Society', requiring the passing of 19 federal laws, together with central direction from Washington as to which local programmes and private institutions should receive funding (Boaz, 1996, p. 32). In other words, the supposedly autonomous sphere of civil society is to be fostered via a highly dependent relationship with the state. Supporting the re-invigoration of non-state organizations may not therefore mean diminishing the state's role, simply finding it a different one. This criticism, of course, may also be put to proposals to establish a government office of civil society.

Furthermore, conservatives' historical accounts of civil society, as arising spontaneously and developing autonomously, may be considered romanticized depictions. As Theda Skocpol documents, the history of voluntary organizations in America has always been one of subsidy and interdependence with the state rather than one of mutual exclusivity (Skocpol, 1996, pp. 297–9). A similar analysis may be presented of the role played by the state in relation to British civil society (Gray, 1998, pp. 7–16).

Importantly, this pattern of dependence remains true in the present. As Salamon and Anheier show in their study of civil society across the developed world, the conservative idea of a zero-sum relationship between voluntary bodies and the state is simply false: for example, in terms of the funding of non-profit organizations, only 10 per cent of income is accounted for by private donations, with over 40 per cent coming from government (Salamon and Anheier, 1997, p. 63). Even in the United States, where private giving is relatively higher than elsewhere, only 19 per cent is from private donations, with 30 per cent provided by the state (the remaining 51 per cent coming from fees and dues). Even were the state able to disentangle itself from civil society, it is far from clear that voluntary activity would be able to fill the vacuum.

A further problem for conservatives is that it is by no means certain that real-world communities fit their idealized image. Michael Kenny takes left-wing proponents of civil society discourses to task for simply assuming that the institutions they support are likely to be benign, or even progressive, in terms of the values they believe them to embody (Kenny, 1996, p. 19); yet a similar point may be put to conservatives. That is, many appear unreflectively to assume that the mediating institutions they wish to foster are bound inevitably to be homes of conservative values. In reality, they are not, and may even be hostile to such values. Particularly striking is that the almost wholly positive image of civil society to be found in conservative accounts does not square well with the picture of seemingly dire cultural and moral malaise also to be found in their writings.

More thoughtful conservatives recognize this tension. Himmelfarb, for example, urges conservatives to realize that many of the beliefs responsible for our present demoralized condition, including affirmative action and multiculturalism, originated from civil society institutions such as universities and private foundations, rather than from the state

(Himmelfarb, 1996b). 'Bad' families and even some churches may also be culpable in the creation of an immoral and permissive culture. Indeed, rather than regarding the whole of civil society as in a state of disrepair, many of its institutions should be seen – regrettably from Himmelfarb's standpoint – as stronger and more influential than ever. Consequently, conservative programmes need to engage with the task not only of reviving civil society's institutions, but the much harder one of their 'remoralization'.

A similar circumspection towards the uncritical enthusiasm of many civil society revivalists is expressed by Robert Browning. Drawing upon new class theories, Browning argues that non-state organizations such as consumer and public interest groups are a part of the problem of the present intellectual climate, in promoting hostility towards technological progress and economic growth (Browning, 1991, pp. 31–8).

Two possible conclusions may be drawn. For Browning, it is to question conservatives' assumptions that civil society is always to be seen as a buffer against the evils of the state, suggesting that many of its organizations are little more than adjuncts of an antagonistic state bureaucracy. Yet, as noted in the previous chapter, the one Himmelfarb draws is that the state itself may have to be entrusted with the task of remoralizing a hostile civil society. What can again be seen is how a focus upon the realm of civil society, seeming to imply an inherently anti-statist perspective, may – in a context in which conservatives have lost faith in the actual character of wider society – lead to even more reliance upon the state.

Notwithstanding the questioning of Devigne's distinction between American and British conservative theory raised earlier, British conservatives often avow more tolerance when it comes to considering the potentially adversarial nature of civil society. For example, Willetts argues that believing in freedom for the institutions of civil society implies having 'to accept that that means not just allowing these institutions freedom to do things you approve of, but freedom to do things you disapprove of' (D. Willetts, interview by author, 22 June 1998). Even so, this more tolerant attitude is as much to do with the fact that he is more confident than many American conservatives that if the state is rolled back 'the institutions and arrangements [which] will thrive and survive will be ones which display strengths which conservatives understand and appreciate'. In other words, it may be less a commitment to pluralism as an end in itself that allows British conservatives to be more accepting of civil society as a realm of diversity, than a less despairing view of their nation's moral condition. It may be wondered as well whether Willetts's liberalism on moral issues must at all be circumscribed by his adherence to a communitarian ethics.

A different problem to that of presupposing too hopeful a view of civil society's 'conservative' orientation arises from the deifying of its institutions. This issue is well highlighted by Scruton, in criticizing conservative politicians who continually assert the value of the family. As he argues, 'the more it is held forth as an ideal and an example, the more it will wither and disintegrate under the strain' (Scruton, 1996a, p. 21). If the value of the institution derives from its spontaneous – possibly even 'natural' – character, then 'it is self-defeating to make the family and family values into an object of policy. For this merely sets the most precious of our institutions in the centre of politics, where it does not belong, and under the pressure of which it crumbles' (p. 25). The same might well be said of all of civil society's institutions.

Yet most serious for conservatives, conservatism is much less well equipped to incorporate communitarian themes than its rivals. If many libertarians are sceptical of communitarian conservatives' liberal credentials, other communitarians are suspicious of conservatives' true commitment to the value of community. Many contend that it is simply not possible for conservatives to answer individuals' aspirations for communal modes of life, since the corrosive effects of free-market policies are a prime cause of civil society's enervated state (Lasch, 1991, pp. 38–9; Wolfe, 1989, pp. 51–77). Even to the extent that conservatives may be willing to acknowledge that unbridled capitalism is a problem, these protestations frequently have little credibility outside conservative circles. Moreover, the very necessity of having to deny that theirs is a philosophy of selfish and unrestrained individualism suggests a defensive confirmation of the fact that they lack a convincing social doctrine.

The notion that there can be a balance between markets and communities is also widely questioned. For example, Gray is unconvinced by Willetts's argument in particular. Although, Gray argues, the belief that the free play of market forces is not disruptive of communities may have possessed some truth in the past, when the authority of cohesive forces such as religion was strong, the absence of such binding moral beliefs today means that communities are largely defenceless when confronted by destabilizing market influences (Gray, 1995, pp. 110–11).

At the root of the problem with conservative attempts to marry free market and communitarian doctrines is the commitment to two incompatible visions of the nature of individual identity. This is well illustrated by Willetts: 'I want my content of what it is to be a British citizen to be deep and embedded and tied up with history and tradition, and

I want my role as an economic agent to be relatively mobile and frictionless' (D. Willetts, interview by author, 22 June 1998). The contradictory results of this desire can be seen in Willetts's own writings, where different emphases are to be found in different contexts.

In an effort to present a community minded face for conservatism, Willetts argues that conservatives have a 'moral obligation' to give – albeit limited – support to the welfare state: 'Regardless of whether people in need have been reckless and feckless or unlucky and unfortunate ... They have a claim on us simply by virtue of being compatriots. The welfare state is an expression of solidarity with our fellow citizens' (Willetts, 1992a, p. 141).

At the very least, this is an unexpected argument from someone who views Macmillan's efforts to theorize a Middle Way in the 1930s as 'striking evidence of how far ... [the Conservative Party] was moving away from its principles' (p. 31). Yet most significant is the fact that elsewhere – when instead wearing his free marketeer's countenance – Willetts argues that it is the mistake of conservatives' opponents to believe that social solidarity may be expressed through state activity (Willetts, 1997, p. 16). The attempt to forge a market-based communitarian philosophy may therefore generate not only critics' scepticism but also internal contradictions.

The *au courant* resonance of communitarian ideas may not so easily be achieved by conservative expropriations for other reasons. Although communitarians may appear 'conservative' in many respects, the conceptions of community they proffer are typically very different to those developed by conservatives. This can be seen by examining Frohnen's attempt to distinguish the conservative doctrine of community from those of writers he terms 'new' communitarians (Frohnen, 1996, pp. 8–17). Two basic charges are levelled against the latter. First, in that their programmes are frequently reliant upon state action, they are no real friends of autonomous institutions. Second, they are too relativistic: while modern communitarians may be willing to oppose some antisocial practices, they nonetheless remain tolerant of many 'vices'. By contrast, the distinguishing feature of conservative critiques of individualism is that they rest upon a reverence for traditional virtues.

Both criticisms are common among conservatives. Willetts also believes that many communitarians are too statist (Willetts, 1996b, p. 84), while others agree that many are too liberal (Attarian, 1994, p. 369; Carey, 1997, p. 30). On the former point, what is regarded as problematic about non-conservative communitarians is that they do not accept conservatives' arguments that the state is to blame for civil society's decline. Nor, therefore, do they realize that the state cannot be an ally in its resuscitation. Of course, to the extent that this is true of other communitarians, it may at least mark a more honest appreciation of the relationship between civil society and the state. Equally, a question of credibility clearly arises in relation to conservatives' own programmes.

Still, it is the second distinction that is of particular interest. Scruton levels the same charge as follows: 'No communitarian has yet come to terms with the fact that the strongest communities in the modern world... are also closed communities – communities which maintain a vigilant hostility towards outsiders and unbelievers' (Scruton, 1996a, p. 12). Upon this basis, he disapproves of communitarians like Etzioni for being too 'sentimental', unwilling to recognize that strong communal bonds cannot be forged at the same time as keeping the luxuries of an open, liberal society.

Frum also believes of communitarianism that 'the essence of it is the fuzziness of its thought and the sentimentality of its aspirations' (D. Frum, interview by author, 4 September 1998). Similarly, William Kristol argues that 'left-wing communitarians end up not being tough-minded enough about what you really have to do' to remoralize society (W. Kristol, interview by author, 20 October 1998). Moreover, Digby Anderson explains that the arguments presented in *This Will Hurt* were precisely aimed at the sort of communitarians who believe that 'we can have all the pleasantness of a community based society without any of the nastiness' (D. Anderson, interview by author, 22 June 1998).

The significance of these claims is that the widespread appeal of communitarianism today derives from its ability not only to offer an alternative to discredited individualistic philosophies, but also to separate itself from any necessary connection with the traditional values and institutions that have also lost much social esteem. For this reason, even the most conservative-seeming communitarians are typically disconcerted at the absolutism of conservatives. For example, Etzioni attacks those on the Right who seek to uphold absolutist moral positions, as being dogmatic and authoritarian (Etzioni, 1995, p. 13). Similarly, MacIntyre sees conservatives as having done a great disservice to the notion of tradition, criticizing Burke for using it simply to defend the status quo; ostensibly, critical debate within a tradition is one of its essential features (MacIntyre, 1988, p. 353).

In other words, modern communitarians attempt to offer a balance between the communal nature of identity and a non-absolutist conception of its character that conservatives – with their commitments to cultural remoralization – cannot. Even though traditionalist conservatism may seem to possess the resources allowing it to adapt well to an intellectual and social climate hostile to individualism, it is nonetheless dependant upon backward-looking notions of tradition and morality that have themselves fallen out of favour. Even when employing much of the same rhetoric as communitarians, conservative community based philosophies still appear outmoded while those of their rivals may seem highly contemporary.

Conclusion

In a number of important ways, the meaning of civil society for present-day conservatives is quite different to those found in historical understandings, construed as it is in terms of their contemporary preoccupations. That is, conceived of as a sphere that promotes moral and cultural 'renewal'. In fact, the often highly instrumental nature of their agendas may imply a greater rather than diminished role for the state, with attendant implications for individual freedom.

Furthermore, although doctrines centred upon the notions of civil society and community may seem to fit naturally within a conservative world-view, in a post-Cold War world in which not only socialism but all determinate ideologies have in many respects lost their purchase, conservative attempts at advancing programmes of social unity face numerous difficulties. Whether or not the writings of communitarians like Etzioni can be considered wholly innocent of authoritarian connotations, there remains an important truth that their understandings of community are different from those of conservatives. Most significant, they need not be tied to the historical values or institutions of conservative conceptions. For this reason, the success garnered by their opponents in articulating community-centred doctrines may not so easily be attained by the more demanding requirements of conservative agendas. The exact nature of the moral and cultural values contemporary conservatives feel the need to defend is the topic of the next chapter.

4
Fighting the Culture War

Within conservative writings since the Cold War's end, the most prominent discussions have been those relating to the spheres of culture and morality, with anxieties about social decline encompassing issues from abortion to multiculturalism and from gay rights to political correctness. This salience arose in the 1990s as a result of the idea that some form of 'culture war' was raging within Western societies, a conflict fought between defenders of traditional standards and values and an array of critics. The rhetoric of war and conflict was embraced especially by American conservatives. Although these debates often possess a lower profile in Britain, many of the same issues are a prime focus of British conservatives' attentions.

However, by the close of the 1990s – even with debate still raging – a number of conservatives had come to believe that this war had in fact been lost. For some, the central issue has since become not how to preserve traditional values but what is the role of conservatives in a culture that no longer believes in them. In other words, the fundamental question of identity is raised, of what being a conservative means in a wholly antagonistic climate.

Other conservatives do not accept that they have been defeated, or at least believe that battle can be rejoined. Whatever assessment is true, the concerns of this chapter are in many respects the most important for understanding contemporary conservatism. As already seen, many of what might be imagined to be essentially political or economic questions – concerning the roles of the state and civil society – are defined by conservatives as at heart moral ones.

A major obstacle to understanding in this area is the sheer quantity of relevant material. A further aim of this chapter, therefore, is to determine what unites the range of concerns that so agitate present-day conservatives.

The real Cold War

While the term 'culture' may possess a variety of meanings, two are most significant for conservatives (Kirk, 1993, pp. 1–6). It may refer, first, to the realm of human creative achievements, including those of art and literature, and, second, to the shared values and customs of a particular society. However, conservatives also believe that conflicts in these two arenas are inextricably linked: for instance, as will be seen, debates around the arts are believed to be as much about ethical judgements as aesthetic ones. Indeed, for contemporary conservatives moral issues are usually the primary concern. For example, Novak asserts that 'The culture wars are fought in moral wars' (Novak, 1996, p. 115).

Of course, the fear of cultural and moral decline has been a perennial theme of conservative writings. The most important post-war American figure within this tradition is Strauss, who was concerned particularly with the rise of historicist and relativistic doctrines (Strauss, 1953, pp. 9–34). His fear was that the ascendancy of such beliefs within the academy would lead to the spread of a corrosive nihilism throughout society. By vitiating belief in objective notions of morality and the political good, the consequence of these doctrines' influence might be the very dissolution of the social and political fabric.

Not least of Strauss's concerns was that the undermining of the foundations of America's liberal polity would pave the way for the victory of totalitarianism. Blaming developments in modern philosophy for our contemporary malaise – beginning with the modern tradition of natural right, as initiated by Machiavelli and Hobbes – Strauss sought the recovery of an older tradition of natural law, that of the ancient Greeks. This tradition, he argued, affirms that there are immutable principles and absolutes, vouchsafed to us by reason and possessing universal compulsion.

Another post-war American writer disquieted at the implications of modern intellectual developments was Bell. According to Bell, the anti-traditionalist anomie of the modernist spirit – unleashed by the rise of industrial capitalism and championed by adversary intellectuals – is responsible for weakening the traditional Protestant ethics of discipline and order, and thus threatening the integrity of capitalist society (Bell, 1978). Although Bell rejected Straussianism, preferring religion to natural law as the hope for effecting the restoration of traditional values,

much intellectual cross-fertilization has occurred between neoconservatives and Straussians, with both being at the forefront of current cultural
debates.

Although the precise origins of the cultural debility afflicting Western
societies may not be agreed upon, a large area of common ground exists
among conservatives as a result of their belief that a sharp acceleration
of detrimental trends occurred in the 1960s (Bloom, 1987, pp. 313–35;
Kristol, 1994; Murray, 1992b). This era's increased acceptance of 'alternative lifestyles', homosexuality, abortion and contraception – together
with changes in their legal statuses – has been held responsible by many
conservatives for every moral and social problem since.

Yet what is striking about more recent times is the prominence of
conservatives' concerns and the sense of urgency with which their
arguments are imbued. While the idea of a culture war is hardly new, the
present phase of especially heated conflict began in the late 1980s, sig-
nalled by the publication of works such as Allan Bloom's *The Closing of
the American Mind* (Bloom, 1987). However, as Jeremy Rabkin observes,
the term 'culture war' did not gain widespread currency in American
politics until the 1990s (Rabkin, 1999, p. 4).

Equally, Martin Durham highlights the fact that during the 1970s and
1980s much of the British New Right took 'relatively little interest in
moral issues' (Durham, 1991, p. 160). Certainly among free marketeers,
although some concern was shown for the norms and traditions that
underpin the market, this was essentially secondary to their interest in
restoring the conditions of economic liberty. Today, conversely, it is
harder to identify conservatives or think-tanks even of the free-market
variety not anxious about moral and cultural issues. As noted in Chapter 1,
many of the most significant publications put out by the Institute of
Economic Affairs in the post-Thatcher era have been writings bemoan-
ing the state of the family and morality (further examples are Davies,
1993; Quest, 1994; Whelan, 1995). Libertarians Duncan and Hobson are
also much interested in themes relating to the moral and cultural
spheres (Duncan and Hobson, 1995, pp. 237–391).

Even so, the explicit according of priority to cultural questions
is undoubtedly most common among American conservatives. For
instance, William Kristol argues that cultural matters are 'more important than the tax rate or whether public housing's been privatized'
(W. Kristol, interview by author, 20 October 1998). Conservatives themselves recognize that this represents a change from the past. For example, at the start of the 1990s, Terry Teachout predicted that, in contrast
to the political and economic ones of the 1980s, 'the great battles of the

'90s will be fought in another arena: that of culture' (Teachout, 1990, p. 230); William Lind similarly felt that for American conservatism the 'new agenda is found not in economics, but in culture' (W. S. Lind, 1991, p. 40). American free-market advocates have also become as concerned with cultural questions and the fostering of morality as their British counterparts (Dorn, 1996; Gingrich, 1995, pp. 71–85, 141–52; Machan, 1998).

One reason conservatives began to prioritize cultural issues after the Cold War's end might simply be that the resolution of earlier economic and political conflicts allowed them to change their focus. As Feulner argues, 'There's a greater interest today than there was say twenty years ago because ... [other issues] were more pressing and higher on the radar screen' (E. Feulner, interview by author, 22 October 1998). Moreover, conservatives may also believe in some form of 'beyond Left and Right' thesis. For example, Podhoretz argues that, rather than conventional divides between Left and Right, the main battle lines in politics today are drawn through cultural issues (N. Podhoretz, interview by author, 11 September 1998).

Explanation may also be found in the search for new enemies, with foes such as feminists and multiculturalists figuring as substitute menaces for conservatives' vanquished socialist adversaries. Thus, at the time of communism's collapse, Meyerson claimed that the greatest ideological threats to Western civilization now came from within the West's own cultural institutions (Meyerson, 1990).

However, more has heightened conservative anxieties than just the conclusion of previous conflicts. What may again be seen is that conservatives recognize that whatever victories have been won have not meant the triumph of their beliefs in every sphere. As Thatcher concedes, 'while we *have* converted our opponents to an extent on economics, we have not done so on much of anything else' (Thatcher, 1997a, p. 36). This being so, she too emphasizes that 'conservatism is not ultimately about economics', but matters such as tradition, the family and education.

At the same time, a number of conservatives have drawn parallels between the Cold War and the culture war, perhaps seeking a similar clarity and unity of purpose. For example, Irving Kristol argued in the early post-Cold War period that

> There is no 'after the Cold War' for me. So far from having ended, my cold war has increased in intensity, as sector after sector of American life has been ruthlessly corrupted by the liberal ethos ... Now that the other 'Cold War' is over, the real cold war has begun. (Kristol, 1993, p. 144)

However, such talk of the Cold War highlights a major difficulty conservatives face in making culture their main battleground. Whereas socialism presented a relatively clear and easily identifiable enemy – even if only as caricature – those within the sphere of culture constitute a more diverse set of antagonists. As Minogue argues, the threat posed by ideologies such as feminism and political correctness is a far more amorphous menace, and therefore much harder to combat (Minogue, 1992/3, p. 83).

To justify their claims that morality is in decline, many conservatives rely upon rafts of quantitative data for support, appearing to take an almost perverse pleasure in the cataloguing of statistics of moral disarray. An exemplar of this approach is Bennett, compiler of an index of 'leading cultural indicators' – including rates of divorce and levels of educational attainment – drawing together every possible measure of American's parlous moral condition (W. J. Bennett, 1994a). Yet despite this reliance upon empirical data in identifying social malaise, by contrast, explanation usually turns upon normative argument. Rather than considering the possibility that material factors, such as poverty, may be responsible for 'antisocial' behaviour, it is moral ones that are typically cited. Indeed, arguments that economic factors may to be blame are given short shrift by conservatives, as does Himmelfarb (Himmelfarb, 1996a, pp. 238–43). Thus, she argues, 'social pathology' – illegitimacy, crime and dependency – is assuredly a function of 'moral pathology', and not the result of economic deprivation.

One consequence of the priority present-day conservatives attach to cultural issues is that conventional politics becomes much less important. Indeed, it may be far less worthwhile for conservative writers to focus their efforts upon influencing politicians. For example, Digby Anderson argues that whereas in the 1980s most of the output of the Social Affairs Unit was essentially addressed to government, in the 1990s a much wider audience needed to be targeted, since it is 'as important to change the way the Archbishop of Canterbury thinks or the way that the medical profession thinks as the way the government think' (D. Anderson, interview by author, 22 June 1998).

Yet believing that those who control the cultural and moral spheres possess more influence than those in political power leads many conservatives to highly pessimistic conclusions. For instance, Bork wrote at the time of the Gingrich-led Republican capture of Congress that he was far from sanguine about its prospects (Bork, 1995, p. 146). The reason for this, he argued, is that politicians are largely impotent in the face of developments such as the spread of political correctness, which are more significant worries than an unbalanced budget. In other words, even when conservative politicians win power, this may not provide a solution to conservative thinkers' worries.

In fact, pessimism among American conservatives is widespread, with declarations of the 'crisis', 'end' or 'death' of Western culture and morality commonplace (Boxx and Quinlivan, 1996; Buchanan, 2001; Kopff, 1996). However, a definite change of tone has occurred since the early to mid-1990s. Typical then was Himmelfarb, who identified the grievous moral disorder of society as representing a state of demoralization (Himmelfarb, 1996a). While ominous prognostications were certainly made – for example, Neuhaus portended that 'cultural warfare may be on the edge of turning into civil war' (Neuhaus, 1994, p. 53) – belief in the possibility that society might be remoralized was nonetheless widespread.

Yet by millennium's end, significant conservative figures had come to believe that they had been decisively, and possibly irreversibly, defeated. For American conservatives, the watershed issue was the Clinton–Lewinsky scandal (though more in confirming what they had for some time feared than itself being the determining factor). For example, Paul Weyrich – co-founder of the Moral Majority – concluded after the failure to impeach Clinton that 'If there really were a moral majority out there, Bill Clinton would have been driven out of office months ago' (Weyrich, 1999). His gloomy assessment was that there remains today only a 'moral minority' and that conservatives 'probably have lost the culture war'. Irving Kristol, after a much briefer period of conflict than the Cold War one with which he had compared it, has also declared the culture war lost, believing that the forces of moral decay have proven largely victorious (cited in Bailey, 2001).

Not all conservatives see the situation as entirely hopeless (see Arnn and Feulner, 1999), yet unqualified optimism is distinctly rare. Despairing sentiments are also expressed by British conservatives, in perceiving the demise of Britain's traditional values, customs and institutions. For example, journalist Peter Hitchens believes that we have witnessed the very 'abolition' of Britain (Hitchens, 1999), while Scruton feels that the only way to speak of English identity today is in the form of an elegy (Scruton, 2001a).

What then is – or was – at stake in the culture war? While space prohibits an examination of every relevant issue, four of the most significant can be explored.

Major issues

Education and the arts

Much of the literature in this area takes its cue from the arguments set out by Bloom, a Straussian defender of traditional educational standards and the Western canon (Bloom, 1987). Conservatives accord educational issues such a high priority because they believe that the 'cultural transmission belt of a free society is education' (Eberly, 1994, p. xxxiii). In other words, because it is a prime means by which a culture reproduces itself (Scruton, 2001b, pp. 132–41). For American conservatives, writings on educational issues constituted a mini-industry in the early 1990s (Bradford, 1992; D'Souza, 1991; Finn, 1991; Kimball, 1990).

Conservatives are troubled by two perceived developments. The first is a decline of educational standards, with many believing that traditional ideals of rigour and application have been eroded by modes of teaching that reduce ambition to the level of the lowest common denominator. Child-centred teaching methods, the downgrading of objective methods of assessment and the displacement of traditional academic subjects by vocational ones are all seen to contribute to a lowering of standards and the eclipse of excellence (Lawlor, 1990, 1993; O'Hear, 1991a, 1991b).

Second, is the belief that schools and universities are now dominated by educators not even motivated by traditional educational ambitions, but by the desire to instil in students politically correct notions about culture and society. Conservatives claim that curricula are corrupted by a disproportionate attention being paid to marginalized groups and non-Western cultures; an over-emphasis upon the negative aspects of Western societies' records on matters such as race and gender; a denigration of great historical figures and their achievements; and a corrosive questioning of traditional values and institutions (Cheney, 1995; Phillips, 1996).

Most serious, the harmful effects of current educational theories can be felt far beyond the domain of education. For example, Lynne Cheney argues that in encouraging students to adopt cynical attitudes towards their own societies and histories, adversary ideologues undermine the foundations of patriotism (Cheney, 1995, pp. 24–30). The major problem, therefore, with ideologies such as feminism and multiculturalism is that their adherents are responsible for politicizing the process of socialization. Indeed, David Bryden believes that 'the struggle in the universities is not really about the curriculum', but about politics (Bryden, 1991, p. 52).

The cross-over between concerns relating to the sphere of education and those relating to the wider culture is also apparent in the distinction conservatives seek to maintain between 'high' and 'low' culture. One of the core components of a traditional education conservatives wish to uphold is the centrality of the Western canon, since this is believed to embody the most important insights of human experience. According to Hilton Kramer, editor of the *New Criterion*, 'the treasured intellectual traditions of the West ... require a vigorous and creative high culture for their survival and renewal' (Kramer, 1999, p. 25).

Concomitant to this defence of the highest is a belief in the inferior status of the lowest. In Kramer's view, 'the fate of high culture ... depend[s] on its ability to marshal a principled resistance to the influence of popular culture'. Taking up this challenge, Scruton seeks to show that classical music and literature are most definitely superior to popular varieties, with the notion that all should be treated as of equal worth met with derision (Scruton, 1998). Popular culture is viewed by conservatives not only as less valuable, but as positively harmful: many argue that the violence and 'obscenity' to be found within popular films and music is causally related to real-life antisocial behaviour (W. J. Bennett, 1994c, p. 21; Will, 1994, pp. 13–15).

The charge commonly levelled at conservatives in defending high culture is that of elitism. This indictment is confronted by Minogue, who argues that 'to criticise a conclusion as elitist is merely to commit a fallacy of irrelevance, an evasion of the issue of truth' (Minogue, 1997, p. 7). In other words, it is a means of sidestepping instead of answering the question of whether one cultural artefact is in fact superior to another. However, a different accusation that may be put to conservatives is not that they are too elitist, but rather that they are rarely 'elitist' enough, that is, it is difficult to view conservatives genuinely as objective defenders of high intellectual standards, since they themselves typically hold highly partial views as to the purposes of education and cultural experience. Conservatives are clearly guilty of aiming at partisan ends, even if they deny that these are 'political'. Many argue, like Cheney, that the fostering of a traditional sense of national identity should be the task of educators (see Phillips, 1996, pp. 313–22). Furthermore, Bennett believes that, to combat the social regression that has occurred since the 1960s, 'we desperately need to recover a sense of the fundamental purpose of education, which is to engage in the architecture of souls' (W. J. Bennett, 1993b).

In other words, conservative defences of a traditional view of education and the arts are frequently motivated not by any passionate commitment to their intrinsic merits, but by the belief that they are useful tools in engineering individuals' moral and social beliefs. As Claes Ryn observes, 'Many supposedly intellectual conservatives seem to consider ideas and cultures from afar' (Ryn, 1996, p. 117), having little real interest in them beyond the instrumental.

Multiculturalism and identity

As seen in the last chapter, many conservatives believe that membership of a society implies the acceptance of common beliefs about its aims and values. Yet, as Ernesto Laclau notes, the post-Cold War world has witnessed a 'proliferation of particularist identities' (Laclau, 1994, p. 1) which do not appeal to any single, common foundations. Indeed, contemporary theories of identity often deem the requirement of a common culture oppressive, instead conceiving the preservation of difference to be crucial.

What conservatives fear about multiculturalism in particular is that society will be hastened down a path of 'Balkanization', with an explosion of disparate identities leading to hostility and conflict. This view especially informs conservative diagnoses of racial conflict. Again, the idea that explanation may be found in material causes is usually dismissed, with blame for racial tensions widely attributed to the fragmentation engendered by multiculturalists' preference for maintaining distinct racial identities against integration or assimilation (Decter, 1992; Murray, 1992a). Sensitive to accusations of racism, conservatives stress that preserving a common culture is not simply for the benefit of a white elite. Instead, it is multiculturalists' encouragement of non-whites to maintain separate identities that, conservatives argue, is precisely what enforces their segregation and lower status within society (Decter, 1991).

Behind the promotion of multiculturalism, John O'Sullivan again perceives the dark hand of the new class at work, having discovered 'that the way to extend its power is to divide Americans into different tribes so that it can then step forward as the mediator of their disputes' (J. O'Sullivan, 1998, p. 23). O'Sullivan also undertakes to distinguish conservative from multicultural and postmodern views of identity, seeing as a major challenge to conservatism the perspective of 'identity politics' (J. O'Sullivan, 1996, pp. 23–43).

For conservatives, he argues, individual identity is relatively fixed. In the first instance, this is largely by the accidents of birth: the family, nation and religion into which we are born. Over time, we may reflect upon the ideas and norms we receive from these sources and modify our identities to an extent, but the influence of our origins should never be eradicated. Individual change should be effected as gradually and cautiously as social change, always retaining the basic essence of our original identity.

By contrast, O'Sullivan claims, contemporary views suggest that there is no such incliminable core to identity, and therefore countenance its wholesale reconstruction. Such fluid views of identity thus reveal a similar hubris to that of the social engineer. Moreover, whereas a conservative understanding incorporates a wide range of sources as responsible for the formation of identity, presenting a multi-faceted vision, the concentration identity politics asks individuals to place upon single aspects of their identities – such as race or sexuality – means that modern understandings offer essentially one-dimensional conceptions.

Accordingly, there are for O'Sullivan a number of problems with modern theories. First, in predicating identity upon a single facet of personality, they offer an impoverished view of individual existence; second, in regarding identity as open to constant revision, this is a decidedly fragile and precarious one; and third, infinitely plastic individual identities provide weak foundations for the maintenance of strong and stable communities.

An important question conservatives have to answer is that of what grounds a sense of common identity. A number of possibilities may be suggested. For example, for Straussians it is the universality of natural rights. However, identifying a universal foundation for common bonds contradicts the particularist standpoint preferred by many conservatives, even though they may also wish to resist the implications of a multiculturalist approach. An answer to this dilemma may be found by conservatives in conceiving of these bonds as formed at the level of the nation-state – as does Scruton (Scruton, 1996a, pp. 27–8) – which thereby avoids the polarities of either an abstract universalism or a fragmentary postmodernism.

American conservatives inevitably feel the challenge of multiculturalism to be especially acute, in the light of the diverse origins of their society. Appealing to the bonds of a common national culture may therefore be more difficult. One strategy is that of writers such as Kirk, who argue that a specifically British cultural heritage is the single most important source of American identity (Kirk, 1953, 1993). Richard Brookhiser similarly emphasizes the priority of a particular cultural perspective for American identity, that of the White Anglo-Saxon Protestant (WASP), although being careful to frame the argument in cultural rather than racial terms (Brookhiser, 1991). In fact, most will go no further than Frum,

who argues that 'the preservation of the existing ethnocultural character of the United States is not in itself an illegitimate goal...with the
emphasis on culture rather than ethnicity' (Frum, 1997a, p. 64). Here
then 'culture' serves another important purpose for modern conservatives, which is to allow them to circumvent the quicksands of controversial racial discussions.

Even so, critics of conservative efforts to uphold the ideal of a
common culture typically highlight an alleged disjunction between
conservative assumptions and the pluralistic realities of modern societies. For example, Gray argues – in seeming agreement with Giddens's
view of modern conservatives and tradition – that 'cultural fundamentalists' like Scruton are mistaken if they believe it possible to recreate in
the modern world traditional shared modes of life, since this overlooks
the truth of 'an ethnic and a religious pluralism that is unalterable and
irreversible in any foreseeable future' (Gray, 1993b, p. 277). Efforts to
override this pluralism are therefore not only intolerant but also imprac-
ticable: modern societies simply are pluralistic ones and no amount of
conservative protestation will change this fact.

However, whether or not Western societies truly have become more
pluralistic, the argument that it is primarily the reality of social diversity
that is the difficulty for conservatives is mistaken. Many American
conservatives willingly acknowledge that their society originated from
a varied range of identities (Ryn, 1993, p. 21); yet this did not mean
that the creation of a common identity was then impossible. The idea
of American citizenship as embodied in the motto *e pluribus unum* –
implying that whatever differences individuals brought with them from
the old world might be pooled in the creation of a shared identity in the
new – is far from entirely a myth of cultural conservatives.

One of the means by which this once took place is highlighted by
Kirkpatrick, in arguing that a traditional model of public education is of
value to American conservatives because it aims to create the common
ties of identity that America's ethnic origins do not (J. Kirkpatrick, interview by author, 16 September 1998). Conservative critics of multiculturalism are at least correct in perceiving that the significant change of
recent times is not increased social diversity itself, but a decreased belief
in the idea that differences can or should be transcended.

The family

One of the most important sources of identity cited by conservatives is
the family (W. J. Bennett, 2001; Morgan, 1992, pp. 35–45; J. Q. Wilson,

1993, pp. 141–63). Indeed, support for the family is often seen as wholly central to a conservative outlook (Scruton, 2001b, pp. 129–31). This centrality derives from the fact that it is the first institution through which the social world is perceived and is therefore crucial in the formation of identity. Its value resides in its establishment of a link between generations: as Murray argues, a Burkean understanding of the world teaches that 'there is an accumulated human wisdom in the evolution of the family across society over the centuries' (C. Murray, interview by author, 22 September 1998). In other words, family relations bind the individual within the web of past and future history.

In cultivating a sense of belonging, the family is believed to act as a natural source of the values of stability, order and continuity that the individual takes with him when relating to wider society; it is thus at the heart of legitimating the conservative belief in a continuing social order. Similarly, because the individual learns in the private sphere that identity is not an artificial construction, he will also recognize the misguidedness of so regarding society. It is thanks to these lessons of family life that 'however vociferously people may declare their attachment to other ideologies, in their most solemn innervations they are naturally conservative' (Scruton, 2001b, p. 131).

Conservatives' preferred model is 'the nuclear family, defined as a monogamous married couple living with their children' (W. J. Bennett, 2001, p. 12). Moreover, according to Bennett, its thriving 'is vital to civilization's success'. The family is responsible not only for the inculcation of a broadly conservative disposition but also for the transmission of specific values. As James Q. Wilson puts it, it is a 'school for moral instruction' (J. Q. Wilson, 1993, p. 163). As a result of conservatives' strong conviction that the cause of antisocial behaviour is personal immorality, a condition of social disorder is traceable back to a state of disorder within the family. For example, Patricia Morgan argues that social problems relating to issues ranging from crime to health to the environment are all 'related to the loosening and breaking of relationships' (Morgan, 1992, p. 43). Consequently, they 'are only amenable to family policy'.

It is because the nuclear family is imagined to perform such key functions that conservatives strenuously resist any threats to it, such as the liberalization of laws and attitudes towards illegitimacy (Murray, 1984, 1990, 1996), divorce (Decter, 1997; Deech, 1994; Mattox, 1995) and abortion (Johnson, 1996a; C. Moore, 1992b; Neuhaus, 1992). However, although libertarians like Murray may be as uneasy as traditionalist conservatives about modern developments, the latter – as shown in the previous chapter – frequently hold the market at least partly responsible for the debased condition of civil society's institutions. This includes the family. For example, Morgan argues of the 1980s that 'In the very decade the traditional family needed support, government – Conservative Government – failed it' (Morgan, 1992, p. 36). In its commitment to prioritizing the individual and attacking the collective institutions of the Left, the Thatcher administration neglected the interests of those collective units, like the family, cherished by conservatives. In this area as well, tensions between varieties of conservative are much apparent.

While the traditional family model has been subjected to numerous intellectual assaults over the years, many conservatives believe that current ideological attacks are especially potent. Two arguments in particular are worth noting. The first is forwarded by Daniel Moynihan, who identifies a phenomenon he terms 'defining deviancy down' (Moynihan, 1993). His argument is that modes of behaviour that would have once been considered deviant, such as childbirth out of wedlock and minority forms of sexuality, have today become accepted as normal. With the category of deviancy greatly contracted, non-traditional lifestyles are now treated simply as equal alternatives to traditional ones. The unique status of the traditional family model has thus been severely eroded.

Yet even more worrying for conservatives is a complementary phenomenon, identified by Charles Krauthammer as 'defining deviancy up' (Krauthammer, 1993). According to Krauthammer, the problem today is not merely that institutions like the nuclear family no longer possess a privileged status, but that they are often treated as the 'deviant' form. The way in which the traditional family unit is discussed by many – particularly feminists – is in largely pathological terms, with the emphasis placed upon negative issues like wife-beating and child abuse rather than its positive virtues. Krauthammer's claim is that, by exaggerating statistics on rape and abuse and attacking the values of masculinity, conservatives' opponents seek ruthlessly to demonize the nuclear family.

However, in relation to the family there are again clear signs of defensiveness among conservatives. Even the most resolute are frequently far less 'hard-line' on family issues than at first sight they appear. Neuhaus, although viewing abortion as wholly and unquestionably immoral, nonetheless argues that what he seeks is 'constructive debate' over the issue, adopting a more conciliatory approach when attention is turned to what he believes is practicably achievable (Neuhaus, 1992, pp. 121–4). Yet the clearest indicator is the attempt by some to accommodate to a world of plural family models. For example, Portillo hopes to stake out territory for a more compassionate conservatism by accepting the reality of different types of family (Portillo, 1997, pp. 18–19).

The problem with such proposals is that it is far from certain that non-traditional families are capable of fulfilling the roles that conservatives expect of traditional ones. This is well illustrated by John O'Sullivan. He argues, for example, that although the gay family model may 'mimic' the form of the conventional one, in that it cannot perform functions such as childbearing, its content is very different and does not possess the same merit (J. O'Sullivan, 1996, p. 39). Moreover, if any type of relationship is considered a family, without requiring the same commitment as a traditional marriage, this inevitably weakens the family's status as an ideal to be esteemed. Yet most crucially, O'Sullivan is concerned like Krauthammer that the way in which gay and feminist identities define themselves is precisely in opposition to the supposedly repressive nature of the traditional family. In other words, there may simply be no possibility of peaceful coexistence between different conceptions.

From a conservative perspective, O'Sullivan's contentions make sense. However, what is also significant today is that the arguments forwarded even by defenders of the traditional family are often not distinctively conservative ones. In regard to this, it is useful to consider the critique developed by Josephson and Burack, who characterize the model propounded by many contemporary defenders of the two-parent biological family as a 'neo-traditional' one, the neo- prefix denoting the fact that its proponents avoid explicit suggestions of male dominance and offer as primary justification for its superiority the well-being of children (Josephson and Burack, 1998, pp. 213–31).

While child welfare has always been a part of conservative arguments, it is today given an especially prominent position. For example, Richard Gill's plaintive plea that support for the nuclear family is necessary 'for the sake of the children' (R. T. Gill, 1992) is repeated by numerous conservatives, who argue that it is the range of emotional, psychological and material needs of children that makes families comprised of two biological parents the best (Joseph, 1991; Raison, 1990). For Josephson and Burack, this emphasis upon child welfare is largely a smokescreen, to disguise the real concern of family values advocates to preserve an oppressive, male-dominated institution. However, what is revealed more than any attempt to hide a covert patriarchal agenda is a reluctance on the part of many conservatives to argue their distinctive case for the nuclear family, instead laying their hands upon whatever arguments may win them ready consensus.

In fact, an almost politically correct concern for the plight of not only children but also women is much in evidence within the conservative literature. For example, Paul Johnson's professed unease about the rise in the divorce rate is that it 'is the prime cause of poverty in Britain today, especially among women and children' (Johnson, 1996b, p. 22). Equally, the feminist critique of masculinity may be given a conservative twist. For example, Duncan and Hobson argue that a key virtue of the nuclear family is that it restrains the 'naturally aggressive' male: 'the demise of the traditional family has spawned a new kind of rogue male, who is young, inadequately socialised, personally irresponsible and lacking in self-control' (Duncan and Hobson, 1995, p. 385; see also Murray, 1994a, p. 26; J. Q. Wilson, 1993, pp. 165–9). There is much in conservatives' arguments, therefore, that might easily find favour even among their adversaries.

The difficulty for libertarians in echoing many feminists' negative opinions of male behaviour – rather than expounding the positive view of assertive individualism one might expect – is that they may simply provide intellectual support to their enemies' demands for increased regulation of the private sphere. Furthermore, as Josephson and Burack argue, child welfare arguments provide weak justification for traditionalists' preferences – if the well-being of children truly is the main concern, prioritizing the nuclear family is far from the only option. For example, Josephson and Burack's own conclusion is that greater resources, including welfare payments and educational and child-care facilities, should be provided to support families of all types. In other words, the 'sake of the children' does not imply the necessity of any particular family model.

Religion

Although there may be no necessary connection between conservatism and a religious outlook, among major ideologies conservatism has always placed the greatest emphasis upon the values of the Judeo-Christian tradition (Nisbet, 1986, p. 68). Indeed, some conservatives do believe that conservatism would be unthinkable without a religious dimension. For example, Quintin Hogg argues that 'there can be no genuine conservatism which is not founded upon a religious view of the basis of civil obligation' (Hogg, 1959, p. 19). In contemporary terms, William Kristol contends that 'it's hard to imagine that there'll be a conservative future that is not also a reasonably religious future' (W. Kristol, interview by author, 20 October 1998).

While many conservatives may be genuinely religious, a highly instrumental view of religion's role is frequently evident. For example, Nisbet believes 'that some bulwark of faith, even if in a body of morality that is falsely credited with divine inspiration, is necessary to human beings' (Nisbet, 1986, p. 73). Similarly, it is as least as much the institutional side of religion that is important to conservatives as its specific teachings. Scruton argues that the Church of England is of value to conservatives, whether or not 'its fundamental doctrines [are] true or false' (Scruton, 2001b, p. 159), because it helps attach citizens to civil life.

The obvious problem for contemporary British conservatives is that neither the Christian religion nor the Church of England any longer possesses much social authority. Gray believes that British conservatives neglect 'one very large and, for them, very awkward fact...that "traditional Christian morality" is for most people in Britain today not even a historical memory' (Gray, 1997, p. 129). This being the case, it is anachronistic to expect Christianity to buttress traditional moral values; as much as the latter have been vitiated in recent years, so has the authority of the former. Moreover, insofar as the Anglican Church continues to have an influence upon social and political life, it is not necessarily a 'conservative' one. The emergence of 'dissident bishops and socialist priests' (Honderich, 1990, p. 168) means that on issues such as gay rights, divorce and abortion, it cannot automatically be depended on to line up on conservatives' side.

While it is not the place here to analyse the Church of England's travails in adapting to a post-traditional world, it is certainly true that established religion does not offer absolutist conservatism the support it historically once did. However, it is not true that conservatives are entirely neglectful of this 'awkward fact'. Scruton accepts that, owing to factors such as social mobility and the role of a cynical media, few young people today possess much knowledge of the Christian faith (Scruton, 1996a, pp. 21–3). He is also aware that the Church itself may not be particularly sympathetic to conservatism.

Nonetheless, although Scruton believes that these developments are lamentable, he argues that even in the absence of belief in a transcendent being, the desire for 'transcendent' bonds of community – those that are not simply the result of contractual choice – retains a strong compulsion (Scruton, 2001b, pp. 158–9). Even in a largely secular context, he maintains, the conservative vision is still more compelling than that of a contractarian liberalism. However, even if it is granted that British conservatism does not necessarily require the support of the Christian tradition, there are still difficulties with Scruton's argument. Secular ties do not sanctify the grounds of political obligation and nor is it certain that community bonds – even transcendent ones – are always grounded in values of which conservatives approve. As discussed in the last chapter, community institutions are not inevitably homes of conservative principles.

American conservatives may appear to be in a more sanguine position – as Irving Kristol points out, church attendance in America remains among the highest in the developed world (I. Kristol, interview by author, 13 October 1998). Indeed, one battle of the culture war Kristol believes conservatives have not lost is the significance of religion in American life (Bailey, 2001). However, this significance is not as straightforward as conservatives may imagine, or critics often fear.

In fact, the level of church attendance says little about the actual character of religious conviction. Bork is likely nearer to the truth than Kristol, in his pessimistic assessment of the modern Catholic Church. Despite the number of its adherents, he argues, it is 'amazing the number who attend but don't subscribe to what the Church teaches, in so far as the Church teaches anything these days … most of the Catholics sitting in the pews choose what parts of the teaching they like and then reject the rest' (R. Bork, interview by author, 10 September 1998). In other words, even the traditional heartland of moral absolutism may not be the last bulwark against moral decay conservatives like Kristol may hope.

Nor is the Religious Right the force it once was. Groups such as the Promise Keepers (which encourages men to come together in public to avow their commitment to God) typify more its contemporary face than organizations like the Moral Majority or the Christian Coalition. Although Kristol sees in the rise of groups like the Promise Keepers evidence of something close to a religious awakening (cited in Murray, 1995, p. 131), its popularity is in reality attributable to the fact that it offers a 'watered down, gushy religion', with meetings characterized by such sentimental indulgences as 'hand-holding and hugging and multiracial sing-alongs' (Rosin, 1997, p. 11). In Hanna Rosin's adroit description, the emergence of such groups more likely represents 'the feminization of the American right', than anything akin to a revival of old-time religious fervour.

Frum's analysis of the failure of the traditional Religious Right to achieve any of its major goals is also relevant: abortion has not been made illegal, gay rights have not been reversed, church and state remain separate and the teaching of multi-faith education continues to be extended in schools (Frum, 1997a, pp. 79–82). Whatever the strength of religious adherence within American society, this devotion rarely translates into political successes for a traditional moral agenda.

The refuge of scoundrels

With conservatives evidently concerned about a range of moral and cultural issues, this raises the question of whether talk should be of a singular 'culture war' or plural 'culture wars'. Neuhaus, for example, defends the former conception, asserting that at the root of cultural conflict is a single issue: abortion (R. Neuhaus, interview by author, 23 October 1998). However, although it may well be that the various disputes are united, it seems arbitrary to pick any single substantive issue as the unifying factor.

For most conservatives, if there is a common culprit in explaining society's descent into moral chaos, then it is relativism – the notion that there are no absolute values or standards, merely different interpretations and perspectives (Cheney, 1995, pp. 15–16; D'Souza, 1991, p. 157; Duncan and Hobson, 1995, pp. 263–73). Whether it is the proliferation of alternative lifestyles or the rejection of the Western canon, what conservatives perceive underlies all culture war disputes is the problem that society not only no longer seems to share their values, but appears to reject the very idea of definite right and wrong.

The centrality of relativism to conservative concerns is well shown by Bloom, who offers as his introductory statement the regretful observation that 'There is one thing a professor can be absolutely certain of: almost every student entering the university believes, or says he believes, that truth is relative' (Bloom, 1987, p. 25). Moral relativism is the form that worries conservatives most. For example, Wilson is shocked to find amongst his students 'no general agreement that those guilty of the Holocaust itself were guilty of a moral horror' (J. Q. Wilson, 1993, p. 8). Equally, Bennett's titling of his book on the Clinton–Lewinsky scandal *The Death of Outrage* (W. J. Bennett, 1998) reveals the widespread concern of American conservatives at the time not just with an issue of supposed immorality, but at least as much with the relativistic lack of censure with which society greeted it.

Relativism also raises British conservatives' ire, notably Scruton's. In moral disputes, he contends, 'relativism is the first refuge of the scoundrel'; indeed, '*vulgar* relativism has no hope of surviving outside the minds of ignorant rascals' (Scruton, 1994, pp. 32, 33). Scruton is well able to pinpoint the logical flaw in the relativist's case: 'in asserting that relativism is true for *him*, the relativist asserts that it is true for him absolutely. He is committed to absolute truth by the very practice of assertion'. That is, even to avow relativism entails a contradiction. Yet despite this identification of its incoherence as an intellectual doctrine, the bluntness of Scruton's condemnation reveals the almost palpable frustration conservatives feel at relativism's seeming prevalence and immunity to rebuttal. Nonetheless, Roy Bland sees saving 'our culture and democracy from the relativist cancer' (Bland, 1996, p. 51) as a key 'cause for conservatives'.

The most common accusation conservatives face in attacking relativism is that of authoritarianism, of seeking to impose their own interpretation of truth while oppressively denying validity to all others. Conservatives usually reject this suggestion, arguing that they support free speech and critical debate (Cheney, 1995, pp. 192–206). Indeed, many argue that it is their opponents who are the real enemies of liberty. D'Souza observes in relation to advocates of political correctness what he describes as 'the paradox of the relativist authoritarian': though they may decry the bigotry of moral absolutists, they are ruthless in their efforts to quash dissenters to their own doctrines (D'Souza, 1991, p. 190). In support of this argument, D'Souza documents numerous alleged cases of students and academics persecuted for failing to abide by the strictures of political correctness.

Unsurprisingly, in apportioning responsibility for the decline of faith in traditional values, at the top of conservatives' lists are antagonistic intellectuals. According to Wilson, the belief that subscribing to a definite morality lacks any rational basis is a proposition 'we have learned, either firsthand from intellectuals or secondhand from the pronouncements of people influenced by intellectuals' (J. Q. Wilson, 1993, p. viii). Similarly, Duncan and Hobson – citing Keynes's view of the power of ideas – blame not only the interventionist state but also all those thinkers who scorn traditional morality, whose beliefs have managed 'to insinuate themselves into the private lives even of uneducated men and women' (Duncan and Hobson, 1995, p. 267).

One difficulty with these arguments is that identified with new-class analyses in Chapter 2, that of attributing too great a coherence and unity to 'adversary' groups. However, another is that it is very much open to question whether hostile intellectuals could ever be solely responsible for widespread changes in society's beliefs. The problem with this notion is not so much that conservatives ascribe too much importance to the power of ideas, but that they treat them as too autonomous a force. That is, in attributing the success of 'antagonistic' ideas simply to the activities of malevolent intellectuals, conservatives neglect the deeper forces that are responsible for undermining traditional values, and which therefore give these ideas resonance.

In terms of these deeper forces, Gray argues that what is truly responsible for the depletion of a common culture is the 'permanent revolution' unleashed by conservatives' own free-market policies (Gray, 1997, p. 48). In that conservatives do not wish to recognize their own culpability, their blaming of a liberal-dominated culture is a form of scapegoating (p. 127). However, although Gray's argument highlights an important truth in emphasizing the role of market forces in undermining tradition, previous chapters have demonstrated that many conservatives are prepared to accept that market forces are responsible for weakening the moral fabric. In fact, as will be explored in Chapter 6, conservative culpability for the undermining of belief in absolute values may reside as much in their own articulations of sceptical and anti-universalist doctrines as in their support for free markets.

Regardless of who or what is responsible for any decline, what needs to be examined next are the strategies conservatives put forward in the hope of reversing moral and cultural degeneration.

The remoralization of society

Although many conservatives are committed to absolutism when it comes to values, a particular difficulty they face today is that uncertainty surrounds even the meaning of the term 'value'. As Wilson observes, while cultural conflict is not new,

> What is new, distinctive, and odd about the contemporary version of this age-old debate is the language in which it is conducted. It is about 'values'. But what do we mean by a 'value'? A taste? A preference? A belief? A moral principle? A binding obligation? Most people flinch from answering that question, at least in public. (J. Q. Wilson, 1993, p. xi)

In attempting to obviate the confusions that appear to have infected even the language of morality, one of the most salient features of contemporary conservative discourses is the resurrection of the idea of 'virtue'. Himmelfarb emphasizes the difference between the definiteness of virtues and the relativism of values. Thus, she argues, a transmutation occurred in the twentieth century – though owing its origins to Nietzsche – whereby 'morality became so thoroughly relativized and subjectified that virtues ceased to be "virtues" and became "values"' (Himmelfarb, 1996a, p. 9). Whereas talk of 'values' seems to imply that morality is mere custom and convention, the idea of 'virtues' lends it a much more resolute character. Following Thatcher's notorious invocation, Himmelfarb believes our virtues should be those of the Victorian era.

The notion of virtue is prevalent within present-day conservative writings (D. Anderson, 1992; W. J. Bennett, 1993a; Machan, 1998; Sommers, 1993). According to Frohnen, 'Virtue is, in fact, the very basis of conservative political philosophy' (Frohnen, 1993, p. 3). Similarly, Shirley Letwin interprets the Thatcherite project not as an essentially economic enterprise but as an attempt to rejuvenate the 'vigorous virtues' (S. Letwin, 1992). Thatcher herself emphasizes that, although she is usually cited as praising Victorian values, she originally stressed Victorian virtues (Thatcher, 1993, p. 627).

Closely related to the desire for the revival of virtue is the appeal for the resurrection of more virtuous forms of identity. Thus, another prominent feature of conservative writings is a concern with individual character (J. Q. Wilson, 1991). Many conservatives wish in particular to see a return of the categories of 'gentleman' and 'lady' (S. Letwin, 1992, pp. 336–7; Minogue, 1997, p. 54; Murray, 1995, p. 132). Even libertarians argue that it is not just any type of individual they wish to see thrive if the state is rolled back. For example, Boaz contends that although libertarians aim at emancipating individuals from coercive government, this does not mean emancipating them from their social responsibilities; the type of character he hopes will flourish in a libertarian society is one imbued with values opposite to those of 'profligacy, intemperance, indolence, dependency' (Boaz, 1997, pp. 146–7).

In terms of specifics, many conservatives present lists of virtues they believe to be the most important. For Letwin the virtuous Thatcherite individual is 'upright, self-sufficient, energetic, adventurous, independent-minded, loyal to friends, and robust against enemies' (S. Letwin, 1992, p. 33); for Himmelfarb, Victorian virtues include 'hard work, thrift, cleanliness, self-reliance, self-respect, neighborliness, patriotism' (Himmelfarb, 1996a, p. 5); while Bennett offers self-discipline, compassion, responsibility, friendship, work, courage, perseverance, honesty, loyalty and faith (W. J. Bennett, 1993a).

An obvious difficulty with such presentations is that they often appear to be platitudinous. While the advocacy of a virtue-centred ethics may seem to offer a solution to the problem of moral relativism, the actual content of conservative conceptions may be so vague or uncontroversial as to fail to distinguish their preferred morality from any other. As Paul Starr comments sarcastically in relation to Bennett, 'I do not know liberals who endorse indiscipline, insensitivity, irresponsibility, hatred, sloth, cowardice, vacillation, lying, disloyalty, and despair' (Starr, 1996, p. 6). Although Murray takes the success of Bennett's *Book of Virtues* – having proven a best-seller – as evidence that a 'partial restoration of traditional society' is underway (Murray, 1995, p. 132), the fact that the virtues Bennett acclaims are ones that only the most determined of relativists would deny positive worth means that its popularity likely proves very little.

If the mere fact of desiring society to be 'virtuous' does not distinguish conservatives, what may is their assertion that the virtues they espouse are in some sense 'tough'. Conservatives typically argue that only they are willing to recognize the need for moral norms that may be difficult, or even painful, to accept. For example, to indicate that we are to understand them in a tough-minded way, Letwin stresses that the 'vigorous' nature of the Thatcherite virtues is in contrast to 'softer' virtues such as kindness, humility and gentleness (S. Letwin, 1992, p. 33). Although the two types may be compatible, Letwin argues, where conflicts arise it is the former that should be prioritized. It is their willingness to embrace this privileging that therefore distinguishes conservatives.

One issue raised by arguments seeking to resurrect the morality of a past era is whether this can be effected without the restoration of that era's social conditions: for example, whether the discipline of Victorian virtues can be revived without also an explicitly hierarchical social system and the consigning of women to the private sphere. Himmelfarb argues that it is possible for Victorian virtues to function in a context that does not require the undesirable social features of nineteenth-century England (Himmelfarb, 1996a, p. 252). Yet this belief can certainly be questioned, as overestimating the extent to which values are separable from their material and social setting, a truth that community minded conservatives at least ought to recognize.

Nonetheless, communitarian conservatives argue that by understanding beliefs as embedded within the shared identity of communities they can eschew relativism in a way that liberal ethical theories cannot. Indeed, a further reason why conservatives seek to revive civil society – constituted, of course, according to their particular understanding – is to recreate the conditions necessary for a common, absolutist morality. Thus, Eberly believes that while contemporary usage 'treats personal and civic virtue as though they are purely private concerns', revitalizing civil society 'will necessitate doing away with a radical, ethical pluralism which holds that no ideal is superior to another' (Eberly, 1994, pp. xxii, xxv).

One of the most widespread criticisms of conservative arguments around virtue and the rejection of relativism arises again from the issues of pluralism and tolerance. For example, for Starr the problem with conservative proposals is that they neglect 'the legitimate demand of different people for equal respect in a society where diversity is not a slogan but a fact' (Starr, 1996, p. 11; see also Morone, 1996). However, from a conservative standpoint the most problematic issue is how in fact to enforce a robust morality.

The common demand of conservatives is for the revival of the notions of shame and stigma, since one of the most pernicious consequences of relativism's sway is that those who transgress against society's norms fail even to acknowledge that they are doing so. For example, Fleming – a conservative who obviously does not believe in adopting any concilia-tory tone – believes about abortion that

> There have always been mothers who killed their babies, born as well as unborn. What is almost unique about our society is that so far from hiding their sin, so far from showing any signs of shame or embarrassment, our latter-day Medeas want not just public monies but public approbation. Instead of slinking into the back alleys where they belong, they march in parades and testify in Congress. (Fleming, 1996b, p. 10)

In other words, even though 'immorality' is not new, at least in the past sinners had the decency to recognize their own moral turpitude. Yet if wrongdoers no longer even accept that they are sinners, there is not even the possibility that they will try to avoid sinning. The fact that today's moral 'deviants' often appear proud of their deviancy – march-ing in parades to draw attention to the fact – is especially galling to many conservatives.

The use of shame to regulate morality is urged by many writers: Anderson, for example, claims that the 'trepidation, circumspection, and anxiety' (D. Anderson, 1995b, p. xvi) caused by the fear of stigma is what best enforces a sense of moral probity (see also Lapin, 1995; Scruton, 2000c). Shame may also work hand in hand with market calcu-lations, suggesting a source of common ground between libertarians who reject using state mechanisms and traditionalists. For example, John Hood (President of the John Locke Foundation) writes in regard to the boycotting campaign organized by Bennett against Time Warner – to force it to stop distributing the records of controversial rap artists – that 'boycott threats and public shaming [are] both perfectly acceptable modes of discourse in a free society' (Hood, 1996, p. 42). However, the linking of economic incentivization with stigma is clearest in Murray's writings, in his argument that individuals can only be expected to recognize their moral failings when they feel the effects – in the form of reduced welfare payments – economically (Murray, 1994b, p. 31).

Of course, it is debatable whether economic incentivization can actually remoralize individual behaviour. Wilson for one queries the belief: 'Over the last two decades, this nation has come face to face with problems that do not seem to respond, or respond enough, to changes in incentives' (J. Q. Wilson, 1991, p. 12). However, even if rational incentives are effective in altering behaviour patterns, distinct from the question of efficacy is that of what type of morality they can regenerate.

For example, although the traditional family might be 'saved' by the elimination of economic support for single-parent families, this salvation would be the result not of individuals coming to recognize the deep and abiding value of the institution, but of their making a utilitarian calculation. Yet preserving institutions in a formal sense is not the same as preserving the values they embody. As Morgan argues, asking individuals to perform cost–benefit analyses in deciding whether to obey moral imperatives will not safeguard the family in any sense that conservatives can applaud, since it is of value precisely because it embodies transcendent bonds of loyalty and respect beyond mere self-interest (Morgan, 1992, p. 44). Indeed, from a traditionalist viewpoint, even to address moral questions from the perspective of individual choice is problematic.

Even so, the charge of failing to appreciate the 'true' value of the family can also be levelled at many traditionalist conservatives, in terms of their dependence upon government to privilege the traditional model. Morgan's attack upon the Thatcher government for its role in the decline of the traditional family is centred upon its removing economic protection, in reducing the pro-family bias of the tax system, and enacting legal changes, such as allowing 'no fault' divorces, that weakened the institution of marriage (pp. 38–9). Yet implying that the strength of the family is dependent upon positive government discrimination suggests as shallow a view of the bonds of marriage – that they are formed to gain tax advantages, or break apart because of the lack of legal constraints – as any utilitarian argument. In theory, conservatives value the family because of its independence from the state; this is frequently contradicted by their reliance upon government to support it.

However, the nature of the contemporary era suggests why cultural conservatives may be particularly inclined to depend upon the state. The difficulty with the 'tough-minded' moral doctrines conservatives propound is that they require very significant demands to be met: not only that individuals understand the difference between right and wrong but also that the majority is willing to enforce these standards, by censuring and ostracizing those who transgress. Yet to suppose the existence of an active moral majority is to suppose a majority informed with the virtues conservatives believe have largely disappeared. Although in traditional societies it may be possible to enforce a sense of shame upon a recalcitrant minority, if the influence of relativism is as pervasive as conservatives claim, then they lack a social basis for implementing their agendas.

As Carl Horowitz points out, while conservatives may see shame as a substitute for state regulation, they commonly fail to recognize 'the messy possibility that it leads to, and reinforces, censorship' (Horowitz, 1997, p. 74). That is, since shame only works as an informal moral regulator when a majority agrees with its strictures, if such social agreement does not exist, it may become necessary to use more formal means to enforce moral codes.

In the past, conservative hostility towards using state mechanisms for this purpose was premised on the belief that, even though the political and intellectual classes might be thoroughly suffused with antagonistic beliefs, the rest of the population, the 'silent majority', were essentially conservative in their values and attitudes (a view that dates back to Burke – Burke, 1968, p. 181). Even if conservatives were isolated intellectually, they could at least imagine themselves in tune with ordinary or commonsense morality. Regardless of whether such a belief was ever correct, it gave conservatives confidence to argue for the state's rolling back, believing that, if individuals were freed from the state's control, people would spontaneously lead 'conservative' lives. Yet today, a distinct worry is evident among many that this is no longer the case.

It is instructive here to examine the analysis presented by Frum. In the 1950s, he argues, it was possible for social conservatives to be anti-statist, and therefore make common cause with libertarians, because at the time America was 'a very socially conservative country' (Frum, 1997b, p. 22). Even during the 1960s, the majority still held to conservative positions on matters such as divorce and premarital sex. However,

> today it's not so clear that the American people, left to their own devices, will behave in ways that a conservative would consider 'virtuous.' In fact, a disconcerting minority of them will choose to smoke marijuana, get pregnant out of wedlock, major in basketweaving at college, wear T-Shirts with obscene messages on them, watch too much television, live on welfare, burn the flag, and play their boomboxes too loud.

The eclecticism of Frum's list – his concerns ranging from the conceivably serious to the largely trivial – indicates well conservatives' sense of

a widespread and diffuse loss of faith in traditional values, many conservatives believing it is more than just a 'disconcerting minority' that
can no longer be relied upon to be virtuous. Moreover, the free market
may be seen as complicit in individuals' loss of moral bearing: it is, Frum
argues, easy to believe the market 'to be egging them on', responsible for
rap music, the Jerry Springer show and internet pornography. Yet if in
their efforts to preserve traditional values conservatives not only face
opposition from adversary intellectuals, but cannot rely upon either
a sympathetic silent majority or the free market for support, then the
only institution upon which they can depend may be the state.

Frum himself, though seeing the logic of the argument, rejects the
conclusion. Yet as seen in earlier chapters, others – like Bork and
Himmelfarb – do not. Here it is worth stressing the consequences of conservatives believing their opponents to be as powerful and influential as
they maintain. For example, DeMuth argues that although he would
prefer to rely upon private rather than state sanctions to discourage drug
taking – such as employers dismissing drug-taking employees and the
disapprobation of friends and neighbours – if it were not illegal, use
of these mechanisms would encounter the resistance of antagonistic
liberals (C. DeMuth, interview by author, 16 October 1998). Employees
dismissed for using drugs would, he argues, be supported by bodies like
the American Civil Liberties Union, who would defend them on the
grounds of discrimination and harassment. Although in an ideal world
conservatives would not have to use the state to enforce moral prohibi-
tions, in this imperfect one they may have to, because of the strength of
hostile forces.

Similarly, if the educational sphere is so much under the control of
adversary educationalists, again it may be necessary to look to the state.
Chester Finn rejects the 'charming but antiquated devotion to "local
control" of schools' of many conservatives, since in practice this preference 'is indistinguishable from maintenance of the status quo under
the thumb of the education establishment' (Finn, 1991, pp. 233–4).
To take power away from hostile educationalists operating at the local
level it may, Finn argues, be necessary to consider measures such as
the introduction of a national curriculum and a national system of
examinations.

However, once more may be seen the danger for conservatives in conceding the legitimacy of using the state to regulate the moral and culture
spheres, in that there is no guarantee that the agenda the state pursues
will be theirs. For example, arguing for a nationally imposed curriculum
for schools does not mean that this will automatically be a conservative

one. As Sheila Lawlor argues in relation to Britain, despite the creation of a national curriculum – as well as the diminution of local education authority control – oppositional educational theorists continue 'to survive, if not dominate, the post-reformed world' (Lawlor, 1992, p. 27). Indeed, thanks to the centralizing measures of Conservative governments, they may simply have gained more powerful means to impose their deleterious ideas upon the whole country.

Puritanism and anti-Puritanism

Undoubtedly the most basic criticism that can be put to conservatives is that the picture they paint of moral and cultural malaise is simply a distortion. That is, the trends they identify are misrepresented and nor are we experiencing any form of fundamental 'crisis' (see M. Lind, 1996, pp. 138–87; J. K. Wilson, 1995). Even if society has become more pluralistic, this need not mean that its moral fabric has been eviscerated by relativism. Such is Gray's belief:

> [I]t is a travesty of our condition to suggest that moral life itself is weak among us. The truth is that we have the makings of a strong and deep common moral culture in Britain today, but its content is rejected by cultural conservatives … it departs not only from Christian values but also from humanism in its concern for the well-being of animals and the integrity of the natural environment. (Gray, 1997, p. 129)

In other words, rather than society having experienced a demoralization, the reality is that its morality has undergone a change in character.

Certainly, conservatives frequently caricature the positions of their enemies in depicting them as thoroughly immoral. In particular, in that a prominent aspect of conservative discourses is to blame the legacy of the counterculture for sexual and moral permissiveness, there is much in the argument of David Wagner 'that the Right (quite intentionally) froze its view of the Left in the late 1960s and early 1970s' (Wagner, 1997, p. 139). Conservatives therefore ignore the fact that the modern Left no longer typically advocates countercultural or bohemian lifestyles. As Wagner observes, the modern Left is more likely to promote what he terms a 'new temperance', a stringent philosophy of restraint founded upon concerns about risks such as AIDS and the imagined prevalence of racial and sexual harassment.

Of course, many conservatives do take account of these newer forms of moral discourse. As examined earlier, writers on education like

D'Souza attack their opponents precisely on the grounds of moral authoritarianism. The significant point is that conservatives thus seem to adopt schizophrenic stances, simultaneously enjoining us to practise greater moral probity in the face of rising licentiousness, while at the same time urging that we reject the constraints demanded by politically correct moralizers.

In terms of this latter face of conservatism, David Brooks is bold enough to declare in the introduction to a collection of writings, entitled *Backward and Upward*, that modern conservatism 'is low on puritanism' (Brooks, 1996, p. xii). The articles that follow celebrate such politically incorrect pleasures as smoking, fast cars and hard drinking. While some of these are merely lowbrow exercises in liberal-baiting – by self-consciously provocative writers like P. J. O'Rourke (pp. 295–7) – in more sophisticated mode Scruton (pp. 91–3) provides a philosophical outlook on the importance of pleasure and Bloom is remembered as a defender of Eros (pp. 176–90).

What is to be concluded from such positionings? One possibility is that the very idea that post-Cold War conservatives have been chiefly preoccupied with prosecuting a culture war to defend traditional values is mistaken. This is argued by Thomas Frank, who claims that – while a 'backlash' against the values of the counterculture predominated from the 1960s through to the Reagan era – from the 1990s onwards, conservatives' main creed has been what he terms 'market populism', a form of market-centred, hedonistic libertarianism (Frank, 2002, pp. 23–39). Indeed, he argues, works like *Backward and Upward* reveal that modern conservatives prefer to distance themselves from traditional culture war themes, such as defending 'order, deference, the past, "family values"' (p. 47). Rather than presenting themselves as 'proudly square', he claims, conservatives instead attempt to embrace 'rock 'n roll street cred', including the attitudes of the counterculture (pp. 32–3).

Evidently, Frank's thesis contradicts much that has been argued in this chapter. For this reason, it is necessary to give it some consideration. To continue with *Backward and Upward*, Frank's argument can only be sustained by ignoring the contributions of writers like Murray (Brooks, 1996, pp. 264–71) and Bennett (Brooks, 1996, pp. 272–8) who do defend 'family values' and the importance of social order (as, of course, does Scruton). More generally, the underpinnings of his argument are severely weakened by his failure to take account of the writings of many of today's leading culture war conservatives – especially their qualified views of free markets – including not only Bennett but also Bork, Himmelfarb and Irving Kristol. In fact, what Frank perceives as a shift away from culture war issues is, rather, conservatives' defensiveness and sense of marginalization in relation to their traditional touchstones. Claiming that this means they have abandoned these beliefs is to offer a wholly one-sided and partial reading of modern conservatism.

Furthermore, insofar as conservatives may strain for greater 'credibility', it is at most the style, and not the politics or morality, of the counterculture that they embrace. Gingrich – who, for Frank, is a key figure in the development of market populism – is as much a critic of the 'immorality' of the 1960s counterculture as Bloom or Kristol (Gingrich, 1995, p. 30). Even among those ostensibly more sympathetic towards the counterculture generation, their diminished hostility is only made possible by the perception that this generation has itself changed. Thus Brooks is able to present a much more cheerful version of new-class theory than is commonly advanced by conservatives, because although he believes that the 'bohemian bourgeoisie' have indeed become the new elite, he also thinks that money and success have transformed them into a dependable, as well as dynamic and ambitious, ruling class (Brooks, 2000). In other words, if a neutered counterculture is no longer a threat to established order – which remains, in any case, a minority view among conservatives – there is much less reason to be fearful of it.

Frank's thesis will be returned to in the next chapter. Yet the paradox noted above remains to be resolved. Frank is not the only one to see conservatives' rejections of politically correct beliefs as revealing a commitment to unrestrained libertarianism. In fact, Scruton's championing of the freedom of smokers caused leading anti-smoking organization ASH (Action on Smoking and Health) to bestow upon him the title of 'high priest philosopher of the British libertarian right' (ASH, 2002). He has also earned the libertarian label for his defence of what in Britain is one of the most politically incorrect of all pastimes, foxhunting (C. Bennett, 2002). Bizarre as these labellings may seem to anyone who has read Scruton's writings, this confusion nonetheless testifies to a widespread belief today that – with much of the modern Left demanding increased restraint and regulation – only extremist libertarians mount principled defences of freedom. However, this tells us more about the changed nature of the Left than it does about the Right.

Closer to the mark is Paul Safier, who identifies the standpoints of contemporary conservatism as entailing a contradiction, with conservatives appearing to want to present themselves as both 'courageously puritanical *and* courageously antipuritanical' (Safier, 1996, p. 50). What this reveals, he argues, is that modern conservatives do not really take morality seriously, but simply adopt whatever position suits their purposes at any one time. However, while it may be legitimate to accuse some conservatives of such opportunism, this argument is too simplistic in the case of more thoughtful writers. In fact, conservatives do provide justifications for assuming different attitudes towards forms of 'puritanism', by distinguishing between traditional and politically correct modes of moral discourse.

Himmelfarb, for example, notes that another label widely used to describe the outlook of political correctness is the 'New Victorianism' (Himmelfarb, 1996a, pp. 259–63); unsurprisingly, she is therefore concerned to distinguish this perspective from Victorianism's 'real' meaning. The difference, she argues, is that whereas for the Victorians morality was 'so deeply embedded in tradition and convention that it was largely internalized', that of today's moralists is 'novel and contrived, officially legislated and coercively enforced' (p. 260). For the Victorians, upholding morality did not mean constructing a set of values afresh, but preserving those that had evolved over time. Consequently, they would have rejected the formality of the regulations – such as codes of conduct governing sexual relations – demanded by New Victorians. Equally, in that they did not believe in paternal or intrusive government, they would have derided the type of moral guardians (regulators and watchdogs) required to enforce a politically correct morality.

A similar understanding is presented by Minogue, who argues that what is distinctive about modern forms of morality is their formal and abstract character (Minogue, 1997, pp. 47–56). In traditional societies, he claims, moral behaviour is part of a complete way of life, organically linked to all other facets, so that individuals acquire a moral character as part of their communal identities. As a result, the individual is capable of practising moral self-reliance. Today, by contrast, since morality is not intimately connected to community and tradition, to persuade people to behave morally requires reliance upon an array of technical mechanisms – such as sanctions, therapy and propaganda. Often, therefore, even seemingly moral behaviour is merely the product of a government-imposed obligation rather than genuinely virtuous.

However, while conservatives may be right to accuse proponents of political correctness of illiberalism, and to argue that its codes represent an artificial imposition upon society, many lack credibility in attacking its authoritarianism. For example, even if Himmelfarb's idealized depiction of Victorian moralists – as neither coercive nor statist – is allowed, it is clearly not a portrayal that fits her own beliefs. After all, she believes that today's disorder requires 'strenuous moral purgatives' (Himmelfarb, 1995b, p. x), which may need to be administered by the state.

What also needs to be understood is that conservatives' anti-Puritanism and moral liberalism usually only surfaces in response to the authoritarianism of their opponents, which far from prevents them propounding fears about cultural and moral decline. This may be illustrated further. As seen, not all conservatives agree with using state mechanisms to promote their moral agendas, though widespread pessimism certainly creates a tendency in this direction. Yet a criticism more generally applicable is that while conservatives are only too ready to condemn the social and moral panics underpinning the authoritarianism of their adversaries – whether about AIDS or other health and environmental risks – many are clearly willing to propagate their own (see Furedi, 1997, pp. 47–8).

For example, while Krauthammer argues that statistics on rape and child abuse are evidently over-reported, because therapists and feminists have raised society's sensitivity to these issues, general crime figures are by contrast under-reported – by as much as two-thirds – because society has become inured to living with crime (Krauthammer, 1993, pp. 20–1). In other words, whatever legitimacy there may be in conservatives' arguments that the statistics employed by their opponents are artificially inflated is compromised by their willingness to endorse the worst possible readings of statistics that support their own anxieties. Once again, it is obvious that rather than any genuine concern for the upholding of truth and objectivity, conservatives' rejections of 'politically correct' arguments are premised upon largely partisan grounds. What is equally confirmed, contra Frank, is their continuing reliance upon the notion of cultural disorder to justify their agendas.

Finally, it is necessary to return to the arguments of those who believe that the culture war has been lost. If they are right, what course is left open to conservatives? Indeed, what does it any longer mean to be a conservative? Weyrich's recommendation is that the remaining moral minority should abandon the campaigning strategies of the past and instead attempt to 'quarantine' itself from the influence of a hostile culture (Weyrich, 1999). That is, it is time to abandon politics altogether and retreat to the margins (see also Thomas and Dobson, 1999). Regarding English culture, Scruton similarly appears to believe that it is not possible to fight for any restoration: 'To describe something as dead is not to call for its resurrection' (Scruton, 2001a, p. 244). A conservative may hope that the memory of English civilization will, like the achievements of ancient Rome, provide inspiration to future generations; yet largely, it seems, all that is left for him to do is 'to mourn, but privately'.

Conclusion

Not all present-day conservatives are entirely pessimistic: an undeniable strand of optimism remains. For example, Brooks presents a largely positive, as well as refreshingly different, version of new-class theory. Likewise, not all conservatives believe in the notion of a culture war (Rabkin, 1999). Nonetheless, these are not typical assessments. Many conservatives plainly believe that traditional morality has been largely marginalized, if not utterly extinguished, by their enemies.

What may also be concluded is that it is correct to understand the culture war in the singular. However, although conservatives understand its common underlying basis as the challenge of relativism, this is only partially true. What they perceive as society's loss of faith in all moral judgement is principally a decline of belief in specifically traditional absolutes. It is right to observe that moral life has not disappeared, but changed; on issues like the environment, it is frequently possible to find assent to very definite moral claims. Potentially, this makes the problem even harder for conservatives: filling a moral vacuum would be easier than having to displace an entrenched 'antagonistic' morality. The question of whether conservatives might themselves embrace notions such as an ethic of the environment, or even a postmodern perspective, will be addressed in later chapters.

5
Embracing the Future: the New Economy, Globalization and the End of the Nation-State

If the notoriety of many present-day conservatives derives from their seeking to defend or revive the values and social structures of the past, a seemingly contrary repute is possessed by those who appear to adopt a future-oriented outlook. Indeed, today the keenest proselytizers for the benefits of new economic and technological developments are typically believed to be conservatives. Moreover, as noted in Chapter 2, one of the strongest arguments of those who believe there has been a decisive shift in favour of a free-market philosophy is that the demands of globalization are not only desirable, but irresistible. Equally, celebrations of these demands provide powerful support to critics who see modern conservatives as all but entirely committed to a form of free-market zealotry.

This chapter will examine these claims with the purpose of highlighting a number of main points. First, that tensions exist with strands of conservatism that remain opposed to a future-oriented vision; second, that even conservative articulations of this vision are not always as confident or straightforward as they may appear; and third, that while the issues under discussion seem to be ones that most clearly polarize conservatives into camps of the 'backward-' and 'forward-' looking, once again it will be shown that it is simplistic merely to describe a divide between traditionalists and libertarians.

What must also be stated at the outset is that it will not be possible to give any indepth consideration to the actual veracity of the notions addressed: for example, whether the ideas of a fully 'globalized' world or a 'new economy' are actually true. Critiques of these notions are, in any case, plentiful, a number of which will be examined below. Rather, the aim of this chapter is to explore how and why conservatives argue what they do, to see what this reveals about the nature of modern conservatism.

The nation-state and identity

Since one of the most significant implications of the changes to be discussed in this chapter is their impact upon the nation-state, it is necessary for a brief digression regarding its importance within conservative thought. In fact, one of the major deficiencies of the literature on globalization when dealing with conservatism is that minimal attention is usually paid to what conservatives believe about the nation-state and its role in shaping identity. In particular, what is generally neglected is that – as seen in earlier chapters – conservatives today believe that their traditional understandings of stable, common national identities are very much under threat. Yet if these identities are insecure, the question of whether the challenges posed by forces such as globalization should be welcomed or resisted is made that much more complex.

This point will be returned to later. To begin, it is necessary to set out some of the basics about conservative understandings. Since, as also already seen, British and American conservatives may be believed to have very different attitudes towards the nation-state and nationalism, each will be considered in turn.

Starting with British conservatism, the standard view is that central to its outlook 'is the idea of the nation-state with fixed boundaries, a clear identity and a particular tradition' (Ludlam and Smith, 1996, p. 5). More strongly, Bill Schwarz argues that 'every philosophical defence of British Conservatism for the past century turns on the potency of the nation' (Schwarz, 1997, p. 15).

Confirmation of these beliefs is provided by Scruton, who believes that the fundamental bonds that tie society together are embodied at the level of the nation-state. His understanding also reveals one of the most important themes of conservative discourses, which is that the 'nation' and 'state' elements of the 'nation-state' should be distinguished, with the former accorded priority. Thus, according to Scruton, 'Nations have an identity through time which is distinct from that of the state, and independent of institutions, even those dearest to its people. A nation can outlast the demise of its system of government, and its ancestral laws' (Scruton, 1990, p. 75). In other words, whatever is meant by the 'nation' is distinguishable from a society's political arrangements, and of deeper significance. What constitutes the pre-political bonds of nationhood is, for Scruton, a common culture.

However, it is important to recognize that there is no necessary connection between conservatism and nationalism (Aughey, Jones and Riches, 1992, pp. 80–1). The undoubted preference of many conservatives for the particular over the universal need not mean that the nation is the particular in question: Burke's affinity for the little platoons or Oakeshott's preference for the familiar may imply an attachment to the immediate locality, but not necessarily the nation as a whole. Indeed, the idea of the nation may be as much a false abstraction of rationalists as any other collective entity.

Certainly from a historical perspective, there has been no easy congruence between nationalism and conservatism. Hobsbawm argues that the ideas of the nation-state and nationalism began life in the late eighteenth century as revolutionary notions, with the nation believed to embody the interests of a united sovereign people against the divisions of particular interests (Hobsbawm, 1990, pp. 14–45). The radical implications of the idea that the nation represents the embodiment of the popular will mean that it is of little surprise that many early conservatives were reluctant to embrace it.

Hobsbawm's is not the only interpretation of the history of these notions, and it is one of the major disputes regarding them whether they are of modern or 'primordial' provenance. However, two of the strongest attacks on the concept of nationalism of recent times come from followers of Oakeshott – Minogue (Minogue, 1967) and Elie Kedourie (Kedourie, 1966) – who agree with Hobsbawm that nationalism is an essentially modern, revolutionary doctrine. Of course, they interpret this fact in a very different light; for Minogue, nationalism is 'a direct enemy of conservative politics' (Minogue, 1967, p. 135).

Scruton also recognizes that nations are not 'natural' and that nationalism may be a distinctively modern ideology (Scruton, 2001a, p. 4). Moreover, nationalism may not only have disreputable origins, but its ideological assertiveness has continued to be the cause of conflict and war ever since. What then of conservatives' allegiance to the nation? The common strategy of conservatives is the one Scruton employs, which is to draw a distinction between nationalism and the more acceptable notion of patriotism: whereas the former is an aggressive 'call to arms', the latter 'is an altogether quieter view of the matter', expressing simply the natural inclination of allegiance we feel to the society of which we are members (Scruton, 2001b, p. 26). Whether or not this distinction convinces, it provides conservatives with a means of distancing themselves from a 'political' conception of national allegiance. Equally important, as Scruton continues, patriotism 'is not simply a stance towards the international world', but represents an appreciation of the nation as a fundamental source of identity.

Considering the case of American conservatism, a different set of issues is presented. As previously seen, there is a strong tradition of American conservatism that argues that individuals' primary attachment should be to the sub-national social unit. However, the implications of this belief for nationalist sentiment need to be interrogated more closely. Among some paleoconservatives, many of whom still cling to the doctrines of antifederalist republicanism, hostility towards nationalism is implied in their vituperative animosity towards federal government. According to Samuel Francis, 'nationalism and republicanism have usually been enemies' because the antifederalist tradition counsels 'resistance to the leviathan state of the nationalists' (Francis, 1992, p. 18). Yet for most modern American conservatives, localism does not imply any such antagonism. For example, Wilfred McClay argues that loyalty 'is not necessarily a zero-sum game' (McClay, 2001, p. 46); consequently, a strong attachment to local institutions does not prohibit a patriotic allegiance to the nation.

However, the main difficulty in understanding American nationalism arises from the idea of exceptionalism, the belief that the American nation differs from European ones in being an artificial, political construct. Thus it is common for American writers – and not solely conservatives – to distinguish between American and other forms of nationalism. For example, Clyde Wilson argues that what separates American from European varieties is that the former has always had about it 'something of the nature of a doctrine, a set of beliefs, as opposed to the allegiances of blood, dynasty, language, history, religion, and territory that form the core of European senses of national identity' (C. Wilson, 1990, p. 17). Allegiance to the American nation is distinctive in that it implies allegiance to a set of ideas, in particular those embodied in the Constitution, rather than to concrete customs and traditions.

Yet with some justification, John O'Sullivan argues that the 'America-as-an-idea' view of national identity is essentially a liberal one – and, in denying the existence of a common culture, in his view a 'Trojan horse' for multiculturalism – since the belief that individuals' allegiances should be to abstract principles is hardly conservative (J. O'Sullivan, 1998, p. 22). In fact, he argues, American identity can be seen as predicated upon a common upbringing and culture: 'The ideas of liberty and equality in the Declaration of Independence were the distilled essence of a much broader and richer culture including songs, stories, poems, customs, folkways, shared historical experience, and the mystic chords of memory.'

Tendentious as the assertion that the origins of Americans' commitment to liberty and equality derive more from custom than principle may be, American conservatives generally believe that a common culture at least developed subsequent to the American Revolution. For example, Will contends that 'a common American consciousness formed in the crucible of revolutionary struggle' (Will, 1994, p. 360) was what led to the creation of a shared culture and political vocabulary. As is evident from the rejections of multiculturalism detailed in the last chapter, most American conservatives believe that at some point in America's history a common culture came into being, whether derived from a British heritage or as something distinctive.

Lastly, consideration must be given to the case of free-market thinkers. Most obvious, anti-collectivism may lead economic liberals to have similar misgivings about the nation-state to anti-rationalist conservatives. For example, Hayek – at least in his earlier writings – distrusts the nation-state because it is the focus of socialists' efforts to organize people along planned lines, and is therefore a collectivist social unit (Hayek, 1944, pp. 103–5, 173–4). By contrast, he claims, an individualist viewpoint demands an internationalist perspective. As will be seen, this understanding would appear to the one favoured by modern champions of globalization. Even so, it must be noted that conservative proponents of free markets have often sought to combine a commitment to them with support for the nation. For example, Willetts stresses that the promotion of free markets and the integrity of the British nation are mutually dependent (Willetts, 1992a, pp. 170–3).

A world without borders, progress without limits

The first issue to examine is that of globalization. Like other contemporary notions discussed in this book, an immediate difficulty arises even in reaching a satisfactory understanding of what globalization is supposed to mean. One reason for this may be that, as Stephen Gill argues, globalization 'is not amenable to reductionist forms of explanation, because it is many-faceted and multidimensional' (S. Gill, 1995, p. 405). Alternatively, the problem may be a more straightforward one, which is that there are as many definitions of globalization as there are writers who employ the term; in other words, its meaning is as (deliberately) ambiguous as ideas of community or the new class.

This notwithstanding, the most prominent theme within discussions is the idea of a fully integrated global economy. This vision is clearly expressed by Kenichi Ohmae, prophet of the borderless world, who argues that the growth of international economic activity means that 'national borders have effectively disappeared and, along with them, the economic logic that made them useful lines of demarcation in the first place' (Ohmae, 1990, p. 214).

Of course, the internationalization of economic activity is not in itself a new phenomenon. What theorists of globalization frequently suggest is that the present represents a qualitatively new phase in capitalism's history, with the global economy integrated to a degree hitherto unseen. For example, Hobsbawm – though more a critic than a celebrant – argues that the distinctiveness of the contemporary era resides in the fact that, since the 1960s, a 'transnational' economy has emerged (Hobsbawm, 1994, p. 277). That is, rather than just an increase in trade between nation-states having occurred, what has developed is 'a system of economic activities for which state territories and state frontiers are not the basic framework, but merely complicating factors'. On this view, as with Ohmae's, the imperatives of capital appear to have rendered the sovereign, territorially bounded nation-state obsolete.

Of most importance here is the standpoint of conservatives, who are usually seen as in the vanguard of championing this development. It will be valuable first to consider their depiction by critics. According to Gray, free marketeers' vision of a fully globalized world is nothing less than the Enlightenment utopia of a universal civilization, in which the 'manifold economic cultures and systems that the world has always contained ... will be merged into a single universal free market' (Gray, 1998, p. 2). The idea of inexorable economic globalization became attractive to the New Right during the 1980s because globalization's imagined logic allowed it to rationalize its assaults upon the Keynesian consensus of the post-war period.

Espousing ideas of an ever-globalizing world, free marketeers could argue that the constraints imposed by growing interdependence in international trade and finance meant that national economies were increasingly faced by realities that could not be ignored. This meant that their free-market programmes could be presented as not only desirable but necessary, demanding abandonment of the belief that the state can effectively manage the economy. On Gray's view, the hegemony of free-market ideas ever since means that this is a project that continues to dominate present-day conservatism. Indeed, American conservatives have become little more than 'ranting evangelists for global capitalism' (p. 104).

A second critique worth noting is that of Hirst and Thompson who, unlike Gray, question the whole notion that globalization is a real phenomenon (Hirst and Thompson, 1996). In a slight variation on Gray's argument, theirs is that the rhetoric of globalization is of value to free marketeers today precisely because of the failure of the New Right's economic programmes of the 1980s (p. 176). Contemporary theories of globalization are thus a 'godsend' to economic liberals because they give a new lease of life to free-market ideology when its bankruptcy might otherwise have been exposed by its real-world failings.

It is useful next to return to Frank, who also paints a picture of ranting free-market evangelism, but set within the broader context of theories of the 'new economy' (Frank, 2002). According to Frank, the new economy is the touchstone for modern conservatives. The major features of this model are: minimal state regulation and taxation; a crucial role for new technological developments, especially those in the realm of information technology; and an increasingly interconnected world system. It is by no means exclusively conservatives who promote the new economy – Frank examines a much wider range of thinkers and economists who do so, including those of the Clintonite and Blairite Left – though here it is his argument's relevance to conservatives that will be explored.

In particular, it is the distinctive features of the new economy's intellectual defences that it will be important to examine. Frank makes a number of claims. First, that until the 1990s free-market ideas were, though present among conservatives, kept discreetly in the background, whereas today they are at the forefront of their arguments. Second, the new economy's ideologues believe that not only the economy but also every sphere of society must accede to the demands of market forces, including those of culture and morality. Third, the entrepreneur – especially the internet entrepreneur – is portrayed as more than just a self-interested capitalist, but as a 'radical' hero, in sweeping away outdated ideas and institutions. Fourth, today's free-market ideology is a 'populist' one – that is, the new economy is presented not just as profiting the few, but as bringing prosperity to all. Moreover, markets are argued to possess democratic virtues, reflecting the popular will much more effectively than elected governments and supporting the interests of the majority by challenging vested ones. This ideology not only incorporates an anti-elitist spirit but also an anti-intellectual one.

All of the above critiques suggest that, surprisingly, conservatives are today leading exponents of change. A point worth noting at this stage is that the belief that capitalism has undergone a qualitative transformation is not itself entirely new among conservatives. If the 'new economy' is the latest favoured term, an earlier claim that society had reached a new stage of development was notably forwarded by Bell, in theorizing 'the coming of post-industrial society' (Bell, 1974).

According to Bell, a postindustrial society is one in which the economy is primarily based on the production of services rather than manufactured goods. As capital and labour are the prime resources of industrial society, knowledge and information are those of the postindustrial. Accompanying the shift from industrial to postindustrial society is the emergence of a new knowledge class of scientists, engineers and administrators. Bell also perceived a growing global interconnectedness. Although he did not believe that there is a necessary connection between postindustrialism and capitalism – and nor was his stance towards the changes he identified wholly celebratory – the features Bell distinguished as characteristic of postindustrial society are very similar to those of more recent free-market laudings of the new economy.

Still, much evidence can be pointed to in support of contemporary critics' arguments. A good example is the case of D'Souza, a conservative who in many respects seems to match Frank's depiction perfectly. Indeed, he appears to personify the change Frank identifies from the era of culture war backlash to that of market populism, having apparently transformed himself over the course of the 1990s from an anxious culture warrior worried about 'illiberal education' (D'Souza, 1991) to a celebrant of the new economy and 'the virtue of prosperity' (D'Souza, 2000).

Ours is, D'Souza asserts, an age of unparalleled affluence. A major revival of faith in free-market capitalism has occurred, with the spirit of capitalist enterprise penetrating every corner of the culture as never before. The driving force behind this new gilded age is technology, particularly information technology, with the entrepreneur – especially the young – the central figure. Furthermore, D'Souza believes, it is right to speak of a single world economy. In relation to all these changes, D'Souza sides himself with capitalism's cheerleaders.

In fact, numerous beliefs argued by critics to be characteristic of present-day conservatism can be identified among both American and British conservatives. For example, many appear to see the era of globalization as representing a qualitatively new phase of development. John Patten argues that, although internationalization is not entirely novel, the challenges of globalization 'are not the international or imperial challenges which a Peel or Disraeli had to deal with' (J. Patten, 1995, pp. 177–8). The irreversibility of these changes is also frequently stressed. For example, Howell argues that 'There can be no going back... To suggest that the globalization system can be undone is like saying that the industrial revolutions of the last two or three centuries can be put in reverse' (Howell, 2000, p. 225). Or, as Stephen Dorrell argues, there simply 'isn't an alternative to global trade' (S. Dorrell, interview by author, 23 June 1998).

The 'no alternative' perspective has important consequences for policy-making. If there is no possibility of undoing the realities of an increasingly open world market, then developing a deregulated, low-cost environment for investors becomes imperative to confront the challenge of international competition. Redwood argues that recognizing the needs of global business means that the aims of 'Taxation, industrial relations and social policies . . . [must] concentrate on ensuring a skilled and flexible work-force' (Redwood, 1993, p. 15), flexibility meaning greater wage-restraint by workers and fewer employment laws. Similarly, Howell believes that 'national governments should understand the game is up' for the belief that it is possible to manage domestic economic affairs; their priority instead should be 'to ensure the best possible environment' for competition in the global marketplace (Howell, 2000, p. 232).

In fact, it seems to be a reflexive habit of many conservatives writing on globalization to maintain that the traditional authority of the nation-state is rapidly disappearing. For example, Gingrich argues that:

> All current economic textbooks are based on the national economy as though that were still the keystone of an understanding of how the world works. Yet the fact is that the world economy is now, in large part, an interconnected system of electronic signals. (Gingrich, 1995, p. 64)

Indeed, William Rees-Mogg predicts that the cyber-economy is soon likely to displace the 'monolithic' nation-state (Rees-Mogg, 1995).

Critics are also right in arguing that the way in which the free market is promoted today is as a popular, anti-elitist force. For example, Gingrich claims that although 'Elite criticisms of the can-do spirit have undermined [the entrepreneurial] ethic', the true American philosophy is that anyone can achieve the American dream through hard work and enterprise: 'the spirit of free enterprise remains at the heart of American civilization' (Gingrich, 1995, p. 43). Equally, the workings of the market do not merely line the pockets of the rich. George Gilder – another key enthusiast for the new economy – contends that 'technological and entrepreneurial progress, impelled by deregulation and low tax rates . . . brings once rare products into the reach of the poor' (Gilder, 2000, p. 157).

There is also a distinct strain of anti-intellectualism in conservatives' arguments. This is evident in Gingrich's desire to emphasize that many entrepreneurs achieve success by by-passing the elite-dominated institutions of academia; for example, he thinks it important to mention that Bill Gates and Steve Jobs (founders, respectively, of Microsoft and Apple Computers) 'were both college dropouts' (Gingrich, 1995, p. 41). This anti-intellectualism not only is in stark contrast to a Straussian academic and cultural 'elitism' but also appears especially odd coming from Gingrich, given his own background as a one-time professor of history. The importance Gingrich attaches to convincing us of capitalism's meritocratic nature is shown by the fact that he attempts to present his own journey from being 'a professor from a small college in Georgia ... to the highest levels of government' as somehow confirming the idea that any one in America can rise to the top, even from the humblest of origins.

Another recurrent theme of writings on globalization during the 1990s was the threat posed by the high-growth, low-cost economies of the East (at least prior to the economic turmoil that swept through them towards the decade's end). That is, to meet the challenge of competition posed by the rising 'tiger economies' the conclusion, yet again, was that it is necessary to create similarly flexible economies (Redwood, 1993, p. 222). However, according to Howell, this confrontation between East and West was as much about values and culture as economics (D. Howell, interview by author, 14 July 1998). Interestingly, therefore, Howell disagreed with those who look to Western writers like Etzioni for inspiration as to how to rejuvenate the moral fabric of civil society, instead urging us to consider the Asian model of values: of order, respect and discipline (Howell, 1995, pp. 20–3). Conservatives worried about demoralization should perhaps abandon the Anglo-centrism of their efforts to revive Victorian virtues and instead embrace the opportunities opened up by globalization for importing the values of a culture that is a living example of how societies should be ordered.

In fact, it is frequently more than just the economic side of globalization that is emphasized. A liberal global vision also has implications for political culture. This, of course, was at the heart of Fukuyama's understanding when he made his declaration of the end of history, in seeing all societies of the world as moving towards not only a single model of market-based economics, but also a single democratic culture: 'for a very large part of the world, there is now no ideology with pretensions to universality that is in a position to challenge liberal democracy' (Fukuyama, 1992, p. 45). A similar belief is expressed, though set within a less overarching historical philosophy, by Howell: 'the trend towards a privatized, globalized world [is] part of a wider pattern of human progress', including the growing recognition of the value of democracy and an open society (Howell, 2000, p. xix).

One of the most important aspects of contemporary espousals of global liberalization is the emphasis placed upon the role of information technology. Gilder in particular propounds a vision of unfettered capitalism centred upon the power of technology. His argument is that the global information revolution has turned the world into a 'microcosm', in which it is at the micro-level – technologically and socially – that the most significant advances occur (Gilder, 1990). Coupled to this vision of the microcosm is his belief that we are entering the age of the 'telecosm', in which the very latest developments are creating a world of high-speed networking and infinite communications capacity, which liberates us from the physical constraints even of the microchip-based revolution (Gilder, 2000).

According to Gilder, although once economic success came to those nations possessing superior stocks of natural resources and heavy industry, today it comes to those at the cutting edge of information technology. Moreover, whereas mills and factories cannot easily be moved, since technology, information and ideas are extremely mobile, an overly regulated economic environment is rendered unworkable because these latter can so easily move elsewhere.

Some of Gilder's views are certainly highly individual, not to mention bizarre, blurring as they do into mysticism: for example, his belief that the information revolution is sweeping away the old 'superstitions' of materialism and rationalism seems, as one commentator puts it, to offer conservatives their own version of New Age spirituality (Wright, 1989). However, more generally, what is obvious is that as much as conservatives' arguments are concerned with upholding the virtues of technological progress, underlying this are political and social concerns. For example, for many libertarians the realm of 'cyberspace' is perceived to be a model for wider society, as a sphere that is decentralized, unregulated and predicated upon the freedom of the individual. Thanks to the affinity of these features with a libertarian perspective, David Shenk argues that 'Cyberspace is Republican' (Shenk, 1997, p. 174).

Gingrich, drawing heavily upon the work of Alvin Toffler and his heralding of the 'Third Wave' (the information revolution), also believes that the expanding role of computer technology is revolutionizing both society and politics: 'While the Industrial Revolution herded people into gigantic social institutions – big corporations, big unions, big government – the Information Revolution is breaking up these giants' (Gingrich, 1995, p. 57). Similarly, Gilder believes that it 'is increasingly eroding the powers of despots and bureaucracies, powers and principalities' (Gilder, 2000, p. 263). Murray is also impressed by the liberalizing potential of the computer revolution: 'as the technology continues to turn a revolution every five years ... the de facto freedom within a society will increase' (C. Murray, interview by author, 22 September 1998).

Although these arguments are strongest among American conservatives, British writers share similar beliefs; for example, Redwood believes that 'The world market is data and communications driven' (Redwood, 1993, p. 12). Howell also draws the conclusion that government regulation and taxation are much less feasible in the information age. The rise of the electronic economy and an increasingly well-informed and mobile citizenry means that 'the state has no alternative but to downsize and alter its priorities ... Information technology and the worldwide web do the work of liberals for them' (Howell, 2000, p. 298). British conservatives also stress the role of communications technology in increasing liberty. For example, Mount believes that 'The newest technologies fragment and disperse knowledge and power far beyond the capacities of lumbering national bureaucracies reliably to track their activities, let alone effectively to control them' (Mount, 1992, p. 239).

Finally, if Gilder offers a peculiarly New Age approach to spirituality, the more traditionally religious may also see their beliefs reflected in the mirror of globalization. In viewing the world as the creation of a single God, and as constituted by a single community of people regardless of territorial boundaries, Christianity possesses strongly universalistic elements. In the middle of the 1990s, Neuhaus perceived with the approaching millennium a growing trend for religious statements to presage a world-wide 'coming together' and a new age of religious renewal (Neuhaus, 1996b, p. 66). Although he argued for circumspection, even his relatively cautious assessment makes the point clear:

> In communications, economics, and interreligious relations, there are hints of an emerging something that might be called a global society, perhaps – stretching the point somewhat – a global community ... [misguided utopianism] should not blind us to the fact that world-historical change does happen, and that such change may be part of God's unfolding purposes in time.

The tenacity of the past

With conservatives depicting contemporary developments not merely as economically beneficial but even.conceivably as part of some divine cosmic plan, critics' portrayals would seem to be confirmed. However, there are three sets of issues that critics largely overlook: that many conservatives question the reality of these developments as well; that traditionalists also emphasize the downsides of globalization and the new economy; and that the standpoints of free marketeers are not always as unambiguously optimistic or 'utopian' as they seem.

Starting with the first of these, a basic reason for conservatives to reject the idea of globalization is that the very nature of conservatism implies that they have a stake in presenting the world as essentially unchanging. This can be seen particularly in the arena of international relations: for conservative 'realists', to uphold the validity of realism itself requires them to deny the reality of globalization. To sustain realism's foundational assumptions – that international relations should be understood through a timeless 'balance-of-power' prism – the claims of globalization theorists must be resisted.

For this reason, Owen Harries, editor in the 1990s of the *National Interest*, asks us to 'View with extreme skepticism the current outpouring of claims that what has been true about relationships between states from the time of Thucydides until yesterday no longer holds' (Harries, 1992/3, p. 109). These include those made about increasing interdependence and the rise of transnational institutions supposedly revolutionizing international politics. The problem with such assertions is that 'They invariably underestimate the durability and tenacity of the past.'

As Harries writes, for the realist the world is divided up 'vertically' into sovereign states, with clear boundaries to control and defend (Harries, 1996, p. 142). Yet for the globalization theorist, this vertical version of the world is being replaced by a 'horizontally' ordered one, a transformation wrought by the mobility of capital, technology and information. Increasingly, these spread horizontally across the globe without recognizing national limits. With sovereignty a myth and the state a fiction, state rivalries and military force make little sense – the realist's viewpoint is an anachronism.

Harries offers four specific arguments against globalization theories. First, there is nothing new in their claims; after all, he argues, a century and a half ago Marx and Engels were predicting the end of the nation-state. Second, the assumption that propinquity automatically produces greater harmony is simply false. Third, the degree of interdependence in the world is in fact no greater than it was at the beginning of the twentieth century, when trade as a proportion of global production was higher than it is now. Finally, the perspective of globalization theorists is a largely 'Western-centric' one. Even if the borders of Western nations have become more porous, this is not true of much of the rest of the world; for example, China, Korea and Japan. In other words, like left-wing critics Hirst and Thompson, Harries believes that nothing fundamental about the world has really changed.

Similarly, Noel Malcolm dismisses a description by *The Times* of a G7 summit meeting as a meeting of the board of directors of 'World Inc' by stressing that in fact it 'was a meeting of the heads of separate national governments: not directors of the same global company' (Malcolm, 1991, p. 8). Such a style of reporting, he argues, is symptomatic of a growing disdain within international affairs towards pursuing the purely national interest, akin to a 'new prudery'. Talk of globalization is thus more about rhetoric than it is about reflecting reality.

Many conservatives question the idea of globalization at least to an extent. Most commonly, even if the benefits of international trade are recognized, the idea that any 'transnational' world order has come into existence is generally denied. For example, William Kristol is typical in seeking to emphasize that while the nation-state may be losing some of its authority this does not mean that it has been superseded: 'There are big forces out there that can't be wished away and in some respects they're healthy forces, they discipline national governments... [but] I don't believe there are these inevitable forces sweeping over the world making nation-states irrelevant' (W. Kristol, interview by author, 20 October 1998). Hurd similarly avers that, although globalization is a reality, the world is still composed of nation-states (D. Hurd, interview by author, 25 June 1998).

Indeed, Feulner argues that although economic activity has become increasingly international, the more fundamental suggestion of trans-national interconnectedness is 'a form of globaloney' (E. Feulner, interview by author, 22 October 1998). Moreover, rather than seeing the nation-state as passively at the mercy of irresistible forces, it is possible to see it as changing to meet the challenges of globalization. DeMuth – though not seeing this development in a wholly positive light – argues that the nation-state 'is proving to be pretty resourceful today in responding to globalization', for example, accruing to itself greater regulatory powers (C. DeMuth, interview by author, 16 October 1998).

Furthermore, actually very few conservatives believe in the idea of a global community. Kirkpatrick contends that 'I don't think we're about to live in a global village' (J. Kirkpatrick, interview by author, 16 September 1998). In fact, she claims, our fundamental view of identity remains unchanged in this supposedly global age. Equally, Dorrell argues that:

> I like the IBM version of this: you trade globally, you live locally ... people don't live in a global community ... they live in much more local communities than that. The nation-state is important in the global marketplace because it is the focus of political accountability, because it's the focus of people's sense of self. (S. Dorrell, interview by author, 23 June 1998)

Nor do many conservatives accept the universalism implicit in Fukuyama's end of history thesis. According to Ian Crowther, Fukuyama's is 'a fanciful vision of global homogenisation' that neglects the strength of particular national traditions (Crowther, 1990, p. 12). Moreover, many identify a contradictory trend to that of globalization theorists, the growth of devolutionary politics. Thus Feulner believes that today 'If you look around the world the trend is clearly towards smaller' (E. Feulner, interview by author, 22 October 1998). Even to the extent that the nation-state is being undermined, this need not mean the emergence of a transnational order, but rather – hope those whose preference is for the world of the little platoons – an increasingly fragmented and localized one.

A final basis for conservatives' scepticism towards globalization and the new economy is their distrust of the purposes to which the language of these notions is put. For example, Clifford Orwin, in developing a critique of multiculturalism, cynically suggests that the reason modern students want educational curricula to include 'a smattering of the "non-Western"' is because they believe that adopting an internationalist outlook is necessary for a successful career in an age in which 'the globalization of the economy' and 'the information highway' are the new 'mantras' of the business world (Orwin, 1996, p. 16).

Most important, globalization theories are frequently perceived by conservatives to be the creations of their opponents. For example, Cowling believes that the term globalization is 'just an intelligentsia catchphrase' (M. Cowling, interview by author, 18 May 1998). Conservatives' suspicion towards theoretical concepts arises from the fact that they see them as 'excuse-making' devices, used to explain away social problems and antisocial behaviour. This also applies to the idea of globalization. For example, Himmelfarb lambasts those who seek to excuse the failings of individual morality by referring to structural factors. Yet in 'this post-cold war era, "globalization" has replaced "capitalism" as the epithet of choice' for those who wish to shift personal responsibilities onto impersonal forces (Himmelfarb, 1995b, p. ix).

In other words, if conservatives' critics perceive globalization theories to be legitimating ideologies of the free market, many conservatives conversely believe that they are ideologies of the Left. Apart from anything else, this reveals very clearly the fundamentally ambiguous and fetishized nature of the concept.

Resisting the globalist tide

According to critics, supporters of untrammelled global market forces disregard the effects they have upon the stability of families and communities, as well as upon national cultures and traditions (Gray, 1998, pp. 24–38). The correct response to globalization is therefore not acquiescence to its imperatives, but to challenge the delusions of free-market fundamentalism (pp. 234–5).

In the light of this, if today's growing army of anti-corporate and anti-globalist groupings – well documented by Naomi Klein (N. Klein, 2000) – have need for a new philosopher, they might consider Scruton for the role. After all, he offers a *cri de coeur* for the 'crisis of identity' engendered by globalization (Scruton, 2001a, p. 246); believes that we should be 'prepared to sacrifice a promise of yet more economic growth for the proven benefits of national sovereignty, local traditions and the common law' (Scruton, 2001b, p. viii); and rejects the policy of 'free market economics, under the aegis of global corporations' (p. 106).

The issue of globalization makes especially apparent the tension between free-market and traditionalist elements within conservative thought. Many traditionalists agree with critics that global liberalism is a threat to national sovereignty and identity. One argument is a paternalist one: for example, Worsthorne argues on behalf of the global economy's victims that the erosion of national sovereignty is particularly 'bad news…for people who need protection from the state' (P. Worsthorne, interview by author, 8 May 1998).

However, particularly vehement critics are Pat Buchanan and other paleoconservatives, who campaign for protectionism and withdrawal from global institutions – together with the restricting of immigration – to defend America's cultural identity and economic security (Buchanan, 1998; Francis, 1993, pp. 170–5). Indeed, Fleming argues that mainstream conservatives' enthusiasm for free trade and open borders for immigrants 'is a leftist position…it's the position of Robespierre' (T. Fleming, interview by author, 2 October 1998). Conservatism, he argues, 'is not a globalist movement, it's not a universal movement'. Clearly, the emphasis traditionalists place upon recognizing limits is contradicted by the commitments of globalization's champions. In this respect, paleoconservatives' criticisms are very much in accord with Gray's scorn for globalists' 'utopianism'.

It is the challenge to the constitutive role played by the nation for identity that troubles traditionalist conservatives most. Fleming again articulates the point well: 'Man is a tribal creature, not a global angel that takes in whole continents at a single glance' (Fleming, 1990, p. 13). Similarly, while others may perceive globalization to bring positive economic benefits, for writers like Scruton the fact that the bonds of national identity transcend 'mere' politics and economics means that the influence of global forces must be seen as more problematic. That is, if community is premised upon a deeply rooted common culture, no amount of economic gains can substitute for a loss of cultural integrity.

Scruton also expresses concern about the role of international regulatory bodies. Although for the Left these are often regarded as bulwarks against the forces of globalization, Scruton takes a very different view. For example, in examining the efforts of the World Health Organization to regulate the global tobacco industry, he appears concerned about the implications this has for democracy and liberty within nation-states. He thus worries that legislative powers are being 'granted to transnational bodies answerable to no national electorate' (Scruton, 2000b, p. 1), with transnational legislation 'curtailing the freedom of law-abiding people' (p. 58).

Scruton's themes are taken up by many conservatives. For example, Minogue does so by introducing yet another variant of new-class argument: the theory of globalization he dismisses as 'a new ideology for an emerging class of internationalists' (Minogue, 1996, p. 38). His argument is that it is by over-emphasizing the significance of global problems like global warming that international regulatory bodies extend their power and leverage over nation-states. What the new internationalist class argues is that sovereign states cannot deal with contemporary problems such as pollution because they do not stop at state borders; moreover, it believes in any case that nation-states are too blind and too selfish to be trusted to tackle them. Even if the global problems used to legitimate this class's authority are usually myths (which Minogue certainly believes), the ideology of internationalization unleashed is real, and dangerous, enough. As Minogue puts it pejoratively, the international world is the natural habitat of instrumental rationality in its extreme form.

Of course, for a writer who believes nationalism to be inimical to conservative politics and who worries about hyperactive statism, it may be wondered why Minogue finds the prospect of the erosion of the nation-state's authority so worrying. Indeed, despite his dislike of international bodies stripping nations of their sovereign powers, he stresses that he is not sentimentalizing the nation-state: 'It is in many ways a vile old brute' (p. 38). However, the point is that even if 'The state is a monster ... it is *our* monster', in that it does possess some sort of accountability. While this does not mean that conservatives should abandon their hostility towards the state, in a world of increasingly powerful international bodies anti-statism may have to be qualified because of the need to combat these even more troubling foes.

Further conservative reservations arise in response to the idea of the information revolution. It hardly needs mentioning that many conservatives are suspicious of 'revolutions' of whatever type. Furthermore, in that libertarians seem to be committed to a form of 'technological determinism' in their dedication to the idea that technology now leads politics and economics (M. Lind, 1996, p. 38), rather than the other way round, it is equally unsurprising that many conservatives are deeply sceptical towards their arguments. For traditionalist conservatives, science and technology have more usually been seen as implicated in man's corruption than as instruments of his enlightenment, providing false expectations for his salvation through reason. According to Kirk, it is a fundamental canon of conservative thought that 'innovation is a devouring conflagration more often than it is a torch of progress' (Kirk, 1953, p. 8). Attitudes towards the global information revolution expose in particularly pronounced form this tension between pessimistic and optimistic orientations within conservatism.

Neuhaus, for example, wishes to nurture 'a healthy skepticism about a digital revolution' (Neuhaus, 1996a, p. 101). His reason for this is that, 'Divorced from the cognitive structure that is knowledge and the reflectively internalized knowledge that is wisdom, information makes us dumb.' The person who gains his beliefs purely from electronic sources is, Neuhaus argues, 'crippled' by a dependency comparable to that of the underclass on welfare. Moreover, Brooks – even though much less disapproving of the bohemian bourgeoisie than other conservatives – is uneasy at the pace of life created by wireless technologies that this class leads (Brooks, 2001, p. 75). Those 'swept along' by the information tide, he claims, do not have time to read books or simply sit and think; yet with these sources of genuine creativity disappearing, ideas produced in the information age are often merely shallow and unoriginal.

Many also see the information revolution as implicated in society's demoralization. For example, McClay includes internet chat rooms

alongside cable television and shopping malls as part of a 'feckless com-
mercial culture' that is weakening the moral fibre of the young (McClay,
2001, p. 57). An especially fretful attack is presented by Kramer. Writing
at the close of the 1990s, his ominous prediction for the new millennium was that the information revolution would be responsible for 'an
acceleration of the merry, mindless, technology-driven surrender' to
nihilism already underway (Kramer, 1999, p. 25).

Indeed, following from his belief – noted in the last chapter – that the
security of high culture depends upon defending against the excesses of
popular culture, Kramer's fear is that 'the telecommunications revolution
will further imperil the already fragile sanctuaries of high culture', since
it is responsible for 'immoralizing and infantilizing almost every aspect
of popular culture'. As an example of this malignant influence he cites
the fact that the progress made in ridding many American cities of the
scourge of sex shops and readily available pornography has been undermined by the fact that 'the vilest forms of pornography are now more
easily accessible on the Internet than they ever were on the streets'.

Yet most fundamentally, the existence of a 'populist' market ideology
has far from suppressed a questioning attitude towards capitalism
among conservatives. In fact, as a reviewer of D'Souza's celebration
observes, conservatives today have not been 'involved in such an
intense internal debate about capitalism' since the late 1970s (Arens,
2001, p. 75). Much of this has already been documented, but it is worth
noting here the number of articles that signal even from their titles that
deliberation over capitalism's morality is a core theme: James Q. Wilson
is concerned about 'Capitalism and Morality' (J. Q. Wilson, 1995);
George Weigel about developing a form of 'Capitalism for Humans'
(Weigel, 1995); and Brian Anderson about 'Capitalism and the Suicide
of Culture' (B. Anderson, 2000). The most noteworthy aspect of this
intense debate is that, whereas when neoconservatives like Bell and
Kristol were articulating their worries in the 1970s it was at a time of
economic uncertainty and insecurity, these more contemporary examinations have taken place against a background of rising prosperity and
the absence of competing alternatives to capitalism. Even these realities
appear not to be enough to prevent many conservatives worrying about
the wider effects of the market's operations upon society.

Not so ranting evangelists

What then of the proponents of a rampant and unregulated form of
global capitalism? It bears repeating that critics like Frank look at a

broader intellectual climate than is possible in this book. Indeed, Frank's skewering of the inanities of management and advertising gurus makes for some of the most arresting passages in his work. Equally, he exposes well the faults and blind spots of the free market's advocates. However, again it must be concluded that his account – like those of many other critics – is highly one-sided. Six points need to be highlighted.

First, Frank very much overstates the novelty of many of market populists' arguments, such as their idealizing of the entrepreneur and the emphasis they place on capitalism's anti-elitist tendencies. Although free marketeers have typically always believed in the ineradicability, and even desirability, of material inequality, they have nonetheless long championed equality of opportunity as a central merit of capitalism. Furthermore, the public face of free-market ideology has rarely been to portray capitalism as an elitist or coercive system: it has always been asserted that its benefits are not just for a rich elite, but trickle down to the whole of society (Hayek, 1960, pp. 39–53). Thinkers like Hayek were also ambivalent about democratic government, while simultaneously casting the entrepreneur as torchbearer of freedom and progress for all of society. Some time before new economy theorists, Hayek was ennobling the role of the capitalist as follows: 'the successful entrepreneur … is led by the invisible hand of the market to bring the succour of modern conveniences to the poorest homes he does not even know' (Hayek, 1976, p. 145).

Second, critics ignore the fact that, beyond writers like Gingrich and Gilder, optimism is far from the only mood to be found among free marketeers. This has already been shown in earlier chapters; for example, David Henderson sees antagonists such as anti-globalists as actually having the upper hand. It is quite possible to argue that – beyond readers of the business press and think-tank pamphlets – critics like Gray, Frank and Klein possess much higher profiles than those who extol globalization and the new economy's virtues. Indeed, one British commentator is so unimpressed with conservatives' abilities to respond to their critics that he is led to ask, 'Where is the cogent, robust defence of world capitalism, the intellectual response to the protestors of Seattle? Where is free-market conservatism's Naomi Klein?' (Freedland, 2001).

This may be felt to be a peculiarly British perspective. Moreover, it clearly is not true that such defences cannot be identified. However, the fact that they can be pointed to – and damning quotations easily pulled from the pages of books by the likes of Gingrich and Gilder – is very different from it being the case that free marketeers actually dominate debates. This is a point they themselves often recognize, including American libertarians.

Illustration of this can be provided by examining a notable example considered by Frank, that of *Reason* magazine, which he urges those obsessed with the culture war should read to discover a prime source of market-populist ideas (Frank, 2002, pp. 299–302, 342–3). The commitment of Postrel, its editor, to the new economy is such that she believes the significant division in the world today is not between traditional political cleavages but between 'the future and its enemies' (Postrel, 1998).

However, although Frank is correct to argue that *Reason*'s libertarianism is strongly argued and largely uncompromising, what he overlooks is that its writers frequently see their own as a minority viewpoint. Not only does Postrel perceive a widespread 'backlash' against free markets (cited in Chapter 2), but in response to critics like Frank himself, one of its reviewers suggests there is a need to be 'brutally honest about the small number of people' who actually subscribe to libertarian doctrines (B. Doherty, 2001, p. 70). Although, this reviewer argues, he wishes the fears of 'leftists' like Frank were true, in reality they are guilty of 'grossly exaggerating the supposed dominance of free-market thinking'.

Third, even conservatives concerned with celebrating the impact of global market forces often also stress their commitment to retaining a nationalist focus. Very few claim that the nation-state has become obsolete. For example, Howell maintains that 'Global economics and well-governed and cohesive nation-state societies are quite compatible' (Howell, 2000, p. 229). It may even be argued that free markets actually require the division of the world into nation-states. Charles Moore argues that this is what Adam Smith believed. The existence of independent nation-states is necessary, partly 'because for free markets to work they have to have competition and nations represent competition as well as individual companies'; and partly because free markets are a cultural development as much as an economic one, and therefore need the historical framework of 'appropriate habits of mind and the rule of law' which only nation-states can provide (C. Moore, interview by author, 14 July 1998).

The non-economic role of nations is also emphasized by Howell, who argues that responding to globalization indeed provides conservatives with a new 'big idea', in terms of establishing what this role is. Precisely because people are frightened of the destruction of local cultures and economic insecurity 'nation-states take on new and very important roles which are not so economic … providing people with a national identity, securing them against crime, instability of all kinds and so on' (D. Howell, interview by author, 14 July 1998). Of course – since conservatives are held responsible for this insecurity – such arguments are unlikely to satisfy writers like Gray; nonetheless, they indicate that, even if wishing the nation-state to be stripped of its economic role, conservatives do not generally expect it simply to whither away.

Even the strongest of libertarians may appreciate the value of the nation. For example, Murray Rothbard argues like Scruton that when reflecting upon the nation-state the 'nation' can be thought of separately from the 'state'; consequently, he affirms, classical liberals may legitimately adopt a different attitude to each. Thus, even while disdaining the state, libertarians recognize that the individual is 'born into a family, a language, and a culture...He is always born into a specific historical context of time and place' (Rothbard, 1994, pp. 1–2). This sounds very similar not only to Scruton's beliefs, but also to Gray's (see Gray, 1993b, p. 259). What is also revealed again is the extent to which contemporary libertarians evidently feel the need to acknowledge the social constitution of individuality.

Fourth, it is relevant to observe how many of those who now number among the ranks of global capitalism's critics are erstwhile supporters. Gray is one example, but he is far from alone in rejecting the 'false dawn' of the globalization age. So does former Reagan advisor Edward Luttwak. According to Luttwak, the present era of an accelerated 'turbo-capitalism' is responsible for causing massive social upheaval, including poverty and crime; by contrast, he would prefer a return to the controlled capitalism that existed from the 1940s to 1980s (Luttwak, 1998).

Similarly, Fukuyama – despite being the most (in)famous celebrant of liberalism's Cold War victory – has subsequently developed a far more circumspect view of liberal capitalism. Not only does he believe that the libertarian impulse is exhausted but also seeks to highlight the social and moral problems not solved by the triumph of market forces. For example, he argues that the information revolution's enthusiasts neglect the fact that, in undermining traditional hierarchies and authority, it threatens to destroy the trust and shared norms that underlie a market society and upon which communities depend (Fukuyama, 1995, p. 24).

Indeed, to venture briefly outside this book's scope, it is pertinent to note that even capitalists can display a distinctly nervous attitude towards the 'self-destructive' tendencies of the system that makes their fortunes, including billionaires George Soros (Soros, 1998) and James Goldsmith (J. Goldsmith, 1994). While no one would expect them to clamour for capitalism's overthrowing, like Gray, Fukuyama and Luttwak they both worry about economic turmoil and social instability, and argue for a more restrained and regulated form of capitalism. It is quite impressive how many of those one would imagine should be among capitalism's strongest defenders have managed to escape free-market liberalism's hegemonic ideological grip.

Fifth, even its theorists are not completely ignorant of the new economy's downsides. Like Bell, who worried that in the postindustrial age increasing interconnectedness and the rapidity of communications would mean that individual societies would be less insulated against external destabilizing forces and might suffer the effects of 'information overload' (Bell, 1974, pp. 314–17), today's heralds of capitalism's new era also display anxieties. For example, D'Souza, although undoubtedly believing that on balance the positives outweigh the negatives, questions whether the new economy has created not only great wealth but also a spiritual vacuum that material success alone does not fill (D'Souza, 2000). Furthermore, not all libertarians welcome entirely the political implications. For example, Murray observes that a consequence of the increasing fragmentation brought about by the information revolution is that it 'defuses all of the political energy to make legislative changes' (C. Murray, interview by author, 22 September 1998).

In fact, although free-market conservatives' visions may be thought to be inextricably tied to an entirely positive and optimistic view of the onward march of market forces, the 'no alternative' perspective may suggest a much more ambiguous attitude towards the beneficence of markets: free-market capitalism not as the best of all possible alternatives, merely the only one that is viable. Howell's formulation of the thesis, that there are 'no alternative escape routes' (Howell, 1995, p. 21), is as likely to inspire dismay among readers as any confidence. In other words, it may not be Enlightenment utopianism that motivates globalization's supporters as much as pragmatic 'realism'. For Howell it is a matter of 'like it or not, globalization now dominates' (Howell, 2000, p. 225); the question of whether it is popular would seem to be secondary.

Nor is it the case that conservatives believe that globalization will always bring rewards. As much as an unregulated global economy may be applauded when it delivers gains, it is no less possible for conservatives to blame it for creating uncertainty and economic insecurity when it does not. The seemingly arcane workings of international currency speculators fit them especially well for the role of the guilty. For example, Patten, who is broadly in favour of embracing globalization, reminds us of 'the devastating effects that gimlet-eyed serial currency-killers at work in front of their screens can bring, as we found on Black Wednesday' (J. Patten, 1995, p. 178). The new economy may therefore provide conservatives with new scapegoats for explaining economic malaise – as with Black Wednesday, which occurred when sterling's value plunged following withdrawal from the European Exchange Rate Mechanism in 1992 – in the absence of socialists and militant trade unionists, as much as it may form the basis for any positive vision.

Lastly, few conservatives are as wholly future-oriented as they seem. Gray contends that it is rarely understood that the project of the free market's disciples is a 'modernizing' one (Gray, 1998, p. 35), and it is certainly not being denied here that, at least historically, progress has been one of capitalism's central imperatives. However, what is more rarely recognized is that although the free market's proponents may appear to face resolutely forward, they continually cast glances backward. For example, Howell justifies his belief that the global marketplace can be 'the breeding ground' of morality on the basis that the Victorians appreciated that commerce and virtue go hand in hand (Howell, 2000, p. 6). Similarly, Gingrich argues that, in fragmenting collective social units, the information revolution is 'leading us back to something that is – strangely enough – much more like de Tocqueville's 1830s America' (Gingrich, 1995, p. 57). In other words, conservatives' ideal of the 'new' economy is as much modelled upon the thriving and virtuous civil society imagined to have existed over a century ago as upon any projected image of the future. However forward-looking they may seem, conservatives' visions are usually imbued with some measure of nostalgic yearning for the past.

In defence of what?

If free-market doctrines come under attack from both the Left and many conservatives, traditional defences of the nation also face difficulties. Conservatives' ability to offer any alternative vision to that of an integrated global system, centred upon the nation-state as the focus of identity, is severely compromised by the fact that their patriotic appeals lack solid foundations.

Although it was established at the outset what patriotism means to conservatives in general terms, the striking feature of contemporary writings is that the question of what is meant by national identity today is one even conservatives have problems answering. This is especially clear among British conservatives. In recognition of the fact that an accepted consensus no longer exists in British society over its meaning, many discussions begin with questions rather than definitive statements. For example, in a book devoted to the subject, Scruton commences his attempt to define English identity as follows: 'What was England: a nation? A territory? A language? A culture? An empire? An idea? All answers seem inadequate' (Scruton, 2001a, p. 1).

Of course, Scruton does try to provide one: his is an England where cricket is played on every village common, the Anglican Church is an authoritative presence and the English gentleman epitomizes its character and values (for Scruton, the idea of a *British* nation is a fiction). Critics of Scruton's argument – and it is noteworthy that his book was greeted with widespread hostility – emphasize two main failings. First, the narrowness of the class viewpoint he adopts; and second, his disregard for the darker side of England's history, the ruthlessness of its imperialist adventures abroad and the exploitation of oppressed groups at home (see Eagleton, 2000). However, what is really significant about Scruton's book is that it is written in the past tense: of whatever else he may be guilty, even Scruton recognizes that his notion of English identity is anachronistic and largely irrelevant.

Another attempt, this time to define British identity, is offered by Moore. After boldly setting out his intention to discuss exactly 'how to be British', he is able to follow this only by delivering a highly anaemic account of the British virtues of decency, pragmatism and a spirit of enterprise (C. Moore, 1995). If once British conservatives could offer specific achievements around which to cohere a sense of national pride – like the creation of an empire – today they are frequently left offering shopping lists of empty banalities. With even conservatives feeling awkward at invoking many aspects of Britain's imperial history, because of the controversies over race and imperialism this will embroil them in, they instead engage in the largely arbitrary selection of qualities that supposedly constitute a unique national character; Moore's conclusion is that the British approach to life is especially 'empirical', 'practical' and 'flexible' (p. 18). Still, he at least confesses that 'I cannot *really* tell you how to be British. No one can' (p. 1).

Nor is there any easy answer today to what being an American means. The problems faced by efforts to reassert the importance of America's British heritage are, of course, compounded by the fact that even British conservatives presently have difficulty asserting this identity. It again seems easier to ask questions than provide answers – John O'Sullivan begins his examination by inquiring 'Is there such a thing as the American people? And if so, what is it?' (J. O'Sullivan, 1998, p. 21). His view is that the challenge of multiculturalism creates the very real possibility that 'the American nation is being replaced by a plethora of little nations'.

Reviving a sense of common patriotism is understood to be no simple task. In McClay's eyes, the degraded nature of America's feckless culture has led to a situation in which the strategies that are usually advocated, such as attempting to educate the young in the virtues of America's founding principles, will simply not suffice: 'there can be no meaningful patriotism in a society whose most privileged young people know nothing, remember nothing, respect nothing, cherish nothing, feel responsible for nothing, and are grateful for nothing' (McClay, 2001, p. 57). As with all the virtues conservatives esteem, there appears to be a pitifully weak social basis for patriotism's vitality.

In fact, a measure of the extent to which conservatives find it difficult to provide a positive vision is that often it is only in relation to negative events that they believe society is able to acknowledge the reality of common bonds. For example, O'Sullivan argues that the 11 September attack on the World Trade Center 'permitted the nation to cast aside the confusions and divisions of "identity politics" and to embrace an old-fashioned common patriotism' (J. O'Sullivan, 2001). Yet if it requires such an event for Americans to reject the perfidious outlook of identity politics, it is less easy to see what permanent basis there is for a secure notion of common national identity.

Conclusion

Compared to the pessimistic, even apocalyptic, outlook of many of the free market's critics – Gray painting a picture of a spiralling descent into anarchy, war and poverty from which there appears little hope of escape (Gray, 1998, pp. 194–208) – there is something undeniably attractive about the enthusiasm of the new economy's champions. One need not be blind to their arguments' flaws to find libertarians' optimism in many ways preferable. Furthermore, the fact that writers such as Scruton and Luttwak are as capable of criticizing global capitalism as Frank or Klein suggests that there is nothing necessarily 'radical' about attacking it: in a context in which capitalism's transcendence is not an option, demands for its greater regulation do not represent a fundamental threat and can therefore be proposed across the political spectrum.

The issues examined in this chapter certainly bring out in particularly sharp relief the differences between types of conservative, between enthusiasts for globalization and the new economy's economic and political benefits and those more concerned at the threat they pose to national sovereignty and cultural integrity. Yet more than just exposing conflicts between strands of conservatism, they reveal the problems faced by all conservatives in constituting their philosophies within a contemporary context. In particular, even though most wish to defend a patriotic allegiance to the nation-state, the foundations of this patriotism appear decidedly weak.

Given the number of qualifications that need to be made to critics' depictions, what must finally be addressed is the question of why they are so often distorted. Gray argues that Hirst and Thompson's questioning of globalization is undertaken for political purposes, to legitimate the viability of their own statist social democratic agenda (Gray, 1998, p. 64). However, the inflation of the strength of free-market ideology by all critics, including Gray, is equally 'political', to justify demands for a more regulated and constrained form of capitalism. The image of a rampantly free-market conservatism allows critics to legitimate their own beliefs, whether in arguing for the revival of traditional left-wing programmes or as part of their critiques of Enlightenment utopianism, but ignores the tensions that exist within conservatism and free marketeers' own insecurities.

6
The Postmodern Alternative

For many conservatives, it is clear that the defeat of Marxism has not meant the end of ideological conflict. Instead, an array of enemies is perceived to have replaced the older socialist menace, from proponents of the Third Way to champions of political correctness. However, a crucial difference between such antagonists and conservatives' traditional ones is that these foes themselves typically define their identities in terms of a rejection of the precepts of Enlightenment-inspired ideologies such as Marxism. In fact, it is possible to identify a seemingly paradoxical reversal of roles. Whereas in the past conservatives were principal critics of the Enlightenment and its associated principles, with their upholders considered to be radicals and revolutionaries, today the mantle of 'radicalism' is more often worn by those who challenge the doctrines first formulated by the eighteenth-century *philosophes*. By contrast, conservatives have become fierce critics of these 'anti-radical radicals'; as has been documented already, many of the former evidently regard themselves as defenders of the values of reason, objectivity and universality.

The objective of this chapter is to investigate this paradox, by considering specifically conservatives' attitudes to postmodern ideas. Its aims are twofold. First, to understand why conservatives have become prime critics of anti-rationalist creeds. Yet second, to evaluate the possibility of conservatives drawing upon their heritage of anti-Enlightenment thinking to create an *au courant* sceptical philosophy of their own. In other words, instead of rejecting contemporary intellectual developments, might conservatives rather accept and adapt to them? Indeed, might some form of 'postmodern conservatism' not be the oxymoronic notion it may at first sight appear?

The postmodern condition

Previous chapters have already considered some of the features often considered to typify the postmodern condition, including the collapse of shared moral certainties. The focus here is to be upon the postmodern stance that sees itself as the appropriate response to a world that can supposedly no longer support the ambitions of modernist ideologies.

The perspective of postmodernism is notoriously difficult to characterize, with a particular obstacle being that no consensus exists even concerning with which thinkers it ought to be identified. Certainly, those most frequently deemed key exponents – such as Lyotard, Derrida and Baudrillard – possess many differences. Equally, numerous issues remain contested. For example, should postmodernity be understood as in opposition to, or instead a continuation of, modernity? Nonetheless, while bearing these caveats in mind, it is possible to identify a cluster of broad notions typically embraced by advocates of postmodern agendas.

One of the most useful encapsulations of the postmodern sensibility remains that provided by Lyotard, who conceives of it as signifying 'incredulity towards metanarratives' (Lyotard, 1984, p. xxiv). That is, it is a stance of scepticism towards those perspectives that attempt a total understanding of society, derived from the aspirations of the Enlightenment and founded upon beliefs in objectivity and rationality since, we are told, it is no longer credible to accept such beliefs, nor can we commit to any project of universal human emancipation.

Rejecting the ambitions of hubristic modernist ideologies, the postmodern concern is instead with the 'little narrative' (p. 60), with the emphasis placed upon the relative and the contingent. The very idea that phenomena possess determinate essences must also be abandoned, with conventional epistemological assumptions – principally, that an objective vantage point for determining truth is attainable – also to be discarded. With no objective reality to be grasped, attention must instead focus upon the 'flexible networks of language games' (p. 17) that embody individuals' subjective representations of the world.

Consequently, postmodernists' intellectual programmes are characterized by projects of anti-foundationalism, deconstruction and the decentring of subjectivity. While not all thinkers commonly assigned the postmodernist label agree with every idea or practice that may shelter beneath a postmodern umbrella, the themes briefly outlined above are recurring ones throughout postmodernist writings, relating to a core rejection of the principles of Enlightenment rationalism. Moreover, these ideas inform a number of the doctrines explored in earlier chapters – such as identity politics and multiculturalism – for whose exponents the search for any universal set of shared or absolute values is commonly regarded as dogmatic and authoritarian. Instead, the stress is upon recognizing, and celebrating, difference.

Before exploring the potential that exists for conservative congeniality towards such a perspective, it is necessary first to examine conservatism's more well-known 'anti-anti-rationalist' face. In fact, it is possible to discern an extended history of conservative engagement with what have become known as specifically postmodern conceits. Indeed, Devigne suggests that modern conservatism may be understood precisely in terms of responding to the challenge of postmodernism. Upon this basis, the two figures he identifies as providing the most important intellectual inspiration for modern British and American conservative thought – Oakeshott and Strauss – were, he argues, led 'to anticipate and fear postmodernism long before it became a fashionable concept in the academy' (Devigne, 1994, p. xi).

Unfortunately, Devigne offers little in the way of developed or in-depth discussion of postmodernism. Nonetheless, although much of his argument concerning this issue remains merely implicit, his basic thesis has much in it to provoke fruitful thought. In particular, Strauss's writings represent an obvious starting point for understanding American conservatives' attitudes.

Strauss's position, as set out in Chapter 4, can readily be taken as representing a rejoinder to postmodern beliefs, since one of his prime interests was to counter the arguments of thinkers like Nietzsche and Heidegger, major intellectual antecedents for many postmodernists. This rejoinder centres upon a number of commitments: to objectivity and universality; to reason as the means of discovering truth; to the possibility of trans-historical knowledge; to moral and political determinacy; and to the superiority of the Western intellectual tradition (Strauss, 1953). Equally, whereas philosophy itself is frequently subjected to a form of decentring by postmodernists, for Strauss the philosopher is deemed to possess a privileged status in relation to knowledge.

A second important analysis to examine is that presented by Bell, whose reading of postmodernism has proved particularly influential upon other neoconservatives (Bell, 1978, pp. 46–55). According to Bell, postmodernism was a product of the social and cultural upheavals of the 1960s. However, he also sees it as representing a continuation of the basic thrust of modernism. Modernism, on his account, is a particular cultural sensibility: a refusal to accept limits, coupled with a continuous thirsting for change. Reaching its apogee in the late nineteenth and early twentieth centuries, the spirit of modernism is held responsible for subverting the traditional bourgeois moral and social values that underpin capitalist society.

While seeing no radical disjunction between modernism and postmodernism, for Bell the distinctiveness of the latter lies in the fact that it carries the anti-traditionalist project of the former to much further extremes. Whereas the modernist temper was confined largely to the spheres of art and imagination, the postmodernist seeks to challenge order and morality in every arena of social life. Furthermore, whereas modernism was largely the preserve of a cultured elite, postmodernism – in disdaining all boundaries – is implicated in the development of a widespread cultural, or rather countercultural, movement.

Considering Strauss's and Bell's perspectives, two different attitudes among conservatives may be distinguished. This distinction is suggested by Jürgen Habermas, who differentiates the position of those he terms 'old conservatives', like Strauss, from that of neoconservatives like Bell. Whereas the former demand a wholehearted rejection of the modern world, seeking 'a withdrawal to a position *anterior* to modernity', the latter accept many of its features, such as the developments of modern science, though nonetheless recommending 'a politics of defusing the explosive content of cultural modernity' (Habermas, 1985, p. 14). In other words, while old conservatives may prefer some form of rolling back of modernity, neoconservatives seek rather to excise the destructive elements within it.

However, although Habermas's distinction indicates a clear truth about the different attitudes that may be held by conservatives towards the modern world, it is necessary to be circumspect in applying it beyond the thinkers Habermas considers. As noted in Chapter 4, despite Bell's rejection of Straussianism, a great deal of shared ground is apparent between neoconservatives and Straussians, both usually espousing very similar agendas on educational and moral matters. As Fleming observes, Habermas displays an over-reliance on Bell for his characterization of neoconservatism (Fleming, 1991, p. 94), problematic since Bell is in many ways atypical, not least in his anti-Straussianism. Equally, later Straussians do not always articulate the same desire to withdraw from modernity that may be attributed to Strauss. Whereas Strauss sought the basis for a binding social doctrine in pre-modern philosophy, his subsequent followers commonly invoke the modern republican tradition as similarly capable of providing its foundations (for example, Pangle, 1988).

What Strauss's and Bell's arguments do share is the fact that both were relatively ignored by non-conservatives until the outbreak of more recent culture war hostilities. As one disciple of Strauss suggests, an article by Richard Rorty (Rorty, 1988) may represent 'the first extended notice that a prominent American philosophy professor has taken of Strauss' (Mansfield, 1988, p. 34). In many respects, Bell's contribution to debates on postmodernism was also neglected until more recently (see Turner, 1990, p. 2).

The arguments of Straussians and neoconservatives concerning postmodernism therefore acquired a wider salience only in the context of the culture war. These more recent writings are what will be considered next. However, as a preliminary, it is necessary to point out two general problems with conservative accounts. First is the fact that, following Bell, postmodernism is typically presented as a type of cultural 'temper', as well as being inextricably linked to the counterculture of the 1960s (see, for example, Kristol, 1994, p. 35). While this clearly suits conservatives' purposes in demonizing postmodernism, it also tends to foreclose debate regarding its nature and origins.

Second is the tendency, even in book-length treatments, to effect a largely uncritical lumping together of different thinkers and schools of thought, as equally guilty of the same offences. That is, the perceived enemy usually figures as a single, undifferentiated bogeyman. For example, D'Souza lists the various 'esoteric' names today's 'fashionable scholars' adopt – 'deconstructionists, postmodernists, structuralists, poststructuralists, reader-response theorists' – with not a word as to what may distinguish them (D'Souza, 1991, p. 157). His claim that they are all embarked upon a shared intellectual enterprise may have validity, but in the absence of any more nuanced discussion or evident close reading of these 'fashionable scholars', conservatives' pretensions to being defenders of high intellectual standards may again seem open to question.

With these problems noted, a number of common themes are apparent in contemporary conservative engagements with postmodernism. In relation to the educational sphere, many of these are once more suggested by Bloom, who is therefore worth quoting at some length. According to him, 'deconstructionism' represents:

> the last, predictable, stage in the suppression of reason and the denial of the possibility of truth in the name of philosophy. The interpreter's creative activity is more important than the text; there is no text, only interpretation. Thus the one thing most necessary for us, the knowledge of what these texts have to tell us, is turned over to the

subjective, creative selves of these interpreters, who say that there is both no text and no reality to which the texts refers. A cheapened interpretation of Nietzsche liberates us from the objective imperatives of the texts that might have liberated us from our increasingly low and narrow horizon. (Bloom, 1987, p. 379)

In other words, with determinate analysis abandoned, and truth and reason suppressed, students are condemned to a world of limited possibilities. However, most troubling for conservatives is that postmodernists' ideas are believed to have spread far beyond the walls of the academy. For example, Cheney argues that the 'progress of postmodernism can be seen in a range of institutions, from museums, to cinema, and even including the practice of therapy' (Cheney, 1995, p. 143). Consequently, postmodernism poses a threat not only to standards within the sphere of education but also to order and cohesion throughout society. According to Will, postmodernists' ideas:

subvert our civilization by denying that truth is found by conscientious attempts accurately to portray a reality that exists independently of our perceptions or attitudes...Once that foundation of realism is denied, the foundation of a society based on persuasion crumbles. It crumbles because all arguments...become arguments about the characteristics of the person presenting a thought, not about the thought. (Will, 1994, p. 135)

The widespread nature of conservatives' belief that postmodernism is a danger to the very foundations of civilization is shown by the range of concerns, from moral relativism to attacks upon traditional conceptions of national identity, that are believed to be undergirded by postmodernists' ideas (Kopff, 1996; J. O'Sullivan, 1996; Windschuttle, 1997). As noted in Chapter 2, a particular concern of American conservatives is the influence the subjective interpretation of texts has upon the reading of the Constitution.

Yet what is especially conspicuous in conservative writings is that it is more than just the intellectual merits of postmodernists' arguments that inspires their odium. D'Souza believes that it is in fact possible to 'overstate the intrinsic importance of the new scholarship', since 'strange and abstruse' theories have always been popular with intellectuals (D'Souza, 1991, p. 182). What is notable, and therefore most worrying, about fashionable ideas today is 'the extent to which they serve the ends of a political movement'. Similarly, Will's concern is that the ascendance of postmodern theories implies 'the displacement of books and all they embody – a culture of reason and persuasion – by politics' (Will, 1994, p. 136).

Many of the above arguments are paralleled within British writings, where similar connections are made between the influence of postmodernism within the educational sphere and its wider implications. For example, one article – examining 'the horrors of post-modernism' and bearing the title of 'The Virus of Evil in Culture' – informs us that literature students today are introduced to 'works that offer only corruption and depravity' (Holbrook, 1994, p. 13). Yet more serious, the whole of Western culture is believed to have been infected by a 'virus of schizoid moral inversion, and it threatens to erode our civilisation' (p. 11). Indeed, it is claimed, 'we are powerfully under the influence of those who have made a pact with the Devil' (p. 13).

Scruton shares a similar perspective. Like Bell, Scruton sees a definite continuity between postmodernism and modernism: 'I suspect that the postmodernizers are really only modernizers in another guise' (Scruton, 1992, p. 3). For Scruton as well, it is the threat to order and tradition that is the menace posed by both: the very 'ruin of meaning... lies on the agenda of those modernists and post-modernists, from Sartre to Rorty, whose world is bereft of all authority' (Scruton, 1994, p. 477). Scruton also appears to believe that a Faustian pact has been entered into by postmodernists, a discussion of deconstruction being placed at the end of a chapter entitled 'The Devil' (pp. 458–79).

Whose Enlightenment is it?

In the light of these frequently scathing attacks, it seems appropriate to raise the question of just where present-day conservatives ought to be placed on any ideological spectrum. In particular, it is necessary to ask whether conservative critics of postmodernism have become defenders of the Enlightenment.

One way in which conservatives may obviate the paradox of seeming to uphold Enlightenment ideals is implied in the suggestion – by those such as Bell and Scruton – of a continuity between modernism and postmodernism. Thus, in calling down a plague on both the modernist's and postmodernist's houses, the latter may be dismissed on the basis of being party to the same faulty mode of thinking conservatives have always sought to expose. For example, Scruton accuses Lyotard of 'a sneaking attachment' to the metanarratives he professes to reject (Scruton, 1992, p. 3).

One problem with this move is that it may easily lead to confused, if not outright contradictory, stances. For example, Bell criticizes the modernist sensibility on the basis that 'it draws from the French Revolution and the idea that men, by their own efforts, should – and can – tear up society by the roots and remake it by design' (Bell, 1985, p. 53), and therefore for its commitment to 'the utopia of the Enlightenment' (p. 54). However, he also wishes to denounce both modernists and postmodernists for their surrender to nihilism and the dictates of immediate impulses, and for placing a premium upon 'pre-rational spontaneity' (Bell, 1978, p. 143). Yet it is hard to see how conservatives can credibly criticize their enemies for being, seemingly simultaneously, Enlightenment-inspired utopians and nihilists swayed by non-rational imperatives.

However, other conservatives argue that postmodernists are not the same as their older enemies on the Left. As Joel Schwartz pointedly writes:

> The irrationalist thinking that appeals to today's academic left … treats the ideas of universality, truth, and human excellence as so many bad jokes. Remarkably, the irrationalist left takes pride in denying to all mankind what an earlier left had criticized society for denying only to the poor. (Schwartz, 1990, p. 30)

With this assessment intended as a criticism, it is apparent that many conservatives today view themselves as defenders of principles and ideals that would once have been more usually articulated by their opponents. Indeed, as one commentator noting the general decline of universalist thinking bluntly remarks, 'only a few cranky groups of the right are trying to make us remember the Enlightenment and Hegel' (Lingis, 1994, p. 10).

Bloom, for example, attempts to do just this, lamenting the fact that, 'As Hegel was said to have died in Germany in 1933, Enlightenment in America came close to breathing its last during the sixties' (Bloom, 1987, p. 314). Similarly, Cheney wishes to resist the attack upon those principles 'associated with the United States and its Western heritage, including, in the last instance, the Enlightenment legacy of scientific thought' (Cheney, 1995, p. 24). In the same vein, Will proudly asserts that 'Our nation is, I passionately believe, the finest organized expression of the Western rationalist tradition' (Will, 1994, p. 139).

Moreover, invocations of objectivity and rationality can be found throughout present-day conservative writings. Most obvious, libertarians' commitment to the free market is predicated upon notions of progress, universality and rational behaviour. There is at least some truth, therefore, in Gray's judgement that 'market fundamentalism, is, like Marxism, a variation on the Enlightenment project' (Gray, 1995, p. 100). Indeed, as seen in earlier chapters, it is Gray's identification of free-market conservatism as one of the most redoubtable remaining strongholds of Enlightenment principles that accounts for its earning so much of his wrath. In particular, the globalist outlook of many libertarians today suggests a commitment to universalism rarely found elsewhere.

However, the value of reason is also lauded by a wide variety of conservatives, and in relation to a whole range of concerns. This may be illustrated by considering one British collection of articles, which seeks to highlight the 'sentimental' and 'irrational' nature of all manner of social, medical and moral panics, from health scares to environmental alarums (Anderson and Mullen, 1998). Typical in tone is an article by Anthony O'Hear in which, reacting to the outpourings of grief prompted by the death of Princess Diana, he expresses disdain for the fact that 'she stood for the elevation of feeling, image and spontaneity over reason, reality and restraint' (O'Hear, 1998, p. 184).

Yet one of the most revealing of contemporary writings is a book review by Roger Kimball, who is moved to ask in its title, 'Whose Enlightenment Is It?' (Kimball, 1996). According to Kimball, although the book's author avows a left-wing standpoint, in attempting to uphold the ideal of a universal common humanity and attacking identity politics he sounds as if he has 'turned over a new, conservative leaf' (p. 6). It is, Kimball suggests, simply not possible both to claim left-wing credentials and to disassociate oneself from notions such as multiculturalism. In other words, defending Enlightenment ideals can today appear presentable as all but wholly the prerogative of conservatives.

Towards a postmodern conservatism?

With many conservatives appearing to have cast themselves as last guardians of the rationalist tradition, it is time to return to the suggestion raised at the outset and explore the potential for conservatives instead to embrace a postmodern viewpoint. Are there not obvious grounds for them to espouse a similar incredulity towards metanarratives?

A major difficulty in answering this question arises from the fact that, as Joe Doherty observes, 'the link between postmodernism and the political right is largely one of implication rather than demonstrable celebration and adoption' (J. Doherty, 1992, p. 214). As will be seen, there are conservatives more ready to recognize this link, yet Doherty's point is largely correct. This being the case, the aim of this section will be as much to draw out implications as to identify explicit avowals.

Certainly, a number of structural parallels between postmodernist and conservative thought may be discerned. Probably the most well-known critic to note these is Habermas, who observes that, in blaming an adversary culture for the ills of the economy and polity, neoconservatives such as Bell reveal a number of shared assumptions with postmodernists regarding the nature of social causation (Habermas, 1985, pp. 6–8, 13–15). That is, by identifying factors such as moral laxity as responsible for undermining economic and political stability, many conservatives implicitly agree with a postmodern idealism that believes explanation for economic and political developments is to be found in the domain of culture. Upon this basis, conservatives' fearful culture-war presentiments of apocalyptic nihilism might be viewed as simply the converse side of those postmodernist accounts that rather revel in its possibilities (compare Novak, 1995, with Baudrillard, 1984).

Furthermore, many conservatives regard themselves as engaged in a largely 'deconstructive' mission: Cowling believes it to be 'an unavoidable fact that a Conservative intellectuality ought to be negative, sceptical and intolerant' (Cowling, 1997, p. 14). Perhaps few postmodernists would agree with the last of these three aspirations, but both they and conservatives are frequently motivated more by the goal of refuting opponents' ideas and programmes than that of offering 'constructive' prescriptions of their own.

Of course, structural congruities do not in themselves point to any necessary similarity in terms of substantive beliefs. Yet beyond formal parallels, the conservative tradition may be seen to share much more with that of postmodernists. According to Habermas, this commonality is a shared spirit of anti-modernism. He thus labels thinkers such as Foucault and Derrida 'young conservatives', to indicate their adoption of a scepticism towards modernity similar to that of both old and neo-conservatives.

To assess whether this attribution is justified, it is necessary to explore the more concrete ways in which a conservative perspective may be in accord with that of postmodernists. The obvious place to begin is with Burke, whose fulminations against the rationalism characteristic of Enlightenment thought have informed the arguments of generations of subsequent conservatives. It would, of course, be a misguided exercise to attempt to pin on Burke any postmodernist label; the aim here is purely to draw out possible points of contact between a Burkean and postmodernist perspective.

Most clearly, Burke offered a similarly modest assessment to that of postmodernists regarding the faith to be placed in individuals' reasoning capacities. In contrast to the perceived reliance of Enlightenment thinkers upon abstract modes of thought, Burke declared that:

> in this enlightened age I am bold enough to confess, that we are generally men of untaught feelings; that instead of casting away all our old prejudices, we cherish them to a very considerable degree ... and the longer they have lasted, and the more generally they have prevailed, the more we cherish them. (Burke, 1968, p. 183)

The prejudices Burke cherished are those generated by man's non-rational faculties, of common sense and intuition. The historical accumulation of experientially derived wisdom, believed to be embodied in traditions and established institutions, was felt by Burke to provide a far surer guide to action than any presumptuous belief in the powers of reason. It is especially fallacious to imagine that the fruits of reason can provide certain enough bases for the radical reshaping of society. Moreover, rather than aspiring to the creation of universal principles, men should look to the particular, the community, for their values and identities.

While the language employed may be very different – for example, few postmodernists offer explicit affirmation of 'prejudice' – a number of areas of agreement between a Burkean and postmodernist stance are clear: scepticism towards rationalistic modes of thought; distaste for the social ambitions of hubristic ideologies; and the prizing of the particular and the contingent.

Yet potentially, Burke's position may also be found to possess similar, though far more rarely recognized, relativistic implications. As one commentator aptly observes, 'One of the ironies of history is that the growth of relativism, to which the right so vehemently objects, has as its intellectual origins the conservative reaction to the Enlightenment' (Furedi, 1992, p. 120). That is, if values and identity are not to be derived from any universal grounding, but formed in the particular of communities, a relativistically historicized view of these might be a logically irresistible conclusion. Indeed, with the 'prejudices' to be found within one society possessing no foundationally justifiable compulsion for any other, the Burkean conservative might be felt to possess little basis for passing judgement upon cultural differences. Moreover, reality itself might slip through a tradition-oriented conservative's fingers as much as those of postmodernists: with no standpoint of universal reason outside of embedded traditions available, objective reality may be as inaccessible to the former as to the latter trapped within the subjectivity of discourse.

Conservatives' revived interest in communitarian themes brings these implications especially to the fore. For example, Willetts is aware of these possibilities, noting that a potential danger of a community centred perspective is that 'We lose all ability to judge anything' (Willetts, 1992a, p. 74). While few conservatives, and certainly not Burke, champion either ethical or epistemological relativism, it is nonetheless not entirely surprising to find Burke treated by a resolute defender of universal grounding and judgement like Strauss as at least implicated – for his downgrading of the role of reason and for supposedly equating the good with the existing – in the descent of modern thought into relativistic ruin (Strauss, 1953, pp. 312–23). As noted in Chapter 4, conservatism itself might be felt to share responsibility for the declining faith in definite values that so troubles contemporary culture warriors.

Further commonalities can be found with other strands of conservative thinking. In particular, the perspective of free-market libertarians may come very close to a postmodern preference for a dispersed and fragmented social philosophy. Indeed, Hobsbawm's suggestion that, in emphasizing the subjective viewpoint of the individual, both free-market liberalism and postmodernism attempt to 'sidestep the problem of judgment and values altogether' (Hobsbawm, 1994, p. 339) highlights the possibility that the former may also be unable to avoid the trap of relativism. While this line of argument has obvious weaknesses – to note again, few free-market thinkers have ever advocated a purely individualist ideology – there is at least a tension regarding their ability to ascribe to either values or identity any straightforwardly fixed or objective status.

The issues documented in the last chapter signify that some conservatives also believe that society has undergone a qualitative transformation akin to that suggested by postmodernists; whether the theory is of postindustrialism, globalization or the new economy, all might be considered postmodern conceits. The enthusiasm of many conservatives for the information revolution in particular suggests as well a strong affinity with the 'postmaterialist' idealism commonly embraced by postmodernists. The fact that so few conservatives recognize any of this is itself significant, revealing as it does the narrowness of their understandings of what postmodernism may mean.

As suggested earlier, most follow Bell in conceiving of postmodernism strictly as a cultural sensibility. Although a major theorist of both postindustrialism and postmodernism, Bell keeps his analyses of each deliberately separate, since one of his key contentions is that changes in one sphere of society need not be related to changes in others. The theory of postindustrialism 'is limited specifically to changes in the techno-economic order ... changes in the social structure do not *determine* either the polity or culture' (Bell, 1978, p. xxx). In other words, economic changes are not the cause of cultural ones; the emergence of a postmodernist temper is not the result of the rise of postindustrial society.

Bell's argument is premised upon conservatives' long-held dislike of thinking of society in terms of a unified system, seen as the 'error' of thinkers like Marx. The same assumption is implicit in contemporary analyses of the new economy, with few conservatives even considering the possibility that – if true – the move to a mode of social organization based principally upon knowledge rather than material production might necessitate broader shifts in society's morality and culture. As with Bell, most wish simply to preserve traditional moral and religious beliefs in any 'techno-economic' context. Yet it is worth commending conservatives like Gingrich and D'Souza to take more seriously today's 'fashionable scholars', as perhaps offering a perspective more appropriate to the supposed contours of the new economic age than that of modernist liberals like Locke or Smith.

Another clear expression of a sharing of perspectives between postmodernists and conservatives is their similar attitudes towards what they decry as totalizing or totalitarian ideologies. In fact, as a corollary to their scepticism towards attempts to understand society in totality, the notion of difference has long played a part in conservatives' discourses of identity, despite their widespread scorning of identity politics. Indeed, the word itself was once far more a part of the vocabulary of the Right than of the Left, especially in discussions around racial identity, which may explain why some now seek to claim it as their own. For example, Aidan Rankin asserts that 'Unlike Liberals, Conservatives welcome difference, whether between individuals or between cultures' (Rankin, 1998, p. 15).

In the light of this, Michael Lind's speculation as to the possibility of a 'multiculturalism of the right' (M. Lind, 1995, p. 2), founded upon the ready acknowledgement of difference, draws attention to an important truth regarding conservatives' intellectual heritage. As Lind recognizes, conservatives today are typically cautious about forwarding views centred upon ideas of racial difference, especially biological ones. Even so, they remain a thread of conservative argument, best exemplified by Murray and Herrnstein's efforts to provide a 'scientific' rationale for the differentiation of racial groups, based upon purported variations in intelligence (Murray and Herrnstein, 1994a). Although Murray and Herrnstein reject multiculturalism, they nonetheless express sympathy for the idea of 'ethnocentrism' (Murray and Herrnstein, 1994b, p. 37), implying similar assumptions about the significance and ineradicability of differences between ethnic groups.

Even among postmodernism's strongest critics, similarities may be identified. For example, Scruton – like many traditionalist conservatives – shares with postmodernists a distrust of science and progress, disparages rationalistic ideologies and values the particular over the universal (Scruton, 2001b, pp. 17–37). Yet what makes Scruton a particularly worthwhile writer to examine is that he shares many of the fundamental assumptions underpinning these beliefs. For instance, he urges his own form of decentring, arguing that the first-person perspective of liberalism, with its presumptions of an autonomous rational self, is deficient; it must be supplemented by considering the standpoint of the other, the third-person perspective (pp. 182–94).

Similarly, Scruton believes in the priority of appearance – that the 'reality of politics is not to be found outside the motives of those who engage in it' (p. 27) – in contrast to the claims of ideologies like Marxism concerning underlying essences. The focus for understanding should therefore be the 'surface' of society, the realm of culture, rather than its supposed material foundations. Like the postmodernist, he is thus drawn to the insights offered by the philosophy of language. Finally, he also affirms a belief in social constructionism: 'The human world is a social world, and socially constructed' (Scruton, 1994, p. 495). Upon the basis of this commitment, it is quite possible to indict Scruton's own philosophy with the charge of relativism (Ireland, 1995, p. 192).

However, most significant is that Scruton's comments on postmodernism indicate an awareness that at least aspects of it may be more agreeable to a conservative than he would likely wish to allow. For example, he confesses agreement with Lyotard's contention that Enlightenment-inspired metanarratives are 'no longer believable' (Scruton, 1992, p. 3). Furthermore, despite his general equation of the ambitions of modernists and postmodernists, he is by no means oblivious to the similarities between the latter's and the conservative's rejection of the former. According to Scruton, the voices of the 'few noble spirits' – including Burke, de Maistre and Eliot – that over the centuries have resisted modernity, have tended to be drowned out by those that believe the process of modernization to be universal and inexorable. However,

> If the announcement of a postmodern condition signals that this view has at last proved to be wrong, and that the world is slowing down or stopping – maybe even going into reverse – then the little

wisdom that has been uttered over the last four hundred years will not have been in vain. (Scruton, 1992, p. 3)

Of course, such an allowance represents only the faintest and most begrudging of approvals. Moreover, Scruton makes certain that there is no confusion between a postmodern position and his own – Lyotard is still chastised, for failing to acknowledge Burke and, as noted earlier, retaining a regard for modernist aspirations.

With even such reluctant recognitions of any kinship with postmodernism few and far between among conservatives, it is to be expected that the actual endorsement of postmodern doctrines is all but non-existent. Yet two writers to present relatively sympathetic treatments worth examining are Gray and Noël O'Sullivan, both of whom draw upon an Oakeshottian understanding of the nature of politics and philosophy.

It is valuable here to return to the argument forwarded by Devigne. Thus, although his attribution of a sense of fearful anticipation of postmodernism may be valid in relation to Strauss, Oakeshott represents a very different case, since the major target of his disfavour is likewise the follies of rationalism. (This is not to suggest that Devigne is not aware of the relevant differences between the two – see Devigne, 1994, pp. 190–3.)

Of particular significance is the fact that Oakeshott is one of the few conservatives to be given by postmodernists either attention or respect. For example, Rorty, although suspicious of the elitist implications of Strauss's thought (Rorty, 1988, p. 28), writes favourably on Oakeshott's anti-rationalism (Rorty, 1980, pp. 389–94, 1989, pp. 57–60). Especially noteworthy is the fact that he draws upon Oakeshott's understanding of a conversation in developing his own understanding of philosophy; that is, Oakeshott's belief that in a conversation 'there is no "truth" to be discovered, no proposition to be proved, no conclusion sought' (Oakeshott, 1962, p. 198). What Rorty contends is that philosophy should be regarded as simply one form of 'conversation' among many, possessing no privileged status as guarantor of the foundations of knowledge.

While it may be as erroneous to attempt to assign a postmodernist label to Oakeshott as to Burke, a number of facets of Oakeshott's writings may be seen to provide resources for the fashioning of a postmodern doctrine. With similar intent to Burke, a preference for knowledge of a practical nature is contrasted with the lamentable favouring by rationalists of 'technical' knowledge (Oakeshott, 1962, pp. 7–13). Practical knowledge is that which is acquired through experience rather than abstract reflection, from the concrete traditions in which people live.

Politics, therefore, 'is not the science of setting up a permanently impregnable society, it is the art of knowing where to go next in the exploration of an already existing traditional kind of society' (p. 58). Unlike Strauss, Oakeshott does not hold Hobbes responsible for the degradation of modern thought, instead approving of the fact that 'His scepticism about the power of reasoning ... separate[s] him from the rationalist dictators of his or any age' (Oakeshott, 1975a, p. 63). It is, in part, by drawing upon Hobbes that Oakeshott develops his model of civil association as constituted by a framework of non-instrumental rules.

The significance of these beliefs for present concerns can be understood by considering Gray's and O'Sullivan's arguments. Starting with Gray, his argument of interest comes from a period when he was seeking to develop a 'post-modern liberal conservatism' as the philosophy appropriate to the needs of an increasingly fragmented society, consciously modelled on Rorty's historicist conception of a postmodern bourgeois liberalism (Gray, 1993b, p. viii). Having come to regard the possibility of a universally valid, rationally grounded liberalism to be a chimera – the misguided nature of this project confirmed by the failings of the universalist, rationalist doctrines of both communism and the New Right – Gray nonetheless believed that as a historical practice liberalism might still be defended, if understood as a time-bound, specifically Western cultural artefact.

By viewing it in this way, we 'initiate a form of post-modern individualism that is fully conscious of its own historical particularity' (p. 259). The place of conservatism in this postmodern philosophy derives from its appreciation of the particular, local character of our experience of individualism, and its ability to rein in liberalism's overweening pretensions. Its value, therefore, is 'in correcting the illusion that we are, or can ever be, dispossessed or unencumbered selves, free-floating sovereign subjects, distanced from all social convention and heirs to no tradition'.

The possibility that traditionalist conservatism might by itself be relevant to our postmodern world is discounted, Gray criticizing conservatives like Scruton for demanding too substantive a notion of a common culture in today's pluralistic world (p. 262). Nonetheless, if conjoined with a duly restrained liberalism, conservatism is a necessary element in the constitution of a suitably humble postmodern philosophy. Moreover, the set of political arrangements Gray believed to be best suited to this circumscribed liberalism is Oakeshott's model of civil association (p. 265).

O'Sullivan presents a similar understanding to Gray. The amenability of a conservative perspective to postmodernism may be traced back earlier in O'Sullivan's writings. His very definition of conservatism, as a philosophy of imperfection committed to 'the defence of a limited style of politics' (N. O'Sullivan, 1976, p. 12), clearly suggests this potential. Moreover, in his analysis of the New Right, an Oakeshottian understanding of 'the role of government as the maker and custodian of non-instrumental law' (N. O'Sullivan, 1986, p. 33), he finds it to be its most valuable theoretical component.

When attention is paid to postmodernism itself, it is therefore not surprising that O'Sullivan should be attracted by its expression of a 'comprehensive dissatisfaction with the western humanist tradition' (N. O'Sullivan, 1993, p. 22). In particular, he identifies three features within postmodernism's deconstructed notion of the self of value in the development of a 'philosophy of modesty' (pp. 31–4). The modest nature of the postmodern self lies, first, in its acceptance of a de-centred cosmic existence, in which contingency is acknowledged as part of the natural order of life; second, in its rejection of the idea of absolute knowledge; and, third, in its repudiation of Eurocentrism, disavowing the idea that Western values must possess a universal significance.

Like Gray (and Rorty), O'Sullivan does not take any of this to mean a necessary abandonment of Western liberalism's values and institutions, but similarly wishes us to recognize their non-universal, foundation-less character (p. 35). A historicized view of the self is thus one that 'acknowledges that the self in question is a specifically *Western* self, rather than man as such'. Explicitly following Gray, he too argues for a Hobbesian view of civil association, seeing in this model the best hope for peaceful coexistence in a world of postmodern pluralism.

However, following from the definition of conservatism O'Sullivan forwards, his argument may imply, more than Gray's, that such a model is *the* conservative one. As noted in Chapter 3, for O'Sullivan the demands for a common culture of conservatives such as Scruton are not only misguided but also in opposition to the fundamental perspective of British conservatism. If this is the case, then perhaps all conservatives – or at least all British ones – ought to find some virtue in a modest postmodern philosophy, since it is in harmony with the basic orientation of their own ideology.

The conservative condition

It is thus possible to see how conservatism may be construed as both antagonistic to and in propinquity with a postmodern perspective. What remains, therefore, is to attempt to resolve this seeming contradiction.

First, it will be valuable to examine more closely Habermas's classification of postmodernists as conservatives. It is certainly not difficult to suggest ways in which postmodernism's claims possess 'conservative' implications. Bloom's argument that deconstruction consigns us to an 'increasingly low and narrow horizon', might well serve as a diagnosis of the potentially conservative consequences of a postmodern perspective as a whole, in its engendering of social and political fragmentation and disallowance of any grounding for large-scale social change. Equally, accepting postmodern contentions may be 'conservative' in terms of a foreclosing of genuine intellectual debate, since with the abandonment of the notions of truth and objectivity it becomes impossible to challenge beliefs – from whatever perspective – at any fundamental level, with all simply sheltered from critique within protective shells of relativistic indeterminacy.

Moreover, it is by no means impossible for postmodernists to draw the same political conclusions as conservatives. Rorty expresses agreement with neoconservatives on a number of issues. For example, writing in 1987, he agreed with Bell that Soviet expansionism continued to pose a serious threat to freedom and democracy, and needed to be combated (Rorty, 1987, pp. 566–7). Without intending to score easy retrospective points, Rorty's exaggerated assessment of this threat during the twilight years of Soviet power – 'it seems likely that the next century will see a steady expansion of Moscow's empire throughout the Southern Hemisphere' (p. 566) – can be traced to a similar inflated apprehension regarding 'totalitarian' ideologies.

Even so, it remains inaccurate to describe postmodernists as being, in the sense Habermas intends, conservatives as such. It is not without value to note that few subscribers to postmodern ideas self-apply a conservative label, even if rejecting conventional left-wing appellations. To its proponents at least, the postmodern turn is typically conceived of as a 'progressive' rather than a conservative one, in representing a challenge to established ideologies and politics. For example, Rorty – despite his confessed agreements with writers like Bell – is 'astonished, and alarmed' (p. 565) at being associated with neoconservatives by critics such as Habermas. Lyotard, too, reacts with great disdain to Habermas's suggestion, subjecting it to a caustic rebuttal (Lyotard, 1984, pp. 72–3).

Yet it is not necessary simply to accept the postmodernists' self-image to understand why assigning them a conservative label may be a mistake. An obvious point concerns the question of lineage. Although conservatives usually take too narrow a view of postmodernism's origins, it is nonetheless correct to recognize that its adoption as a widely employed paradigm is traceable to issues that emerged from within the Left. Specifically, it may be attributed to a loss of faith in traditional left-wing ideas and programmes: from a sense of disillusionment following the failure of the 1968 student revolts, the later retreat of socialist movements and parties throughout the West, and the decline of Third World liberation movements. Most recently, the demise of Soviet communism has further accelerated interest in postmodern themes, as part of the Left's search for alternative agendas. One problem, therefore, in labelling postmodernists conservatives is that it obfuscates postmodernists' true genealogy. Furthermore, most postmodernists do not, at least in theory, construe their ambitions in purely 'conservative' terms: any task of deconstruction is usually presented as the necessary prelude to some form of later reconstruction. That such claims may be regarded with scepticism should not in itself detract from the fact that no simple equation can be made between postmodernists' and conservatives' goals. Indeed, insofar as the implications of postmodernists' contentions are conservative, they are likely to be no more so than Habermas's, in the light of the meagreness of his allowances for the possibility of fundamental change (Mészáros, 1989, p. 42).

Yet most importantly, assigning the conservative label to postmodernists is problematic for then understanding why so many conservatives are hostile towards postmodernism. The following observation of Rorty's is to the point:

> Habermas has said (in an interview) that he knows himself to be on the right track in his ethical universalism because that is the doctrine that brings the loudest squeals from the German political right ... I had taken for granted, on the basis of my (admittedly limited) experience with the American political right, that what made the right squeal was any *doubt* about ethical universalism, any suggestion of historicism. (Rorty, 1987, pp. 573–4)

In other words, while 'anti-modernism' may be a shared theme of postmodernist and conservative writings alike, emphasizing this commonality obscures the fact that many conservatives – including, to take those Habermas himself cites, Strauss and Bell – conceive the problem of modernity as precisely the *opposite* disorder to that typically suggested by postmodernists, that is, as entailing a disastrous collapse of belief in absolute, universal values, rather than any over-commitment to them.

There is thus good cause for caution in applying the conservative label too widely. Nonetheless, the above does not explain why conservatives may be read divergently in terms of their relationships to a postmodern perspective. One way of explaining this may again be in terms of a split between British and American traditions. To return to Devigne's argument cited in Chapter 3, it might be argued that American conservatives, with their strong commitment to the maintenance of a substantive social and political unity, must necessarily reject postmodern assumptions, whereas British conservatives, possessing a more sceptical attitude towards this aspiration, might be more amenable to a postmodern outlook. Habermas's likening of postmodernists to conservatives would certainly be more convincing if the comparison is made with British thinkers like Oakeshott rather than American ones like Strauss.

In relation to present concerns, support for Devigne's distinction may again be found. In particular, an Oakeshottian perspective can be argued to be solely the preserve of British conservatives. For example, this is evident from Gordon Graham's bold expression of parochialism, that Oakeshott's philosophy 'is a decidedly English doctrine with little appeal and no following in other countries … [since] only English and hence British political institutions have ever been decent enough to allow a decent man to be conservative' (Graham, 1986, p. 188). While Oakeshottian arguments have influenced a large number of British conservatives – including (as well as Gray and O'Sullivan) Cowling, Minogue and Shirley Letwin – far fewer of their American counterparts have embraced them.

In fact, Himmelfarb expresses a disquiet common among American conservatives, at what she believes is Oakeshott's failure to provide sure enough grounding for making value judgements:

> Oakeshott is right to criticize the Rationalists for subverting all habits, the good together with the bad. But so long as he provides us with no means for distinguishing between good and bad, let alone for cultivating a disposition to do good rather than bad, we are obliged to look elsewhere for guidance – to invoke mind, principle, belief, religion, or whatever else may be required to sustain civilization. (Himmelfarb, 1989a, p. 228)

In similar vein, William Kristol argues that it is a mistake to believe that 'true conservatism is an Oakeshottian acceptance of whatever's going on and you can't actually appeal to principles' (W. Kristol, interview by author, 20 October 1998). Indeed, if Graham believes that the uniqueness of British institutions is what makes Oakeshott of only local interest, Irving Kristol contends that it is the nature of America's 'exceptional' conservatism, with its strong and certain religious commitments, that means Oakeshott's arguments are of little relevance to Americans (Kristol, 1995, pp. 373–86). Leaving aside for the moment how fair any of these appraisals of Oakeshott actually are, what they reveal is the general suspicion felt by many American writers towards varieties of conservative doctrine that appear to offer insufficient security to a common social philosophy.

However, attractive as the solution Devigne's dichotomy provides may be, the distinction it depends upon must again be rejected as too simplistic, the result of an over-emphasis on the respective significance of Oakeshott and Strauss for modern British and American conservative traditions. Many British conservatives clearly do work with highly determinate conceptions of truth and political practices, Scruton being an obvious example. Similarly, by no means all American conservatives are enamoured of a Straussian perspective. Although Strauss may have seen Burke as implicated in the degradation of modern thought, the identification writers such as Kirk make with a Burkean philosophy places them instead in a particularist, anti-rationalist tradition.

Frohnen, a contemporary upholder of Burkean principles, is critical especially of the emphasis Straussians place upon the role of reason (Frohnen, 1993, pp. 149–52). Nor is he as sanguine regarding the possibility of objective judgement: 'There is no true external, Archimedean point possible from which society may be judged' (p. 19). In fact, Frohnen expresses far more sympathy for Oakeshott's attacks upon the fallacies of rationalism (pp. 156–60) than he does for Strauss's writings.

Moreover, Rorty's use of Oakeshott may suggest something of what is problematic about regarding Oakeshott's philosophy as relevant only to the British context. Indeed, Rorty's historicist defence of liberalism, drawn upon by Gray and O'Sullivan, might be even better suited to appropriation by American conservatives, if only by those who acknowledge that the American tradition is largely premised upon liberal foundations.

In other words, while there clearly are differing attitudes towards the demands of substantive authority – political and moral – among conservatives, again these differences do not provide the basis for easy typologizing. To understand better how these attitudes relate to conservative engagements with postmodernism, it is necessary to explore in more detail conservatives' understandings of the notions of reason and tradition. In fact, although these two concepts are usually understood as in opposition, even the staunchest upholders of tradition and particularism do not typically reject reason per se, while conservative defenders of reason (and even the Enlightenment) are rarely advocates of any straightforward rationalist optimism.

As already seen in the cases of Burke and Oakeshott, conservatives do not see a commitment to tradition as implying the negation of reason, but as suggesting the superiority of a practical, experientially grounded variety over any purely abstract one. By viewing reason in terms of a deference to the accumulated wisdom of the ages, rather than promoting utopian hubris, what it counsels is precisely the preservation of tradition. At the same time, few conservatives have ever been defenders purely of whatever happens to exist, or believed that circumstance alone is all. Thus, even many traditionalist conservatives accept that there are sources of principle that exist beyond the movement of history, such as religion or natural law.

Indeed, one strategy employed by conservatives, popular particularly among his American followers, to rescue Burke from suspicions of being simply a defender of the status quo – and thereby from the charge of relativism – is to regard him as a natural law thinker, committed to at least certain universal and eternal verities (Stanlis, 1958). Scruton also accepts that some beliefs must be justified from outside the perspective of particular communities, the notion that there are forms of allegiance prior to the creation of political bonds itself being one that is 'not of this or that community, but of the essence of civil life' (Scruton, 2001b, p. 36). Further bonds believed to transcend the vicissitudes of history are those of the family.

In other words, a conservative may espouse beliefs and principles that cannot be reduced to purely historicist foundations. Upon this basis, Willetts feels he is able to refute the accusation of relativism that may be levelled at communitarian conservatives, arguing that it is possible for conservatives to appeal to definite criteria in judging institutions, such as their durability or how far they embody the 'deeper traditions and values' of a society (Willetts, 1992a, p. 76). Like most conservatives, Willetts studiously avoids adjectives such as 'abstract' or 'objective' in describing these criteria; even so, traditions are, he argues, definitely not 'irrational'.

Similarly, Frohnen argues that, although reason is a limited capacity, it has a role in uncovering non-historical truths: 'God gave reason to man – to be used in order to discover and follow His will' (Frohnen, 1993, p. 19). In fact, conservatives may believe that it is the emergence of humanist doctrines that is responsible for the rise of relativism. According to Weaver, the abandonment of faith in transcendental values and universals undermines the belief that 'there is a source of truth higher than, and independent of, man' (Weaver, 1948, p. 2). The consequence of this denial is that 'there is no escape from the relativism of "man the measure of all things"' (p. 4).

More generally, no form of conservative anti-rationalism usually goes as far as a postmodernist variety in denying the validity of evaluative judgement. This may be illustrated by comparing Rorty's use of Oakeshott's notion of a conversation to Oakeshott's own. Although Rorty uses this conception to conclude that philosophy possesses no especial claims in comparison to other modes of knowledge, Oakeshott draws no such conclusion. For him, philosophy is a distinctive discipline, which should be privileged as a higher mode of understanding (Oakeshott, 1962, p. 200). Similarly, it is a mistake to suggest that Oakeshott offers no basis for discrimination. His belief that 'intimations' flowing from a deep practical knowledge of a tradition allows us to distinguish between the authentic and inauthentic (pp. 125–6) clearly suggests a desire to offer such a basis, even if this may not satisfy more demanding conservatives like Himmelfarb.

In other words, even the most avowedly anti-rationalist forms of conservatism typically contain core substantive commitments. Yet equally important to appreciate is that for conservatives such as Strauss, the role of reason is not entirely unrelated to that perceived by anti-rationalist conservatives, that role similarly being to maintain continuity with the wisdom of the past. Although Straussians have far more confidence that the principles reason divines possess a universal and eternal validity, this is very different to believing reason to be a creative force in the sense imagined by 'rationalists', as a faculty to be employed to overcome the burden of established tradition. For Straussians, belief in the importance of tradition is crucial; and since reason is not seen as antagonistic to tradition at the same time it is not intended to underpin any utopian immodesty.

Among contemporary conservatives, it is quite common to find them defending tradition and reason simultaneously. For example, O'Hear, although articulating a preference for reason and reality to feeling and spontaneity, also invokes Burke and the value of tradition as a means of restraining these latter sentiments (O'Hear, 1998, pp. 186–7). While it might be speculated as to what Burke himself, as one who cherished 'untaught feelings', would have made of the expressions of spontaneous emotion O'Hear condemns, it is clear that for present-day conservatives reason is at least as often viewed as a force capable of buttressing order and authority, as it is as a source of challenge to them.

This still leaves to be answered the question of what conservatives mean when they profess to be defenders of the Enlightenment. American conservatives are undoubtedly more comfortable employing a philosophical vocabulary inherited from the Enlightenment, since this language informs their own society's founding doctrines. However, here again efforts are usually made to avoid being mistaken for rationalists (even if some, like Will, appear happy to affirm a commitment to the rationalist tradition). In the same way that they typically distinguish between the characters of the American and French Revolutions, American conservatives also distinguish between the intellectual groundings of these two events.

Consequently, Irving Kristol condemns the utopianism of the 'Continental Enlightenment' – the tradition of Voltaire and Diderot – while acclaiming the meliorism and respect for custom to be found within the 'Anglo-Scottish Enlightenment', the tradition of Locke, Hume and Smith (Kristol, 1983, pp. 141–52; see also Himmelfarb, 2001). Drawing upon the same distinction, Kirkpatrick also cites the importance of the specifically 'Scottish Enlightenment' for understanding America's intellectual foundations (J. Kirkpatrick, interview by author, 16 September 1998).

In fact, rather than being either straightforward anti-modernists or Enlightenment enthusiasts, most contemporary conservatives appear to share Digby Anderson's view that the legacy of the Enlightenment represents a 'mixed inheritance' (D. Anderson, interview by author, 22 June 1998). Although we have benefited, he argues, from the advances of science and the wealth generated by a market economy, we have also suffered because of the damaging questioning of authority that has accompanied these developments. This then explains the tension within contemporary conservative writings noted at the end of Chapter 4: whereas health and environmental alarums appear to undermine the positive achievements of the Enlightenment, and thus need to be challenged, conservatives' own inflated anxieties in relation to moral and cultural malaise are the result of the perceived threat posed to authority by modernism's anti-traditionalist thrust.

A similar assessment to Anderson's is made by James Q. Wilson, who believes that the Enlightenment has left us an 'ambiguous legacy' (J. Q. Wilson, 1993, p. 215). Wilson's attempt to identify an inherent moral sense is worth considering further, as it reveals with particular clarity how conservatives' ambivalence manifests itself even within an individual writer's arguments. Thus, on the one hand, Wilson acknowledges agreement with Enlightenment thinkers that there is a universal human nature, since this allows us to counter moral relativism by affirming that there is a universal moral sense. Yet, on the other, he also wishes us to recognize that these thinkers took a far too optimistic view of how far this nature can be understood, wary that a too sanguine view of human beings' capacity for self-knowledge implies conceding ground to utopian schemes of social engineering. In other words, it is necessary to perform a careful balancing act, to uphold a positive view of humanity's ability to perceive universal absolutes, while at the same time warning against drawing too ambitious conclusions from this.

It is conservatives' efforts to mediate between these two requirements that accounts for the difficulty in understanding the relationship of conservatism to postmodernism, incorporating as conservatism does two conflicting impulses: the desire to defend the values of reason and universality, because of the threat their debasement poses to absolute standards of morality and authority; and the contrary need to remind us of humanity's more fallible side, to counter the equal danger presented to traditional values and order by an overweening belief in reason. Moreover, as seen, it is not possible simply to identify either impulse with a particular 'type' of conservative, since many evidently feel some affinity for both.

Nonetheless, this does not mean that the overall question cannot be resolved, since it is typically the case that one of these impulses is given priority. What determines this prioritizing is context, and may be understood by examining further Himmelfarb's analysis of Oakeshott:

> Skepticism is innocent enough, even attractive, in an age suffering from a surfeit of principles and enjoying a plenitude of good habits... But when those habits become insecure or fall into disuse, the conservative must look elsewhere for the civilized values he has come to enjoy. (Himmelfarb, 1989a, p. 228)

In other words, in the past – when the major threat to order came from rationalist liberals and socialists – the need to highlight the dangers of a presumptuous rationalism was conservatives' paramount concern. However, since at the present time the main ideological enemies are foes like postmodernists, appealing to definite principles is the more urgent need. For critics of rationalism like Burke and Oakeshott, it was possible to take for granted a common fabric of shared basic values to preserve social stability, with much less need for their explicit justification. Yet in the absence of 'a plenitude of good habits', adopting too strong a sceptical attitude is likely simply to compound the problem of demoralization,

in undermining conservatives' own ability to re-establish their foundational authority. The keen sense many conservatives have of these
good habits having fallen into 'disuse', also explains why their primary
concerns are with the wider social and political significance of postmodernism rather than issues of theoretical validity.

Even conservatives with whom it is possible to identify some amount
of shared theoretical ground with a postmodern outlook may believe
that the need to combat the real-world implications of such a perspective constitutes a more important priority than acknowledging any
commonalities. As Scruton argues, the response of the Right to the challenge of postmodernism should be to attempt 'to redraw across the
unbounded landscape of permission the old lines of authority, duty and
responsibility' (Scruton, 1996b, p. 431).

Indeed, such conservatives may be willing to sacrifice theoretical
integrity for perceived social utility. This is especially apparent in relation to the issue of relativism. As Scruton also argues:

> Of course, no conservative will be happy to see the spread of rela-
> tivism, since people need values and have them only to the extent
> that they believe in their authority. It is a philosophical question
> whether relativism is *true*. Politically speaking, however, it is better
> that few men believe it. Like Plato, a conservative may have to advo-
> cate the 'Noble Lie'. He might in all conscience seek to propagate the
> ideology which sustains the social order, whether or not there is a
> reality that corresponds to it. (Scruton, 1984, pp. 139–40)

Of course, if it requires the advocacy of a Noble Lie to disavow relativism, then perhaps it is not, philosophically speaking, simply the
refuge of scoundrels, as Scruton contends; or at least, not solely of non-
conservative ones.

Not many conservatives are willing to own so openly to such an opinion, and Scruton himself has excised the above passage from the
updated edition of the work in which it appeared (Scruton, 2001b).
Nonetheless, Straussians likewise believe that philosophers should
refrain from revealing too widely the ambiguities and uncertainties that
may arise from reflection upon moral questions, for the dangers this
poses to social stability (Strauss, 1953, pp. 152–3). In other words, even
those aware that their own standpoints may not provide the surest bases
for defending absolutes and universals often believe that sustaining the
social order is more important than accepting the destabilizing conclusions that may flow from an overly sceptical or modest philosophy.

Conclusion

One conclusion that may be drawn from this chapter's discussion is that a key reason for there being so much contestation over definitions in debates concerning modernism and postmodernism is that these debates are largely shaped by the broader – and conflicting – agendas of those who define their terms. The aim of many is clearly to imply guilt by association: of postmodernists with the sins of modernists by conservatives like Bell and Scruton, and postmodernists with those of conservatives by critics like Habermas. For this reason, it is not surprising that agreement on the meanings of terms is rarely forthcoming.

What examining the example of postmodernism also shows is that the ideologies of many of conservatives' culture-war opponents share much more with conservatism than either they or conservatives commonly recognize. The benefit for conservatives in acknowledging this would be that it would allow them to adopt a much more sympathetic attitude to a world that has become suspicious of moral and cultural absolutism.

However, although there may be clear theoretical affinities between conservatism and postmodernism, scope for any harmony remains limited, principally because it is not possible for conservatives to accept the practical implications of postmodernist agendas. In particular, in a contemporary context in which traditional values and institutions no longer possess unquestioned acceptance, the need to articulate definite principles becomes especially pressing.

7
The Green Alternative

Despite conservatism's victory over its traditional ideological rivals, it is clear that many conservatives perceive the present social, cultural and intellectual environments to be unsympathetic to their doctrines. If many therefore feel less than enthusiastic about conserving much within these spheres, a realm that might be imagined to command far greater respect is that of nature. As a final topic to explore, this chapter will consider how feasible it is for conservatives to forward an 'eco-conservative' perspective, as a means of revitalizing their ideology.

Today, particularly, there is good reason for conservatives to emphasize their long tradition of valuing nature: with concern for the natural environment having acquired widespread favour throughout both academic and broader discussions, highlighting conservatism's 'green' face may offer them one of their most opportune avenues for reclaiming intellectual authority. Indeed, environmentalism itself is one of the few contemporary ideologies, apart from communitarianism, for which it is possible to identify any significant (if still limited) support among conservatives. Furthermore, while there may be no Habermas to label greens young conservatives, a number of commentators argue that environmentalism belongs on the same end of the ideological spectrum as conservatism. For example, Joe Weston considers green thought to fit 'within the broad framework of right-wing ideology' (Weston, 1986, p. 24).

Even so, it is common for all parts of the ideological continuum at least to pay lip service to a concern for the environment. A key question for this chapter is whether it is possible for conservatives to go beyond a merely superficial adherence. What will be demonstrated is that there is in fact a great deal of shared ground between conservatives and greens, much more than is usually recognized. Nonetheless, examining this issue will ultimately prove valuable because it will again be shown that even where there is the greatest potential for harmony with resonant contemporary ideas, barriers remain for conservatives to benefit from a 'conservative' climate.

Towards a green conservatism?

A central issue for this chapter to explore is to what type of green philosophy conservatives might subscribe. One commonly used distinction is between 'deep' and 'shallow' ecological perspectives. Whereas the former implies a fundamental questioning of humanity's relationship to the environment and the nature of modern industrial societies, the latter is concerned merely with particular issues and immediately available solutions. This type of understanding may indicate the need to question the very way in which terms are conventionally employed. For example, Andrew Dobson contends that 'environmentalism' and 'ecologism' – despite the common identification of the two – are qualitatively different notions (Dobson, 2000, pp. 2–3). Thus, environmentalists argue for a managerial approach to environmental problems, simply seeking technical solutions, whereas ecologists assume more radical stances, being willing to reject present patterns of consumption and production and to recognize that the non-human world possesses intrinsic value.

These distinctions may appear to offer an obvious answer to the question of how to classify conservatives who display a concern for environmental issues. That is, it may be thought that such conservatives can simply be placed on the shallow end of the ecological spectrum; or, in Dobson's terms, be regarded as at best environmentalists, but never true ecologists. One aspect of conservative writings that may lend credence to this suggestion is that conservatives generally employ only the environmentalist label. Indeed, some American writers have adopted the self-description of 'conservative environmentalists' (Dunn and Kinney, 1996; Durnil, 1995). Similarly, it is rare to find any explicit recognition of the difference between shallow and deep perspectives.

However, as this chapter will show, conservatives cannot be straightforwardly mapped on to any shallow/deep spectrum, with conservative writings displaying both 'shallow' and 'deep' qualities; nor can these simply be attributed to different varieties of conservatism. (For this reason, and because conservatives themselves rarely use the term ecologism, environmentalism is to be employed here as an umbrella term for green perspectives in precisely the way writers such as Dobson dislike.) This being the case, the way to proceed must be by investigating in detail how conservatives relate to specific green principles.

The best place to begin is with a consideration of how the relationship between conservatism and green philosophies is conventionally presented. Within the literature on environmentalism, the affinities between green and conservative doctrines are frequently noted, yet rarely dwelt upon in any depth. This is perhaps unsurprising: despite regularly disavowing conventional Left/Right labels, environmentalists nonetheless typically operate on intellectual territory at least once occupied by the Left, only with some reluctance admitting to sharing ground with the Right. Instead, the most valuable writer with whom to start is Gray, who – in an effort to develop an 'agenda for green conservatism' – presents one of the most significant attempts to elaborate a green conservative philosophy (Gray, 1993a, pp. 124–77). Although Gray has subsequently become far less confident about this project, his argument remains among the most illuminating.

The first element of the standard view presented by Gray is the belief that contemporary conservatives are largely antagonistic towards environmentalism:

> It is fair to say that, on the whole, conservative thought has been hostile to environmental concerns over the past decade or so in Britain, Europe and the United States. Especially in America, environmental concerns have been represented as anti-capitalist propaganda under another flag. (p. 124)

Yet second, although conservatives are believed *in fact* to be hostile to environmental concerns, Gray perceives a strong theoretical affinity between environmentalism and a particular strand of conservatism. Rather than possessing 'a natural home on the Left', concern for the environment 'is most in harmony with the outlook of traditional conservatism of the British and European varieties'. Indeed, Gray suggests, the orientation of traditional conservatism aligns it specifically with the perspective of deep ecologists (p. 128).

What Gray also emphasizes is the importance of distinguishing traditional conservatism from economic liberalism, underscoring the distinction by arguing that the points at which the former and a green perspective converge are 'the very points at which they most diverge from fundamentalist liberalism' (p. 136). Indeed, the issue of the environment, as with that of community, is one that provokes much venting of antagonisms towards market liberalism among traditionalist conservatives. For example, Vinson happily endorses the views of environmentalists who 'despise' free-market conservatives and urges traditionalists to seek unity with the former rather than the latter (Vinson, 1996, p. 30). In other words, concern for the environment may represent another contemporary issue likely to exacerbate fault lines within conservative alliances.

Among greens and conservatives alike there is relatively widespread recognition that traditionalist forms of conservatism share much intellectual ground with environmentalism – although not necessarily deep perspectives – whereas free-market doctrines are fundamentally hostile. For example, Jonathan Porritt, while also sceptical towards 'Thatcherite' economics, recognizes that 'there is much about green politics that is instantly and deeply appealing to a certain kind of Tory', that kind being a traditionalist (Porritt, 1984, p. 231; see also Young, 1990, pp. 156–7).

There is undoubtedly some truth in these depictions. Nonetheless, it is far from wholly true. In fact, in comparison to other potentially conservative doctrines, such as postmodernism, it is relatively easy to find approbation among conservatives for some form of environmentally aware philosophy (Paterson, 1989; C. Patten, 1990). Moreover, it is a mistake to perceive American conservatives as especially suspicious towards environmental concerns. For example, John Bliese believes that 'a traditionalist conservative today should be an environmentalist' (Bliese, 1996, p. 148).

Yet even more interesting to note is the attitude of the free market's defenders. Rather than merely dismissing or ignoring environmental issues, a number have sought to incorporate aspects of green ideology within their own, in propounding notions of 'free-market environmentalism' (see Eckersley, 1993; Taylor, 1992). For example, one writer contributing to a symposium on what should constitute the key components of conservatism in the 1990s, argued strongly for the inclusion of free-market environmentalism (Andrews, 1990, p. 5). Similarly, Thatcher maintains that 'The core of Tory philosophy and the case for protecting the environment are the same' (Thatcher, 1990, p. 10). Equally, Gingrich avers that he has been a life-long advocate of environmental protection (Gingrich, 1995, pp. 193–4).

Many commentators regard such avowals with cynicism, questioning the depth of free marketeers' commitments. For example, John McCormick finds Thatcher's conversion to environmentalism 'surprising' and asks how well 'pro-environmental statements sit against a background of ardently anti-regulation Thatcherism' (McCormick, 1991, p. 2). However, when the specific parallels between green and conservative beliefs are considered, it can be seen that it is far from solely with traditionalist varieties of conservatism that these may be drawn. It is

therefore necessary to evaluate these in some detail. To do so, ten potential bases for harmony between conservatism and environmentalism
may be highlighted:

1. A desire to conserve; to respect limits

In the light of the shared etymological roots of the words 'conservative'
and 'conservationist', probably the most obvious basis for a commonality of outlook between conservatives and greens is a desire to conserve.
In the light of this, Hurd argues of an environmentally aware philosophy that it 'fits in with the conserving side of conservatism' (D. Hurd,
interview by author, 25 June 1998).

Even so, defining conservatism simply in terms of the desire to
conserve is, as discussed in Chapter 1, flawed. While a straightforward
preservationism may be manifest in relation to specific causes – whether
this be the conserving of a particular tradition or historic building – at
a more general level few conservatives typically defend the arresting
of change altogether. Rather, what they tend to invoke is some notion of
limits as to what change is acceptable, that which does not overstep
'sensible' boundaries; indeed, as also already seen, it is possible to argue
that conservatism should be defined in terms of a respect for limits.

In conservative writings on the environment, this is revealed most
clearly in the recurrence of words such as 'caution' and 'prudence'. For
example, Bliese asks us to remember when thinking about the natural
world that 'the most important virtue in politics is prudence' (Bliese,
1996, p. 152). This prudence, he argues, should impress upon us the crucial need to halt uncontrolled meddling with the world's climate and to
protect biodiversity.

Greens offer similar, though more theorized, formulations of the idea
of limits in terms of such notions as risk aversion and the 'precautionary
principle' (O'Riordan and Cameron, 1994). Since the world's eco-system
is highly complex and ever changing, when considering new technological or social developments it is better to err on the side of caution
because the full consequences of their impact are unforeseeable and, if
unforeseeable, dangerous. Yet long before any sociological embroidery
of this perspective, the belief that the natural world is beyond full
human comprehension has been a commonplace within the conservative tradition. For example, over half a century ago Weaver warned that:

> [N]ature reflects some kind of order which was here before our time
> and which ... defies our effort at total comprehension ... to meddle

with small parts of a machine of whose total design and purpose we are ignorant produces evil consequences. (Weaver, 1948, p. 172)

It is more then than simply a bare notion of limits that greens and traditionalist conservatives share, but the view that what defines these limits is deficiencies in human understanding. Yet this being the case, it is also possible for a free-market perspective to be in tune with an environmentalist one. Thus Anderson and Leal employ an essentially Hayekian epistemology, predicated upon a belief in the limits of the human capacity for knowledge, in favour of their free-market environmental strategy. Since our knowledge of nature is diffused rather than concentrated, and because ecosystems depend upon a complex number of interacting elements which cannot be grasped in totality, it requires the unconscious workings of the market rather than the centralized power of the state to manage the environment (Anderson and Leal, 1991, p. 4).

In fact, many free-market writers claim that the existence of private property rights and the operation of market forces provide the best hope for conserving the natural environment (see Brittan, 1989; Thatcher, 1990, pp. 16–17). This is because, they contend, the market spontaneously utilizes resources in the most efficient – or 'conservationist' – way possible. Furthermore, market discipline rather than state intervention is commonly argued to be a better means of regulating companies that harm the environment, via the mechanisms of consumer choice. As Gingrich puts it: 'To get the best ecosystem for our buck, we should use decentralized and entrepreneurial strategies rather than command-and-control bureaucratic efforts' (Gingrich, 1995, p. 196). Similarly, Willetts believes that the British water industry is much better placed to achieve ambitious environmental standards since privatization, because government Ministers are constrained by a range of political considerations that may conflict with this objective (D. Willetts, interview by author, 22 June 1998).

2. A scepticism towards the claims of science and the idea of progress

A further prime aspect of much green writing is scepticism towards the developments of science and technology, for their roles in degrading the natural and human environments. For example, Porritt is dismissive of 'unimpeded technological development' and the 'viewpoint of narrow scientific rationalism' (Porritt, 1984, p. 44). Moreover, because both capitalism and socialism are committed to the 'super-ideology' of industrialism, greens should be critical of each. It is for this reason, according to Porritt, that they should reject the politics of both Left and Right.

Yet many traditionalist conservatives are just as sceptical towards the viewpoint of 'scientific rationalism' and the idea of progress. Burke's forceful railings against a 'spirit of innovation' (Burke, 1968, p. 119) embody a sentiment that appears regularly within conservative writings, as seen in earlier chapters. Equally, Scruton has much to say about the alienating and dehumanizing effects of industrialization (Scruton, 2001b, pp. 109–10, 116–17). Of course, the idea of progress is central to any free-market vision, as is the role of technological advancement. Nonetheless, even Thatcher is led by her reflections upon environmental issues to concede that progress may not be a wholly unalloyed good (Thatcher, 1990, p. 6).

At the same time, neither most traditionalist conservatives nor greens believe that the advance of science should be halted completely. Rather, what they share is an ambivalence towards the virtues of scientific and technological advances, and the belief that it is necessary to diminish its presumptive status. In this vein, Gray argues that although a green conservatism should not be anti-technology per se, we should reject 'scientific fundamentalism' and temper our enthusiasm for modernity's technological fruits (Gray, 1993a, p. 126). Similarly, the idea of progress is not completely rejected, but what is stressed is that as much as the passage of time brings material improvements, these are always accompanied by costs in the form of lost values and traditions (p. 139).

Although conservatives and greens are hardly alone in repudiating the negative and alienating effects of industrialization, what they also typically share is the belief that what is problematic about science and technology is so inherently, rather than because of their place within a particular social context. As David Pepper points out, green critiques of technology are generally ahistorical, rarely relating it to a specific context of production arrangements (Pepper, 1993, pp. 143–5). This is evident from Porritt's regard for industrialism as some form of 'super-ideology'. Yet Scruton likewise rejects the idea that the evils of the industrial process are related to its capitalist context and would therefore disappear outside of it (Scruton, 2001b, pp. 116–17). In other words, both conservatives and environmentalists tend to believe that science and industry are to be regarded with suspicion whatever the social system they exist in.

3. A scepticism towards unfettered capitalism

If their critiques of science are often ahistorical, greens are nonetheless also often critical of capitalism specifically. For example, Robyn Eckersley believes that it 'is undoubtedly the case that the expansionary dynamics of capital accumulation have led to widespread ecological degradation' (Eckersley, 1992, p. 121). Similarly, Porritt blames increasing GNP for a multitude of ills, including not only pollution but also rising crime and expanding bureaucracy (Porritt, 1984, p. 121). While traditionalist conservatives by no means reject capitalism, they too have always been sceptical of a purely free market form. For example, Kirk criticizes capitalists for their 'glorifying in ruthless competition' (Kirk, 1962, p. 36).

One of the most distinctive features of green economic concerns is a preoccupation with the idea of resource finitude, which Dobson describes as 'an article of faith for green ideologues' (Dobson, 2000, p. 62). That is, the belief that, sooner or later, humanity will simply exhaust the earth's available resources. Often presented in contrast to liberal economic models, ones centred upon a notion of 'sustainable development' are instead advocated, founded upon the belief that the long-term view requires resource conservation to be a priority alongside development. Yet this belief is also very much in accord with a traditionalist conservative perspective, which likewise advocates moderation in economic policy. Thus Bliese embraces the idea of resource finitude and supports an economics of sustainability (Bliese, 1996, p. 152).

Clearly, economic liberals do not view capitalism negatively. Nor do they attribute primary responsibility for economic degradation to the workings of the market. Nonetheless, even on economic issues there are points of contact between environmentalism and free-market ideology, with Thatcher also professing to believe in 'the concept of *sustainable* economic development' (Thatcher, 1990, p. 8). There is, of course, no question that sustainability might require any fundamental questioning of capitalism, or even any significant fettering of market forces. Even so, it has already been seen that economic liberals may argue that capitalism actually provides the best mechanisms for conserving resources, and while many greens are sceptical towards this claim in general harmony is identifiable in relation to economic liberals' views of government spending specifically.

Regarding this, Thatcher's famous paralleling of the management of the nation's accounts with careful household budgeting appears to strike a chord with many greens. For example, John Young believes that it is a useful contribution to green thought 'to think of national finance in pre-Keynesian terms analogous to good housekeeping' (Young, 1990, p. 156). Porritt also emphasizes that 'Managing the household budget *is* important' (Porritt, 1984, p. 231). Although Thatcher's administration was beset by numerous critics demanding that government spending be increased, it may have taken comfort in the fact that environmentalists represented one group willing to endorse its commitment to reining in unsustainable profligacy.

Still, what lies at the heart of many greens' concerns about economic growth is not merely the possibility of imprudence, but the idea that there is a basic immorality about 'consumer capitalism'. In other words, even were consumerism and materialism 'sustainable', they would still be unethical. For example, Porritt scorns a 'materialist ethic' and suggests that we do not really need all the frivolous extravagances produced by modern capitalism (Porritt, 1984, p. 44). Rather than indulging in ever increasing levels of consumerism, we should instead adopt a life of 'voluntary simplicity' (p. 204). However, as shown in previous chapters, many conservatives share this attitude, with one of the major apprehensions of traditionalist and neo-conservatives regarding capitalism being that a consumer culture will have a deleterious effect upon traditional values and customs. According to Fleming, 'Materialism and consumism retard the development of the human person' (Fleming, 1996a, p. 12). Indeed, we are reminded, the latter 'was the religion of Sodom'.

Within this point may be considered the question of elitism. Young ascribes to conservatives the belief that 'Consumerism of the popular kind is distasteful, indeed conspicuous consumption by those unused to it is what conservatives call "vulgarity"' (Young, 1990, p. 156). However, although such an elitism may be more apparent within conservative discourses, a basic contempt for the material aspirations of ordinary people may be felt as much to permeate green rejections of the 'extravagances' of consumer societies.

4. A belief in non-material values; that nature possesses moral claims

With greens and traditionalist conservatives alike disparaging the morality of consumer capitalism, what both frequently avow instead is a preference for non-material, spiritual values (Porritt, 1984, p. 231). For conservatives these are likely to be those of the Judeo-Christian tradition, whereas for greens a much wider range of beliefs may be endorsed, including New Age doctrines. Even so – and leaving aside Gilder's peculiar brand of high-tech mysticism – a bridge between conservative and green spiritualism is provided by the perspective of conservative-minded environmentalist Edward Goldsmith, who emphasizes the value of strong religious commitments in the maintenance of stable and well-ordered green communities (E. Goldsmith, 1988).

Particularly distinctive in green writings is the belief that the natural world possesses moral claims, possibly even rights. The highly moral dimension of green thought is often obvious in the very tone adopted, as when Porritt writes indignantly that nature does not exist simply to be conquered by man (Porritt, 1984, p. 44). However, conservatives express similar sentiments. For example, Gingrich believes that 'human beings have a moral obligation to take care of the ecosystem' (Gingrich, 1995, p. 196).

Even more strongly, greens may argue not only that nature should be accorded moral respect but also that it possesses inherent moral virtue. Robert Goodin implies this in his development of a 'green theory of value': the more 'natural' are a thing's properties, the more valuable it should be deemed (Goodin, 1992, pp. 19–83). Yet a similar belief is evident among conservatives, as indicated by Weaver's claim that 'creation or nature is fundamentally good' (Weaver, 1948, p. 172). In other words, greens and conservatives may share not only a benign moral attitude towards the natural world but also a belief that virtue actually inheres within it.

5. A belief in fundamental holism and harmony

A further presumption often shared by greens and conservatives is the belief that the natural condition of the world is one of stability. Where this is perhaps clearest in green thought is in the Gaia hypothesis, which promotes the notion that the whole planet is in some form of holistic harmony. As James Lovelock contends:

> [T]he entire range of living matter on Earth, from whales to viruses, and from oaks to algae, could be regarded as constituting a single living entity, capable of manipulating the Earth's atmosphere to suit its overall needs and endowed with faculties and powers far beyond those of its constituent parts. (Lovelock, 1979, p. 9)

Two major points are here asserted: first, that the constituent elements of the earth's ecosystem exist in a condition of mutual balance; and, second, that the whole constitutes an entity in its own right. While by no means all greens support the Gaia hypothesis, a belief that nature possesses some balanced or equilibrium state is common. In other words, a Darwinian understanding of the natural world as a domain of perpetual struggle and conflict – 'red in tooth and claw' – is typically rejected.

Yet such conceptions are paralleled in conservative understandings of society, which similarly downplay the roles of change and conflict. Burke's understanding of society bears striking similarities to Lovelock's conception of the world's ecosystem:

> Our political system is … a permanent body composed of transitory parts; wherein, by the disposition of a stupendous wisdom, moulding together the great mysterious incorporation of the human race, the whole, at one time, is never old, or middle-aged, or young, but in a condition of unchangeable constancy … (Burke, 1968, p. 120)

It is not surprising therefore that Gray should urge both greens and conservatives to embrace the Gaia hypothesis (Gray, 1993a, p. 138). At the very least, Thatcher accepts that the world's environmental systems possess a 'fundamental equilibrium' (Thatcher, 1990, p. 6).

In fact, it is again possible to perceive a free-market perspective as also mirroring that of an environmentalist one, despite the central role played by competition. Thus Nisbet classifies Adam Smith as an 'ecological' thinker (by which he means a believer in cohesive interdependence) because of Smith's belief in a 'natural', spontaneous economic order, in which the overall product of individuals pursuing their own self-interests is harmonious equilibrium (Nisbet, 1974, pp. 352–4). It is perhaps necessary to observe here that although free-market writers scorn consciously created social orders, they do not typically believe in 'disorder'. As Hayek contends, the operation of market forces is 'the only way in which so many activities depending on dispersed knowledge can be effectively integrated into a single order' (Hayek, 1973, p. 42). That is, diversity and conflict at one level become integrated into a whole at another. Indeed, upon this basis, free marketeers' conceptions of spontaneous order may parallel more closely an environmentalist's model of nature than do those of authority-centred conservatives.

6. A belief that the natural world should serve as a model for the social

A conservative view of society may not only correspond to that of a green view of nature, but may treat the natural world as a model.

For example, Burke believes that we should regard our constitution as 'working after the pattern of nature' (Burke, 1968, p. 120).

One of the most notable ways in which this is apparent is the frequent recurrence of organic metaphors. Such references are multiple not only within Burke's writings but also within those of traditionalist conservatives in general, most commonly in their rejections of the idea that society is an artificial – that is, political – contrivance (as discussed in Chapter 3). Quinton argues that organicism is one of the key principles of conservatism, contending that we should view society as 'a unitary, natural growth, an organized, living whole, not a mechanical aggregate' (Quinton, 1978, p. 16). Similarly, Rossiter avers that 'Society is a living organism with roots deep in the past' (Rossiter, 1962, p. 27).

In fact, traditionalist conservatives are as likely to attribute some type of emergent existence to society as a whole as proponents of the Gaia hypothesis do to the planet. For example, Scruton believes that 'a society is more than a speechless organism. It has personality, and will. Its history, institutions and culture are the repositories of human values – in short, it has the character of end as well as means' (Scruton, 2001b, p. 13). By imputing to society a personality and interests of its own, in the same way that greens warn against treating the natural world in a purely instrumental fashion, conservatives repudiate so treating society. If society is indeed akin to a living organism, then change must be slow and organic, evolutionary rather than revolutionary. As Rossiter continues, 'men must forbear to think of [society] as a mechanical contrivance that can be dismantled and reassembled in one generation' (Rossiter, 1962, p. 27).

Economic liberals also often employ natural metaphors to serve their purposes. For example, Anderson and Leal seek to legitimate their belief that entrepreneurialism is 'natural' in precisely this way (Anderson and Leal, 1991, pp. 4–6). The operations of the market are deemed natural because they mirror the way in which when a 'niche' in an ecosystem appears, a new species takes advantage of the 'profit' opportunity opened up, with the activity of 'self-interested' plants and animals benefiting the system as a whole. In other words, looking to nature as a model may be as useful for free-market writers as traditionalist conservatives in validating their views of social organization.

7. A preference for community-based modes of life

Also common within green writings is a rejection of the belief 'that big is self-evidently beautiful' (Porritt, 1984, p. 44) and an expressed preference for the life of the small-scale community. Conservatives' similar attachment to these ideals has been discussed in earlier chapters, so here their specifically environmental aspects will be examined. As seen above, libertarians like Gingrich believe that decentralization is as beneficial for the environment as it is for the economy. Yet a conjoining of community and environmental concerns is more widely apparent. For instance, Nisbet highlights as an important strand of communitarian thinking conceptions centred upon the idea of the 'ecological community', which take as their regulative ideal the natural world's supposed harmony and simplicity (Nisbet, 1974, pp. 319–82). Similarly, Vinson argues for the 'revival of rural community' to act as a counterweight to the sterility of city life (Vinson, 1996, p. 31).

In terms of green thought, Eckersley suggests the term 'ecocommunalism' to describe those strands of anarchist and utopian argument that believe small-scale co-operative communities to be the ideal mode of human existence, living in a harmonious relationship with nature (Eckersley, 1992, pp. 160–70). As Eckersley notes, a common theme is the desire for a disengagement or withdrawal from corrupted political and social life, which is echoed by the contempt for politics and ideology articulated by many conservative communitarians (Scruton, 1996a, pp. 13–17).

In noting the importance of communitarian themes for both traditions, Gray again emphasizes their common aversion to liberal tenets, in their rejecting 'the shibboleth of liberal individualism', the idea that only the individual has value (Gray, 1993a, p. 136). That is, both question the failure of the liberal tradition to understand individual identity as embedded within a fabric of social relationships. Yet both may also therefore share many of the illiberal aspects of much communitarianism. For example, Gray considers under the rubric of an environmentalist opposition to laissez-faire the necessity of restricting immigration – though without the vehemence of paleoconservatives like Buchanan – since unfettered it may lead to 'undoing settled communities' and 'mixing inassimilable cultures' (p. 126). In other words, the problematization of immigration may be justified by the need to preserve the environmental integrity of communities as much as any conservative desire to preserve a traditional notion of national identity.

One of the most explicit exemplars of the illiberal approach to ecological communitarian thinking is Goldsmith, who admires the stability and cohesion of primitive tribal communities, as well as the Indian caste system. Yet this requires accepting, in similar fashion to conservatives like Scruton and Frohnen, that 'a community must be relatively closed', with the admission of outsiders only to take place in a climate of wariness (E. Goldsmith, 1988, p. 203).

Many – indeed, probably most – green writers appear uneasy at such explicit illiberalism, yet the necessity of a closed conception of community might seem to flow logically from a commitment to an ideology of limits. In fact, following from their commitments to resource conservation and the need to curb growth, many greens do draw similar conclusions to Goldsmith, even if supplementing them with more liberal qualifications. For example, Porritt – although counselling sensitivity and opposing discrimination – affirms that 'The strictly logical position, as far as ecologists are concerned, is to keep immigration at the lowest possible level' (Porritt, 1984, p. 191).

8. A belief in the need for authority and regulation

If decentralization represents one strategy favoured by conservatives and greens alike, at the same time many see the pressing urgency of addressing the environment's parlous condition as necessitating increased authority and regulation. In the same way that many conservatives' prognoses of dire cultural and moral malaise lead them to prescribe a bolstering of the centralized authority of the state, the notion of environmental malaise leads some greens to argue the same. For example, William Ophuls believes that 'the steady-state society will not only be more authoritarian and less democratic ... [but also be] much more oligarchic' (Ophuls, 1977, p. 163). Others, including Robert Heilbroner, also believe that there is little alternative to using a strong state to achieve environmental, and human, salvation (Heilbroner, 1974). Suggested strategies range from the relatively mild, such as the increased regulation of industry, to the more demanding, such as population control and the enforced rationing of the world's resources.

However, even libertarians – regardless of any belief in the efficacy of free-market solutions – may not be entirely averse to the state playing a role in environmental protection. As Stelzer notes, although libertarians generally reject the use of economic regulation to fulfil wider social goals, preserving the environment appears to represent an exception (Stelzer, 1997, pp. 94–5). For example, although Murray argues a principled case against regulation in general, contending that government actions typically cause more harm than good, in the case of enforcing air and water standards he accepts that these constitute an area where the state has an important role to play (Murray, 1997, pp. 115–19). Equally, DeMuth argues – despite being a strong advocate of decentralization – that private communitarian efforts have limitations in areas like environmental protection (C. DeMuth, interview by author, 16 October 1998).

Of course, few free-market thinkers have ever maintained that markets provide spontaneous solutions to every problem. Thus conceding that examples of 'market failure' such as pollution may warrant regulation need not take them outside the boundaries of their ideology. That is, with pollution being an externality – its costs borne not solely by those consuming the goods that produce it – this means that regulatory mechanisms may be justified to account for the additional social cost. Nonetheless, this does therefore cause market liberals to concede some ground in their hostility to the state, even if they are unlikely to concur with the prescriptions of writers like Ophuls or Heilbroner.

9. A concern for absent generations

One of the most lauded aspects of conservative thought by greens is the fact that conservatism takes a 'multi-generational' perspective (Gray, 1993a, p. 136; Eckersley, 1992, p. 21). As Burke contends in his oft-cited description, society is 'a partnership not only between those who are living, but between those who are living, those who are dead, and those who are to be born' (Burke, 1968, pp. 194–5). A multi-generational outlook obliges us not to damage or despoil the world inherited from our ancestors, since this would imply abusing the partnership between generations. For example, Thatcher believes that: 'No generation has a freehold on this Earth. All we have is a life tenancy – with a full repairing lease' (Thatcher, 1990, p. 10). Similarly, Scruton warns us not 'to plunder our inheritance, as though it were our exclusive property' (Scruton, 1996a, p. 17).

The deeper implications of this perspective are usefully brought out by Gray, who argues that, unlike liberals, conservatives and greens appreciate that 'individuals can never achieve their full humanity as islands in time' (Gray, 1993a, p. 136). Identity is embedded within not only a wider social context than liberals allow but also a broader temporal one. This understanding is, Gray suggests, inherently conservative, because it necessarily forswears any 'project of making the world over anew … the gnostic delusion that beset Paine, Robespierre and Lenin'. Scruton appears to believe the same, arguing that one of the major mistakes of the 'Leninist revolutionaries who destroyed civilisation in Russia' was their failure to appreciate the bonds between generations (Scruton, 1996a, p. 19).

In other words, invoking the imputed interests of absent generations is a powerful means of limiting change in the present. Interestingly, Scruton acknowledges that whereas society's 'natural' concern for absent generations was once most commonly found within a traditional religious perspective, today it is within the environmental movement that this is so (p. 22). Again, a clear affinity may be suggested between environmentalism and the conservative tradition of anti-radicalism.

10. A rejection of Enlightenment humanism

Finally, concomitant to the elevated status of the natural world within green and conservative thought is a widespread belief in the necessity of downgrading that of human beings, to disabuse humanity of its 'arrogant' presumptions regarding its capacities and importance. In fact, the rejection of humanism suggests the most fundamental way in which green and conservative philosophies are in kinship.

For conservatives, it is the humanistic rationalism born from the Enlightenment quest for total understanding and control which is most often the target, with conservatism by contrast stressing man's inherent imperfection. For greens, this rejection is usually manifested as an attack upon anthropocentrism: for example, Porritt argues for the displacement of an 'anthropocentric' perspective in favour of a 'biocentric' one, which implies that humanity does not occupy a privileged position in the natural world (Porritt, 1984, p. 206). Indeed, the rejection of anthropocentrism is what Gray praises as the fundamental characteristic of deep ecological thought (Gray, 1997, p. 195).

Many greens also share the disquiet felt by conservatives since Burke towards the Enlightenment revolution in Western thinking. Eckersley argues that what is distinctive about 'ecocentric theory' is that 'it represents a new constellation ... of post-Enlightenment political thought' (Eckersley, 1992, p. 129). Certainly, broader philosophical questions are at least as central to green thought as a concern for the natural environment. For example, Porritt contends that he is as interested in 'explaining why the old mechanistic world view of Bacon, Descartes and Newton is now wholly redundant ... [as] arguing the merits of flue gas desulphurization' (quoted in Dodds, 1988, p. 201). At least some greens are therefore drawn to the postmodern alternative, Dobson highlighting the fact that there are obvious grounds for them to take on board 'postmodern celebrations of difference, diversity, foundationlessness and humility' (Dobson, 2000, p. 150). As seen in the last chapter, conservative celebrations of difference, diversity, foundationlessness and humility long predate those of postmodernists. Furthermore, in the light of this shared scepticism towards rationalism and political hubris, Eckersley notes the commonalities between conservative and environmentalist critiques of totalitarianism (Eckersley, 1992, p. 21).

With the rejection of humanism, therefore, the most fundamental commonality between green and conservative thinking, this also makes it the strongest basis for envisaging convergence between the ideologies. As Vinson argues, 'it is hard to see why some environmentalists lean toward varieties of leftist thinking which strain and mold life into tight ideological dogmas. Nothing could be so foreign to the rich, organic vitality of nature' (Vinson, 1996, p. 31). In other words, to be true to their own philosophical perspective, environmentalists ought rather to lean to the Right. Dobson at least acknowledges that adhering to a green philosophy may imply 'siding with Edmund Burke against Tom Paine' (Dobson, 2000, p. 78).

Obstacles to a green conservatism

For the above reasons, the potential for the development of some form of 'green conservatism' would seem strong. Yet despite this, there are a number of grounds for caution in imagining any unproblematic convergence between conservatism and environmentalism.

One of these is that, regardless of any green claims to the contrary, conservatives perceive environmentalism to be fundamentally an ideology of the Left. Indeed, it may be presented as a form of 'unmasking' to expose environmentalists as really socialists in disguise. For example, Will believes that (at least some) 'environmentalism is a "green tree with red roots." It is the socialist dream – ascetic lives closely regulated by a vanguard of bossy visionaries – dressed up as compassion for the planet' (Will, 1994, p. 192).

For some conservatives, environmentalism has simply taken the place of socialism for the Left following the Cold War's conclusion. For example, Dunn and Kinney believe that, 'with the failure of communism and socialism, [the Left's] socialistic utopian ideal no longer made sense. The intellectual idealists then substituted the concept of ecological utopia' (Dunn and Kinney, 1996, p. 203). Dunn and Kinney believe that conservatives' dispute with left-wing environmentalists should be located within the paradigm of the culture war, arguing that greens consciously distort the facts about the environment to fit their political agendas. Similarly, Irving Kristol seeks to link the promotion of environmental concerns with a new class analysis (Kristol, 1991, pp. 146–52).

Yet Dunn and Kinney go even further, suggesting that a core group of environmentalists – including organizations, spokesmen and academics – may be operating conspiratorially, working to achieve the goal of undermining civilization that the communist parties of the past failed to accomplish (Dunn and Kinney, 1996, pp. 217–23). At the very least, this suggestion reveals once more the difficulty conservatives have engaging with contemporary enemies, the patent absurdity of comparing networks of environmentalists with those of Soviet agents indicating a mind-set still fighting old battles. More fundamental, such a conspiratorial view underestimates the extent to which green ideas possess widespread currency, not merely representing the ideology of nefarious green cadres.

However, of most significance are the variances of principle between greens and conservatives. A number may be identified:

The rejection of environmental pessimism

Regardless of the affinities identified above, many on the Right are evidently sceptical towards environmentalists' claims. The most prominent of such critics are undoubtedly supporters of the free market, some of whom obviously possess little sympathy even for a free-market environmentalist vision. For example, Julian Simon vigorously contests the empirical claims of greens: marshalling a wealth of quantitative data, he argues that fears about impending resource depletion and population growth are simply mistaken (Simon, 1990).

It is not possible here to adjudicate on the empirical side of these disputes. In any case, most important to highlight is the differences of principle underlying them. Thus Simon – in contrast to what he perceives to be the unfounded pessimism of many environmentalists – propounds a self-consciously optimistic vision: regarding resource finitude and life expectancy, the real facts are 'irrefutable happy' ones (p. 4). Moreover, underpinning his position is a very different view of humanity, one that believes human beings 'create more than they destroy' (p. 2). From this standpoint, population growth should be regarded 'as a triumph rather than as a problem', increasing economic opportunities and accelerating the rate at which knowledge is created (p. 222).

Simon's questioning of eco-pessimism is to be found throughout conservative writings. In fact, as much as it is possible for both free marketeers and traditionalists to espouse a green philosophy, so may both be critics. For example, Will – noting how many predicted environmental catastrophes have failed to materialize – mockingly observes that although 'Various reasons for gloominess come and go … the supply of gloominess is remarkably constant' (Will, 1994, p. 192).

The rejection of green arguments has been made a priority by many right-wing think-tanks, such as the Institute of Economic Affairs

(Bate, 1994; Morris, 1997; Whelan, 1999) and the Social Affairs Unit (Berger and Kristol, 1991; Le Fanu, 1994; O'Hear, 1997). Many conservative journals also question the factual validity of environmental anxieties, from the scale of pollution to global warming (Ehrman, 1994; T. G. Moore, 1995). Good illustration of the stance usually taken by conservative publications is the widespread support given to the controversial work of Bjørn Lomborg (Lomborg, 2001), whose findings endorse many of Simon's contentions (see Jewett, 2001; Ridley, 2002).

One of the greatest concerns of many writers is the support environmental pessimism lends demands to strengthen the power of the state. For example, James Le Fanu argues that environmentalists' efforts to advance the 'greater good' provide powerful legitimation to the state by requiring it to be legislator of this good (Le Fanu, 1994, p. 7). The way in which the promotion of risk aversion may also bolster the authority of the state has already been examined in Chapter 2. However, for conservatives a heightened sensitivity to risk may be seen to have other problematic implications.

While for Giddens this greater sensitivity implies that societies have become more reflexive, Neal and Davies argue that the dominance of risk-centred ideologies such as environmentalism means that modern societies are actually less reflexive than they once were, since assumptions about risks – from anxieties concerning food additives to fears about nuclear energy – typically exist within the public consciousness as rigid and unquestioned dogmas (Neal and Davies, 1998, p. 44). Thanks to a fixed presumption of always presupposing the very worst about human activity, there is, for example, an unwillingness to consider the reinstatement of banned chemicals, even if further testing reveals them to be safe. The real consequence of the success of ideologies like environmentalism, therefore, is that they have displaced any genuinely critical or 'reflexive' outlook.

Indeed, many writers reject embracing the precautionary principle, instead championing the potential benefits of modern science and technology (Miller and Conko, 2001). Furthermore, a Hobbesian understanding of the state of nature may suggest why modern civilization ought to be preferred to living close to nature. Upon this basis, Charles Moore dismisses the romanticization of primitive tribes, arguing that it is nonsense

to revere their superior understanding of their environment and contrast it with our own rapacity. In fact, these tribes are pathetic. Their lives are solitary, poor, nasty, brutish and short. They have no freedom, no law, no architecture, no literature, no universities, no churches, not to mention all the rather more mundane things which make life more pleasant, like public transport and lavatories that flush and electric kettles. (C. Moore, 1992a, p. 8)

In other words, living in a natural state is not to live in the harmonious or pacific world envisaged by many greens.

O'Hear attacks in particular the sentimentality of environmentalism, also strongly defending the value of modern civilization. Although many in the West may bemoan the loss of more simple modes of life, he argues, 'people in the underdeveloped world can think of no fate more desirable than to enjoy the fruits of scientific, technological and economic development' (O'Hear, 1997, p. 9). O'Hear also attacks many of the beliefs about nature deployed by green thinkers. It is, he claims, arbitrary to presume that the present set of balances in nature is either ideal or permanent. In fact, in important ways nature must be understood as in a state of imbalance: without continual change – for example, the extinction of moribund species – evolution could not occur (p. 8). Equally, the notion that what is natural equates to pure and moral, and the artificial to impure and corrupted, is also flawed, illustrated by such counterexamples as the facts that naturally occurring radiation overshadows that produced by power stations and that many of the most toxic poisons are produced by nature rather than man (pp. 17–18). In fact, the distinction commonly drawn by greens between natural and artificial is, O'Hear argues, incoherent and untenable, with conservation itself seen to be 'highly intrusive and anything but natural' (p. 6).

The credibility of free-market environmentalism

Yet what of conservatives who profess sympathy for green perspectives? It is first necessary to examine free marketeers' attempts to address environmental issues. To the free market's green critics, unfettered economic activity is inextricably linked to environmental exploitation. Typical among such writers, Eckersley rejects the perspective of free-market liberalism on the basis that it is culpable for unleashing the very forces responsible for environmental degradation (Eckersley, 1992, pp. 22–3). For similar reasons, the perceived hegemony of free-market doctrines within modern conservatism is the key reason why Gray no longer sees conservatism as the appropriate vehicle for environmental concerns (Gray, 1995, pp. 87–119).

There certainly is a question of credibility to be addressed by proponents of free-market environmentalism, since it is difficult to deny that the operation of market forces is responsible for significantly altering the natural environment, regardless of whether this is seen in destructive or creative terms. Even if market discipline does encourage firms individually to be conservative of raw materials – which may, rightly, be doubted – in terms of capitalism as a whole, it is impossible to ignore the fact that capitalism's expansionary imperatives impel it towards the ever greater mastery and exploitation of the natural world.

Moreover, although the parallels that may be drawn between the natural world and a model of the market conceived in spontaneous, self-equilibriating terms may have some validity, this is clearly so in only limited respects. The type of equilibrium that is produced by the competitive pursuit of self-interest in a capitalist economy is hardly equivalent to the harmony envisaged by environmentalists. Indeed, scepticism towards such paralleling leads Allison to describe Nisbet's classification of Smith as an ecological thinker as 'wilfully perverse' (Allison, 1991, p. 15).

Yet the most serious problem for free marketeers is their inability to recognize the extent to which the contemporary resonance of green ideas is bound up with a more general antagonism towards the tenets of Enlightenment humanism. For example, Eckersley is disturbed by the fact that the classical liberalism of Locke and Smith treats the nonhuman world in instrumental terms and implies that natural resources are worthless until human labour valorizes them (Eckersley, 1992, p. 23). There is equally a 'shallowness' in free marketeers' beliefs that the answers to environmental problems largely reside in scientific and technological solutions (Gingrich, 1995, pp. 198–200; Thatcher, 1990, pp. 16–20). In other words, although green critics often fail to note the many parallels that do exist with their philosophy, they are right to observe the fundamentally humanistic foundations of free market doctrines.

The depth of traditionalist conservative environmentalism

Of course, the tensions between free market and green doctrines are the easiest to identify. Yet it is also possible to argue that even traditionalist forms of conservatism are not truly compatible with a green outlook. Three specific differences are usefully suggested by Dobson (Dobson, 2000, pp. 175–8). The first of these relates to what greens and conservatives respectively value in terms of the forms of 'common life' in which individuals are believed to flourish. For greens, Dobson argues, 'it is *natural* history that counts', while for conservatives it is '*human* history in the form of tradition and culture' (p. 175). That is, ecologists place a value on nature itself, whereas for conservatives nature is understood as part of the cultural landscape, with their visions of community being primarily historical. By the same token, conservatism is 'irredeemably anthropocentric' in its outlook (p. 176).

Second, there is a crucial difference between conservative and green invocations of a multi-generational perspective, which is that whereas conservatives are largely 'interested in the conserving and preserving *of the past*', greens are principally concerned with doing so *'for the future'* (p. 177). And third, while both may share a scepticism towards Utopianism, in the sense of a common belief in limits and the fixed nature of the human condition, greens nonetheless retain 'a Utopian sense of what is possible within those limits' (p. 178), that is, a belief that substantial change – the fundamental transformation of our acquisitive and instrumental relationship with nature – remains possible.

However, there are problems with these suggestions. Considering Dobson's first point, it is not so obvious that conservatives do not see nature as possessing intrinsic value. As has been seen, conservatives may view the natural world as fundamentally 'good' and also regard it as a model for understanding human society. Nor are conservative ideas of community purely rooted in culture and tradition. According to Scruton, 'when war or other crises forced the English into consciousness of their historic ties, it was the country that was the object of their intensest feelings of community' (Scruton, 2001a, p. 234). Most important, there are believed to be intimate connections between the land itself and identity (pp. 72–7). Furthermore, as Vinson observes, throughout the ages 'a prominent strand of conservative thought has been love of the land and attachment to the soil' (Vinson, 1996, p. 29).

The issue of anthropocentrism will be returned to below. Yet considering Dobson's second contention, this too must be questioned. Certainly, conservatives display a particular concern for history and tradition. However, it is with some justification that Scruton rejects the accusation that this is because conservatives 'dwell on the past' (Scruton, 1996a, p. 19). Rather, he argues, their concern arises from seeing the present as part of a continuum. The point, therefore, is that our responsibility to absent generations is – as Burke's notion of a partnership between the living, the dead and the unborn suggests – a responsibility not only to those of the past but also to all on this continuum. In other words, to future generations as well. Similarly, Vinson claims that it is 'for the sake of lifetimes to come' that we should be concerned about damaging the environment today (Vinson, 1996, p. 29). Moreover, invoking the supposed interests of either past or future generations may equally be used to place limits on what is possible in the present (Scruton, 2001b, p. 30).

The third of Dobson's arguments touches upon probably the most common type of criticism raised by green writers, that is, conservatism's lack of radicalism. Eckersley also contends that the green tradition differs from conservatism in that it is able to recognize the need for profound transformations in society's patterns of production and consumption (Eckersley, 1992, pp. 22, 30). By contrast, conservatism is resistant to both cultural innovation and social and political experimentation. In fact, greens commonly accuse conservatives of only being interested in the conservation of a traditional landscape, without addressing fundamental political and economic issues.

In this vein, Mike Robinson argues that '"greenness" for the Conservatives appears as little more than a cosy, nostalgic feeling about countryside past-times and thatched cottages' (Robinson, 1992, p. 220). Similarly, Young believes that conservative environmental concern remains 'for the most part parochial. Conservatives campaign in favour of favourite causes, rare species, special bits of countryside, hedgerows or old buildings' (Young, 1990, p. 157).

In other words, there is a superficiality to conservatives' beliefs. Clearly, traditionalist conservatives do not argue for any comprehensive undoing of capitalism (though nor do many greens). Moreover, Scruton's preoccupation with the disappearance of the English hedgerow and country house (Scruton, 2001a, pp. 237–42) may appear to offer ready ammunition to critics like Robinson and Young. Equally, as suggested in earlier chapters, it is certainly legitimate to label conservatives' visions cosy and nostalgic.

However, it is also possible so to describe greens': Berger's description of the green utopia as one of 'happy peasants, jumping through the grass' (Berger, 1991, p. 30) is hardly any less fair to greens than Robinson and Young are to conservatives. Furthermore, it has already been shown that a conservative environmentalism can extend to more than a simple preservationism: conservatives may also be committed to a more fundamental philosophy of limits; may be critical of industrialization in general and consumer capitalism in particular; and may support favoured green notions like sustainable development. Indeed, Scruton himself derides efforts aimed simply at preserving the landscape's traditional appearance – 'through such exercises in taxidermy as the National Trust' (Scruton, 2001a, p. 242) – that do not take account of the countryside's more fundamental role (which, for him, is to serve as 'the backcloth to the English religion' – p. 234).

It must, of course, be recognized that conservatives would never sub-scribe to Dobson's 'Utopianism' or Eckersley's desire for social or politi-cal experimentation. While conservatives are always sceptical towards *experimental* change, however, *restorative* change – returning the world to some previous (if only imaginary) natural or social order – is often far more acceptable (Scruton, 2001b, p. 11). To the extent then that green radicalism envisions a restoration of pre-modern modes of life, there may not be such a degree of incompatibility. The point, therefore, is that, while unlikely to support the 'radical' means possibly required to achieve this, traditionalist conservatives may be far from unsympa-thetic to greens' more 'fundamental' questioning of modern industrial societies.

However, two very clear points of difference between conservatives and greens are raised by Young's charge of parochialism. First is the fact that, alongside a stated preference for the small-scale, greens are also generally committed to a global perspective (Eckersley, 1992, pp. 176–7). Yet this suggests a tension with the particularism, and specifically nationalism, of traditionalist forms of conservatism. For example, Fleming disdains the fact that a global environmentalist ethic is 'more concerned with the interrelationship between an Illinois landfill site and the greenhouse effect' than with 'local, and national loyalties' (Fleming, 1990, p. 13). Not least of his concerns is the legitimacy a global ethic provides to international regulatory bodies in overriding the sovereignty of nation-states. As noted in Chapter 5, Minogue also worries about the legitimation phenomena such as global warming pro-vide to internationalist ideologues (see also Rabkin and Sheehan, 1999). Furthermore, Scruton displays a firmness in his attachment to the significance of national identity rarely found within green writings.

Second, what may also be distinguished is the fact that while tradi-tionalist conservatism is rooted in a 'parochial' rural perspective, mod-ern environmentalism is typically an urban ideology. Although conservatives like Vinson may believe that society 'desperately needs the perspective of a self-reliant rural class' (Vinson, 1996, p. 31), this is usually the last social group greens seek to represent their perspective. Thus, although within the green literature there is much argument over who should be the bearers of an environmental ethic – suggestions rang-ing from salaried professionals to the members of new social movements (Dobson, 2000, pp. 145–62) – it is rarely imagined that it might be the countryside inhabitants of conservative visions. Indeed, members of this group, those who actually live closest to nature, are more com-monly cast as part of the problem than of any solution. Farmers and hunters are more frequently prime targets of greens' wrath – for embracing modern agricultural methods and failing to share their sentimental views of animals – than seen as potential allies (McCormick, 1991, pp. 69–87).

Yet undoubtedly the most serious obstacle to any convergence with deep ecological thought is that there remains a basic difference concerning how man's place within the natural world is conceived. In this regard, Dobson's accusation of irredeemable anthropocentrism hits the mark.

In particular, the specifically Judeo-Christian perspective of conservatives has a number of important implications. Gingrich, for example, takes his cue from biblical authority: 'As the book of Genesis says, we have an obligation to cultivate that which God has given us' (Gingrich, 1995, p. 195). Of most significance is the fact that conservatives therefore understand man's position vis-à-vis the natural world in terms of a custodial or guardianship model. For example, Bliese – believing that creation is part of God's entail to man – argues that 'we are always to act as trustees, as faithful stewards of all that we have inherited' (Bliese, 1996, p. 151). Similarly, according to Thatcher, conservatives 'are not merely friends of the Earth – we are its guardians and trustees' (Thatcher, 1990, p. 10).

Yet this suggests a very different view to that held by radical greens. As Goodin points out, the theological notion of custodianship implicitly presupposes man to possess a higher status than the rest of nature, in having been given a unique role in its protection (Goodin, 1992, p. 6). In other words, a traditional religious perspective is, if hardly 'humanistic', nonetheless more 'human-centred' than that of radical green thought.

In fact, a belief that concern for the environment should be understood largely in terms of human interests is the norm among conservatives. For example, Dunn and Kinney declare that 'our effort is primarily anthropocentric: we regard the world first in terms of human needs' (Dunn and Kinney, 1996, p. xiii). Equally, Fleming believes that 'Man is ultimately the proper subject of any discussion of the environment' (Fleming, 1996a, p. 12). Where this human-centredness is especially apparent is in relation to the idea of animal rights. Thus, according to Scruton, animal rights activists fail 'to understand the deep differences between animals and humans', in that human beings possess 'free-will' and 'a rational soul' (Scruton, 2000a, pp. ix–x). Although in the past 'people were sure of their status as the highest order of creation, made in God's image', the ideology of animal rights proponents has deleteriously eroded this understanding (p. 3).

What is revealed by such passages is that the character of conservative 'anti-humanism' is of a qualitatively different nature to that of radical greens. That is, the anti-humanism historically so central to conservatism is fundamentally concerned with rejecting the hubris of other ideologies' *social* visions. This need not imply that man does not possess a privileged position in the natural world. In other words, while conservatives would certainly balk at being given the humanist label, their ideology remains human-centred in a way that is inimical to deep green perspectives.

Conclusion

Deliberately avoided in the above assessment has been the general charge often levelled against greens and conservatives, that of romanticism, which greens at least are usually keen to reject (Dobson, 2000, pp. 11–12). Instead, by focusing upon particular points of principle, it has been demonstrated in very specific ways that the common ground between environmentalism and conservatism encompasses much greater territory than is usually appreciated. For this reason, it is not possible for greens simply to dismiss 'conservative environmentalists' as purely shallow in their commitments. Nor can green thought be seen as the wholly distinct post-Enlightenment ideology some adherents may presume it to be: much of the critique of modernity articulated by greens (and others) today has been forwarded many times before by conservatives.

Moreover, although green thought is most clearly in tune with traditionalist conservatism, it is not entirely without legitimacy for free marketeers to incorporate environmental concerns within their agendas. Although there is much that may be deemed shallow, there are more basic ways in which economic liberal understandings parallel those of greens. Nonetheless, there remain important variances of principle between green and conservative philosophies. Principally, despite their own anti-humanist commitments, conservative doctrines are essentially those of a human-oriented ideology. Indeed, it is largely for this reason that many adopt the stance of critic. The historical irony, therefore, is that – in contrast to the ideological conflicts of the past – conservatives have discovered an enemy even less human-centred than themselves.

Yet finally, today especially, conservatives are far less likely to embrace the fundamental philosophical orientation of deep ecologists. As seen in the last chapter, conservatives have become much less concerned with rationalist foes than with combating all varieties of modern 'irrational-ism'. For this reason, Cheney rejects green thinking on the grounds that it 'is about more than ecology, it is about how the great thinkers of the Enlightenment have led us astray' (Cheney, 1995, p. 97). Again, this does not mean that conservatives have become wholehearted devotees of Enlightenment rationalism. Rather, what is once more indicated is their fear that contemporary anti-rationalist ideologies represent more press-ing threats to traditional order and authority than do rationalist ones.

Conclusion

Before offering a final assessment, it is necessary to draw together the threads of argument that have been developed. To do so, it will be useful to return to the propositions set out in Chapter 1.

Conservatives no longer possess any significant defining purpose, either enemies to fight or 'big ideas' to promote

Clearly, conservatives have been able to find ideas to promote even after the resolution of the conflicts of the Cold War era. A number of these have been identified: revitalizing civil society, fighting a culture war and extolling the merits of globalization and the new economy. Similarly, they have found no shortage of foes to line up as replacement menaces, including politically correct moralists, risk-averse regulators and utopian internationalists. However, a number of problems for conservatives relating to these enemies and agendas have also been highlighted.

First, the antagonists conservatives confront today are more disparate. Whereas socialism presented a relatively easy to identify target, the array of -isms contemporary conservatives seek to tackle – from feminism to multiculturalism – does not constitute a single, unified threat. Although conservatives often pay scant regard to the differences between their adversaries, it is even less credible to group all of these within a single category than it is to place together all varieties of traditional left-wing ideologies. Equally, specifying exactly who constitutes any 'new class' without resorting to vague 'knowing them when one sees them' characterizations is evidently no easy task.

Second, understanding the nature of their contemporary enemies seems difficult for conservatives. Many assume that present-day enemies are simply socialists or counterculturalists in different guises, refusing to alter the view of the Left conservatives have held to since at least the 1960s, if not the 1920s. They often fail to recognize that their modern adversaries frequently advocate diametrically opposite views, on issues like sexual permissiveness, to those of their past antagonists, leaving them fighting caricatures rather than real opponents.

Third, contemporary enemies may not represent as convincing threats as those of the past, and are thus less capable of providing conservatives with either wider support or internal cohesion. Although some conservatives may attempt to draw parallels between the Cold War and present-day cultural warfare, it is difficult to present the politically correct academic as a threat comparable to the red menace. Comparing environmentalists to Soviet agents or presenting postmodernists as in league with demonic forces merely demonstrates a lack of perspective.

Fourth, in attributing the influence of antagonistic ideas all but solely to the activities of degenerate intellectuals, conservatives neglect the deeper forces responsible for undermining traditional values and institutions. They ignore what for them is the more difficult possibility, that the spread of relativism or 'alternative lifestyles' is not merely the result of the efforts of malignant ideologues, but reflective of wider social changes.

Fifth, the tenets of those whom many conservatives wish to treat as enemies are not as easily distinguishable from conservatives' own as socialist ones. It is quite possible to see a strong affinity between conservative doctrines and those of ideologies like environmentalism. Although there are also significant differences, there is nonetheless far less clear water between conservatism and 'adversary' ideologies than many culture warriors acknowledge.

Finally, in relation to many of the standpoints conservatives adopt – like rejecting political correctness and upholding traditional educational standards – their efforts to present themselves as disinterested and objective are compromised by the fact that they typically hold highly instrumental and partisan views of the purposes of education and cultural experience. Consequently, it is difficult for conservatives to claim to be standing upon any higher moral or intellectual ground than their opponents.

Despite the absence of viable alternatives to capitalism, free-market conservatism is bankrupt

Strong reason for believing a market liberal ideology to have been pre-eminent since the Cold War's conclusion is that it no longer faces fundamental ideological challenge. Moreover, beliefs in such notions as globalization and the advance of the information revolution are widely deployed in support of the contention that unfettered capitalism simply has to be embraced. A number of determinedly free-market agendas can be identified, like Duncan and Hobson's idea of 'liquidating' the state and Gilder's championing of a technology driven global capitalism.

However, what has also been shown is that free-market beliefs are not free from challenge in the post-socialist context. If arguments to reject capitalism have diminished, ones demanding its constraint and greater regulation have proliferated: to promote social justice; to manage risk; to preserve the integrity of communities and the natural environment; and to protect national cultures.

While free-market writers do offer arguments to meet these challenges, they are compromised in a number of ways. For example, the credibility of anti-statist agendas is clearly undermined by the records of past conservative governments, not only in failing to roll back the state but also in further expanding its scope. Furthermore, many conservatives appear defensive, in readily accepting concerns about the integrity of communities and the market's effects upon values and customs, and in therefore seeking to temper commitments to any 'pure' economic liberalism.

Even if this is not with the intention of accepting that markets are responsible for all the problems critics claim, qualifying their doctrines undoubtedly weakens free marketeers' grounds for rejecting these criticisms. Writers who attempt to combine free-market and communitarian commitments also open themselves to the charge of contradiction. As seen with Willetts in Chapter 3, whatever intellectual legitimacy there may be in siding with Hegel against Kant in rejecting the idea of individual autonomy, this inevitably raises the question of how well this rejection sits with the liberalism of a free-market perspective.

What actually saves capitalism's intellectual defenders from appearing bankrupt is that, despite the prevalence of anti-capitalist sentiments, no fundamental alternatives are on offer. Even so, *positive* free-market visions have become marginalized. Probably the most significant fact confirming this is that even many of the free market's strongest supporters recognize that their beliefs enjoy nothing like an intellectual hegemony.

The main focus of conservatives' concerns has shifted away from economics and politics to issues concerning the social and cultural fabric

Although free-market beliefs have not disappeared from within conservatism, the idea that they are dominant must be questioned. Many conservatives demonstrate very little interest in following market liberals' prescriptions, including their ambitions to roll back the state. Moreover, the antagonism of traditionalist conservatives appears to have been heightened by contemporary issues: many clearly prefer to side with critics in holding free-market doctrines responsible for damage done to the natural and social environments. The effort to rediscover more social conservative doctrines must be understood, therefore, as resulting from conservatives' desire to distance themselves from the free-market agendas of the past.

Similarly, there is undoubtedly strong evidence to support the idea of a 'cultural turn', with numerous conservatives explicitly avowing the importance of focusing upon cultural questions. Yet in relation to these, conservatives' perspectives are frequently highly pessimistic, with institutions from the family to universities perceived to be in a state of grievous moral disorder. If economic decline was once conservatives' key concern, today this is more commonly overshadowed by fears of moral and cultural decline. Indeed, some conservatives believe society to be so demoralized that they are no longer confident even that a 'silent majority' shares their values, let alone adversarial elites.

One significant consequence of conservatives' pessimism is a greater willingness to countenance the use of state mechanisms to remoralize society. Even so, it is also often recognized that in dealing with cultural malaise, politics is largely impotent. For many, it is hoped that civil society will be able to provide the solution. However, given that many sectors of civil society are today far from hospitable to conservatism, the expectation that, if only the state were to withdraw, it will spontaneously function as a breeding ground of conservative values is not well founded. Among the more radical elements of American conservatism, some appear willing to question the very legitimacy of their own regime, with this standpoint – though marginal – indicating the depth of disquiet felt by conservatives regarding the current state of morality. Yet even mainstream conservatives are prepared to acknowledge that they have lost the war over culture and that when discussing traditional values only the past tense can be used.

Despite a social and intellectual climate hostile to radicalism, traditionalist conservative doctrines lack purchase

If aversion to individualist and free-market beliefs characterizes many of the ideologies that enjoy the greatest resonance in the post-Cold War world, there are clearly grounds for believing that traditionalist conservatism possesses the resources to gain much wider intellectual sympathy and credibility. Its sceptical perspective may be in accord with postmodernists' rejections of metanarratives, environmentalists' hostility towards progress and communitarians' critique of individualism.

However, what has also been demonstrated are reasons why the scope for stable alliances is limited. In the case of postmodernism, despite a number of suggestive parallels between their philosophies, conservatives' concerns to resist challenges to traditional values ultimately preclude their acceptance of a perspective that does not provide solid grounding for moral absolutes. In relation to environmentalism, although both conservatives and environmentalists may share broadly 'anti-humanist' beliefs, these are nonetheless of different orders; conservative thought remains largely human centred. Furthermore, regarding the wider appeal of postmodernism and environmentalism, while scepticism towards rationalism and progress may be of benefit to conservatives in undermining the authority of progressive ideologies, widespread social cynicism worries conservatives because it may lead to a lack of faith in all definite beliefs, including their own.

Moreover, as demonstrated by their antipathy towards 'softness' and sentimentality, conservatives' prescriptions are typically much more demanding than those of their opponents, however compassionate they may present themselves as being. Conservative absolutists face not only the charge of being intolerant fundamentalists but also the problem that much more challenging requirements need to be met to sustain conservative communities than is the case with other communitarians' conceptions. Communities must be willing to shame and ostracize transgressors – though in the absence of any clear majority willing to perform this shaming and ostracizing, conservatives' desires seem unlikely to be fulfilled.

Another failing of conservatives is their inability to recognize that the changes that have occurred in Western societies over recent decades do not necessarily imply that morality or belief in tradition has declined, but that they have changed in character. In many respects, modern conceptions may contradict ambitions for radical change, yet are nonetheless opposed to the values of conservatism. The problem this poses for conservative moralists is that rather than simply facing the task of remoralizing a society denuded of all values – difficult as such an undertaking might be – they face the much harder one of combating widely subscribed to alternative moralities.

In other words, even in a 'conservative' climate, conservatism may still be irrelevant.

Contemporary conservatism is characterized by increased factiousness and disunity

A number of areas of agreement between contemporary conservatives do exist. For example, most are antagonistic towards the welfare state, with conservatives' finding common ground in possessing both economic and moral anxieties about the 'dependency culture'. Similarly, a preference for the sphere of civil society is displayed by most varieties of conservative. Indeed, the agenda of regenerating civil society is believed by some to be capable of providing a unifying glue similar to that of the Cold War. The willingness of many present-day libertarians to recognize the importance of the moral and cultural supports of the market also offers the potential for unity.

Nonetheless, there are at least as many bases for disharmony, with the specifics of the contemporary context producing particular fissures within conservatism. For example, the implications the idea of globalization has for national sovereignty exacerbates the conflict between free market and traditionalist conservatives, between the latter's preference for the local and the particular and the former's universalist outlook. Furthermore, with the Cold War over, traditionalist conservatives feel able to be more open in declaring their antagonisms towards liberal individualism, without the fear of providing ammunition to capitalism's mortal enemies. Yet many other schisms are apparent, in relation to programmes of remoralization or to rolling back the state, which are not always simply splits between 'types' of conservative. Even when conservatives agree on shared ambitions, such as the reinvigoration of civil society, conflicts nonetheless arise as to how goals are to be achieved. The increased willingness of some conservatives to use the state to achieve their ends widens existing gaps even further.

Final assessment

The circumspection expressed in the introduction towards abstract typologies of conservatism has been vindicated by the illustration of a range of issues in which conservative commitments do not correspond to straightforward or predictable divisions. For example, although the expectation that communitarian or environmentalist arguments are most in accord with a traditionalist conservative perspective has been broadly confirmed, many free-market writers today also appear to wish to embrace them.

What has also been shown is that commentators often paint highly distorted pictures of modern conservatism. One of the commonest ways in which conservatives' beliefs are misrepresented is by the conflation of free-market conservatism with conservatism as a whole. In the case of critics like communitarians and environmentalists, it is hard to escape the suspicion that, for many, this is to allow them to reject conservatism without having to acknowledge the existence of more compatible elements within conservative ideology. For many more critics, the image of a hegemonic free-market conservatism is used to justify their own agendas, to allow them to argue for the necessity of extending the state's authority to rein in the free market's excesses.

Yet should conservatives be seen as recognizing the need for more caring, compassionate doctrines? And how do these ideas square with calls for the resurrection of shame and stigma? In fact, the tendency of modern conservatives is to oscillate between two poles: that of more 'socially aware' beliefs, to which they are drawn because they recognize the present climate requires them to be more accommodating, and that of 'hardline' beliefs, to which they are attracted because they fear that only tough-minded remedies can cure deep demoralization. That conservatives seem unable to decide which of these poles to remain at, simply confirms the fundamental lack of affinity their doctrines have with the values of the post-Cold War world.

Good reasons have also been seen for agreeing with the idea that Left and Right are inadequate as labels for describing contemporary ideological positions. The number of conservatives seemingly ready to defend the Enlightenment and objectivity, reject the 'irrationality' of postmodernists and attack the illiberalism of political correctness – together with the hostility of many of conservatives' critics towards notions like progress – shows that contemporary ideological divides do not correspond to traditional Left and Right divisions.

Indeed, one of the most striking aspects of many disputes between conservatives and their opponents is that whereas the latter appear to advocate highly cautionary stances regarding human endeavour and individuals' self-determining capacities, the former appear much more ready to champion optimistic views of these. Rather oddly, given the depth of their despair regarding the cultural and moral spheres, they often seem to have much more optimistic views of the benefits of science, technology and modern medicine; and, as shown by conservatives' engagements with environmental pessimism, it is not solely market liberals who defend the achievements of the modern age.

For these reasons, conservatives' relation to the idea of limits has become much more complicated in a context in which their enemies are as likely, if not more so, to articulate risk-averse, caution-centred doctrines. Conservatives have not become Enlightenment-inspired utopians – they still counsel caution against ambitious social projects. Rather, it is more the changes that have taken place among their ideological adversaries that makes them appear to be last defenders of the Enlightenment's legacy.

Nonetheless, to the extent that there is something right about seeing Enlightenment values as residing largely outside the Left today, some aspects of conservatives' arguments can be appreciated. The optimism of free marketeers and their commitments to ideas like progress and universalism are refreshing in comparison to the pessimistic viewpoints of many of their critics, whatever the limitations of their ideology may be. Similarly, their defences of liberty are not without merit, particularly when contrasted with the illiberalism of many of their adversaries. Indeed, Ellen Willis makes the point regarding the term 'libertarian' that the modern Left 'seems content to cede both the word and the concept to the right' (Willis, 1997, p. 111). As seen, this ceding appears to have gone so far that even Scruton, who at best defends particular freedoms and certainly does not offer any general principled defence of liberty, can appear in critics' eyes to be a libertarian.

Of course, all conservatives possess very narrow conceptions of what freedom means, in many cases as meaning little more than the freedom of the marketplace. Furthermore, conservatives' liberalism often emerges only in response to the authoritarianism of their opponents, while rapidly disappearing in other contexts. Even so, their perspectives can insulate them from the illiberalism that has infected much of the contemporary Left, allowing at least some to reject, for example, feminists' demands for censorship or communitarian erosions of individual rights.

Valuable arguments may also be presented by conservatives in regard to cultural issues, not least in rejecting the sentimentality and irrationalism of many contemporary doctrines. On educational matters, E. D. Hirsch argues that educational conservatism is the necessary underpinning of political liberalism, seeing a traditional model of education as actually more progressive than supposedly 'progressive' ones (E. D. Hirsch, 1997). It is those at the bottom of society who are disadvantaged most by the denigration of traditional standards and the value of 'high culture', since this leaves them ill-equipped to understand the world, let alone to change it. While much cultural conservatism remains unpalatable, being authoritarian and instrumental, Hirsch's points are good ones.

Many books on conservatism conclude with calls for the need to mount a renewed response to conservative doctrines. Today, this barely seems necessary. Critics preoccupied with the idea of market liberalism's intellectual dominance would do well to consider the number of writers who attack undiluted free marketism to have emerged from conservatism itself – like Gray and Luttwak – as well as the many conservatives – such as Worsthorne and Scruton – who have long challenged them within. This is not to mention the anti-individualism of communitarian conservatives like Schambra and Eberly and authoritarian moralizers like Bork and Himmelfarb. Although it is important to recognize that the 'anti-capitalism' of conservatives actually has little to do with economics, reflecting more their sense of dislocation from the contemporary social world, the fact that free-market beliefs are far from uncontested even among conservatives ought to give pause to theorists of a free-market intellectual hegemony.

As for cultural conservatism, the very shrillness of many conservatives' contributions to culture war debates indicates not so much an enemy to be feared, as conservatives' insecurities. Even among those who do not believe they have already lost the culture war, there is a patent lack of confidence in the ability of traditional beliefs and institutions to resist challenge. As Berger astutely observes of educational conservatives, their often hyperbolic over-reactions to the introduction of even modest amounts of non-Western materials into educational curricula reveal that they 'frequently seem to have very little confidence in the capacity of the West to prevail in any kind of cultural contestation' (Berger, 1992, p. 64). Indeed, for all that conservatives may decry the 'dumbing down' of culture, such lacks of perspective suggest that they cannot be seen as free from culpability for any intellectual decline. Evelyn Waugh famously complained of the Conservative Party that it had not managed to put back the clock a single minute: for all the bluster apparent among cultural conservatives, nor have they.

What, finally, should be concluded? An important difference with socialism's demise is that no single, dramatic event has made conservatism's exhaustion so obvious. Nor are conservative thinkers as likely to engage in the same search for new labels as has the Left of recent times. For these reasons, some form of ideology bearing the 'conservative' name is likely to remain in existence for many years hence. However, whether the content of this ideology will remain the same is another question. The likelihood is that conservatives will continue to oscillate between efforts to adapt to contemporary realities and attempts to reassert their older values. Either way – and regardless of the electoral fortunes of either the Conservatives or Republicans – it is difficult to see conservatism securing much in the way of intellectual resonance, at least not without substantially redefining what conservatism means. Conservatives should perhaps recognize the need to write an elegy not only for traditional values and identities but also for their own ideology.

References

Abramowitz, J. (1993) 'The Tao of Community', *Public Interest*, No. 111.

Abrams, E. (1999) 'Is There a "Third Way"?', *Commentary*, Vol. 107, No. 4.

Albert, M. (1993) *Capitalism against Capitalism* (London: Whurr).

Allison, L. (1984) *Right Principles* (London: Basil Blackwell).

Allison, L. (1991) *Ecology and Utility* (Leicester: Leicester University Press).

Anderson, B. (2000) 'Capitalism and the Suicide of Culture', *First Things*, No. 100.

Anderson, D. (ed.) (1992) *The Loss of Virtue: Moral Confusion and Social Disorder in Britain and America* (London: Social Affairs Unit).

Anderson, D. (ed.) (1995a) *This Will Hurt: the Restoration of Virtue and Civic Order* (London: Social Affairs Unit).

Anderson, D. (1995b) 'Introduction and Summary: Rediscovering the Sources of Social Order', in D. Anderson (ed.) *This Will Hurt: the Restoration of Virtue and Civic Order* (London: Social Affairs Unit).

Anderson, D. and Mosbacher, M. (eds) (1997) *The British Woman Today: a Qualitative Survey of the Images in Women's Magazines* (London: Social Affairs Unit).

Anderson, D. and Mullen, P. (eds) (1998) *Faking It: the Sentimentalisation of Modern Society* (London: Social Affairs Unit).

Anderson, T. L. and Leal, D. R. (1991) *Free Market Environmentalism* (San Francisco: Pacific Research Institute for Public Policy).

Andrews, Jr., J. K. (1990) in 'Symposium: The Vision Thing', *Policy Review*, No. 52.

Arens, E. (2001) 'The Anxiety of Prosperity: Review of Dinesh D'Souza's *The Virtue of Prosperity*', *Policy Review*, No. 104.

Arnn, L. P. and Feulner, E. (1999) 'Conservatives Should Stay the Course', *Los Angeles Times*, 16 March.

ASH (2002) 'Roger Scruton High Priest Philosopher of the Libertarian Right Defrocked and Exposed as "Grimy Hack" for Tobacco Industry', http://www.ash.org.uk/html/press/020124.html (24 January).

Attarian, J. (1994) 'Sham Vision and Bogus Transcendence', *Modern Age*, Vol. 36, No. 4.

Aughey, A., Jones, G. and Riches, W. (1992) *The Conservative Political Tradition in Britain and the United States* (London: Pinter Publishers).

Bailey, R. (2001) 'The Voice of Neoconservatism', http://reason.com/rb/rb101701.shtml (17 October).

Barnes, F. (1991) 'The Politics of Less: a Debate on Big Government Conservatism', *Policy Review*, No. 55.

Barone, M. (1997) in 'Symposium: Is There a Worldwide Conservative Crack-Up?', *Weekly Standard*, 1 September.

Barry, N. (1996) 'Economic Liberalism, Ethics and the Social Market', in J. Meadowcroft (ed.) *The Liberal Political Tradition* (Cheltenham: Edward Elgar).

Barry, N. (1997) 'Conservative Thought and the Welfare State', *Political Studies*, Vol. 45, No. 2.

Bate, R. (1994) *Global Warming: Apocalypse or Hot Air?* (London: IEA Environment Unit).

Baudrillard, J. (1984) 'On Nihilism', *On the Beach*, No. 6 (Spring).

Bell, D. (1974) *The Coming of Post-Industrial Society* (London: Heinemann).

Bell, D. (1978) *The Cultural Contradictions of Capitalism* (New York: Basic Books).

Bell, D. (1985) 'The Revolt against Modernity', *Public Interest*, No. 81.

Bellah, R. et al. (1985) *Habits of the Heart: Individualism and Commitment in American Life* (Berkeley: University of California Press).

Bennett, C. (2002) 'Keep Up the Good Work, Roger', *Guardian*, 31 January.

Bennett, W. J. (1993a) *The Book of Virtues* (New York: Simon and Schuster).

Bennett, W. J. (1993b) 'Quantifying America's Decline', *Wall Street Journal*, 15 March.

Bennett, W. J. (1994a) *The Index of Leading Cultural Indicators: Facts and Figures on the State of American Society* (New York: Simon and Schuster).

Bennett, W. J. (1994b) 'America's Family at Risk: Politics and the Quest for a Civil Society', *Rising Tide*, Vol. 1, No. 4.

Bennett, W. J. (1994c) 'Revolt against God: America's Spiritual Despair', *Policy Review*, No. 67.

Bennett, W. J. (1998) *The Death of Outrage* (New York: Simon and Schuster).

Bennett, W. J. (2001) *The Broken Hearth: Reversing the Moral Collapse of the American Family* (New York: Doubleday).

Berger, P. (1991) 'Towards a Religion of Health Activism', in P. Berger and I. Kristol (eds) *Health, Life-Style and Environment: Countering the Panic* (London: Social Affairs Unit).

Berger, P. (1992) *A Far Glory* (New York: Free Press).

Berger, P. and Kristol, I. (eds) (1991) *Health, Life-Style and Environment: Countering the Panic* (London: Social Affairs Unit).

Berger, P. and Neuhaus, R. (1977) *To Empower People* (Washington, DC: American Enterprise Institute).

Bland, R. (1996) 'Against Relativism: a Cause for Conservatives', *Salisbury Review*, Vol. 15, No. 1.

Bliese, J. R. E. (1996) 'Richard M. Weaver, Russell Kirk and the Environment', *Modern Age*, Vol. 38, No. 2.

Block, W. (1994) 'Libertarianism and Libertinism', *Journal of Libertarian Studies*, Vol. 11, No. 1.

Bloom, A. (1987) *The Closing of the American Mind* (New York: Simon and Schuster).

Blumenthal, S. (1986) *The Rise of the Counter-Establishment* (New York: Harper and Row).

Boaz, D. (1996) 'Conservative Social Engineering', *Policy Review*, No. 75.

Boaz, D. (1997) *Libertarianism: a Primer* (New York: Free Press).

Boaz, D. and Crane, E. H. (eds) (1993) *Market Liberalism* (Washington, DC: Cato Institute).

Bork, R. (1990) *The Tempting of America: the Political Seduction of the Law* (New York: Simon and Schuster).

Bork, R. (1995) 'Culture and Kristol', in C. DeMuth and W. Kristol (eds) *The Neoconservative Imagination* (Washington, DC: American Enterprise Institute).

Bork, R. (1996) *Slouching towards Gomorrah: Modern Liberalism and American Decline* (New York: Regan Books).

Boxx, T. and Quinlivan, G. (eds) (1996) *Culture in Crisis and the Renewal of Civil Life* (Lanham, MD: Rowman and Littlefield Publishers).

Boyte, H. C. and Kari, N. N. (1997) 'The Commonwealth of Freedom', *Policy Review*, No. 86.

Bradford, M. E. (1991) 'The Monstrosity of Big Government Conservatism', *Policy Review*, No. 57.

Bradford, M. E. (1992) *Against the Barbarians* (Jefferson City: University of Missouri Press).

Bradford, M. E. (1994) *Original Intentions* (Athens: University of Georgia Press).

Brittan, S. (1989) 'The Green Power of Market Forces', *Financial Times*, 4 May.

Brookhiser, R. (1991) *The Way of the WASP: How It Made America, and How It Can Save It, So to Speak* (New York: Free Press).

Brooks, D. (ed.) (1996) *Backward and Upward: the New Conservative Writing* (New York: Vintage Books).

Brooks, D. (2000) *Bobos in Paradise* (New York: Simon and Schuster).

Brooks, D. (2001) 'Time to Do Everything Except Think', *Newsweek*, 30 April.

Browning, R. (1991) 'Who Are the Health Activists?', in P. Berger and I. Kristol (eds) *Health, Life-Style and Environment: Countering the Panic* (London: Social Affairs Unit).

Bryden, D. P. (1991) 'It Ain't What They Teach, It's the Way That They Teach It', *Public Interest*, No. 103.

Buchanan, P. (1998) *The Great Betrayal: How American Sovereignty and Social Justice Are Sacrificed to the Gods of the Global Economy* (Boston: Little, Brown).

Buchanan, P. (2001) *The Death of the West* (New York: Thomas Dunne Books).

Burke, E. (1968) *Reflections on the Revolution in France* (London: Penguin).

Cannadine, D. (1994) 'John Major, Just an Undertaker on Overtime', *Spectator*, 16 April.

Carey, G. (1995) *In Defence of the Constitution* (Indianapolis: Liberty Press).

Carey, G. (1997) 'A Good Communitarian Is Hard to Find', *Chronicles*, Vol. 21, No. 1.

Chambers, W. (1952) *Witness* (Washington, DC: Regnery Gateway).

Cheney, L. (1995) *Telling the Truth* (New York: Simon and Schuster).

Coats, D. (1996) 'Can Congress Revive Civil Society?', *Policy Review*, No. 75.

Coats, D. and Santorum, R. (1998) 'Civil Society and the Humble Role of Government', in E. J. Dionne (ed.) *Community Works* (Washington, DC: Brookings Institution Press).

Cohen, J. and Arato, A. (1992) *Civil Society and Political Theory* (Cambridge, MA: MIT Press).

Conservative Party (2001) *Renewing Civil Society* (London: Conservative Central Office).

Cowling, M. (1978) 'The Present Position', in M. Cowling (ed.) *Conservative Essays* (London: Cassell).

Cowling, M. (1997) *A Conservative Future* (London: Politeia).

Crowther, I. (1990) 'Is Nothing Sacred?', *Salisbury Review*, Vol. 9, No. 2.

Davies, J. (ed.) (1993) *The Family: Is It Just Another Lifestyle Choice?* (London: IEA Health and Welfare Unit).

Decter, M. (1991) 'E Pluribus Nihil: Multiculturalism and Black Children', *Commentary*, Vol. 92, No. 3.

Decter, M. (1992) 'How the Rioters Won', *Commentary*, Vol. 94, No. 1.

Decter, M. (1997) 'Affluence and Divorce', *Public Interest*, No. 127.

Deech, R. (1994) *Divorce Dissent: Dangers in Divorce Reform* (London: Centre for Policy Studies).

DeMuth, C. (2000) 'Why the Era of Big Government Isn't Over', *Commentary*, Vol. 109, No. 4.

Dennis, N. and Erdos, G. (1992) *Families without Fatherhood* (London: IEA Health and Welfare Unit).

Devigne, R. (1994) *Recasting Conservatism: Oakeshott, Strauss, and the Response to Postmodernism* (New Haven: Yale University Press).

Dionne, E. J. (1996) *They Only Look Dead* (New York: Touchstone).

Dionne, E. J. (1998) 'Introduction: Why Civil Society? Why Now?', in E. J. Dionne (ed.) *Community Works* (Washington, DC: Brookings Institution Press).

Dobson, A. (2000) *Green Political Thought* (3rd edn) (London: Routledge).

Dodds, F. (ed.) (1988) *Into the 21st Century* (London: Green Print).

Doherty, B. (2001) 'Laissez-Faire Fiction', *Reason*, Vol. 33, No. 2.

Doherty, J. (1992) 'Postmodern Politics', in J. Doherty, E. Graham and M. Malek (eds) *Postmodernism and the Social Sciences* (London: Macmillan).

Dorn, J. A. (1996) 'The Rise of Government and the Decline of Morality', *Freeman*, Vol. 46, No. 3.

D'Souza, D. (1991) *Illiberal Education: the Politics of Race and Sex on Campus* (New York: Free Press).

D'Souza, D. (1997) *Ronald Reagan* (New York: Free Press).

D'Souza, D. (2000) *The Virtue of Prosperity: Finding Values in an Age of Techno-Affluence* (New York: Free Press).

Duncan, A. (1995) Interview, *New Statesman*, 19 May.

Duncan, A. and Hobson, D. (1995) *Saturn's Children: How the State Devours Liberty, Prosperity and Virtue* (London: Sinclair-Stevenson).

Dunn, C. W. and Woodard, J. D. (1996) *The Conservative Tradition in America* (Lanham, MD: Rowman and Littlefield Publishers).

Dunn, J. R. and Kinney, J. E. (1996) *Conservative Environmentalism* (Westport, CT: Quorum Books).

Durham, M. (1991) *Sex and Politics: the Family and Morality in the Thatcher Years* (London: Macmillan).

Durnil, G. K. (1995) *The Making of a Conservative Environmentalist* (Bloomington, IN: Indiana University Press).

Eagleton, T. (2000) 'An Old Fogey at Silly Mid-off', *Irish Times*, 14 October.

Eberly, D. (1994) 'Introduction: the Quest for a Civil Society', in D. Eberly (ed.) *Building a Community of Citizens: Civil Society in the 21st Century* (Lanham, MD: University Press of America).

Eberly, D. (1996) 'The New Demands of Citizenship', *Policy Review*, No. 75.

Eberly, D. (1998) 'Civic Renewal vs. Moral Renewal', *Policy Review*, No. 91.

Eckersley, R. (1992) *Environmentalism and Political Theory* (London: UCL Press Limited).

Eckersley, R. (1993) 'Free Market Environmentalism: Friend or Foe?', *Environmental Politics*, Vol. 2, No. 1.

Ehrenhalt, A. (1995) *The Lost City* (New York: Basic Books).

Ehrman, R. (1994) 'Falling for the Green Fraud', *Spectator*, 30 July.

Etzioni, A. (1994) 'Restoring Our Moral Voice', *Public Interest*, No. 116.

Etzioni, A. (1995) *The Spirit of Community* (London: Fontana Press).

Feulner, E. (1998) *The March of Freedom* (Dallas: Spence Publishing Company).

Finn, C. (1991) *We Must Take Charge: Our Schools and Our Future* (New York: Free Press).

First Things (1996) 'Symposium: The End of Democracy? The Judicial Usurpation of Politics', No. 67.

First Things (1997) 'Symposium: The End of Democracy? A Discussion Continued', No. 69.

Fleming, T. (1990) 'Short Views on Earth Day', *Chronicles*, Vol. 14, No. 8.

Fleming, T. (1991) 'Review of Jürgen Habermas's *The New Conservatism*', *Society*, Vol. 28, No. 3.

Fleming, T. (1996a) 'Man, Man, and Again Man', *Chronicles*, Vol. 20, No. 6.

Fleming, T. (1996b) 'Shame and Science', *Chronicles*, Vol. 20, No. 10.

Fleming, T. (1997) 'Hanging with Our Friends', *Chronicles*, Vol. 21, No. 5.

Francis, S. (1992) 'Nationalism, Old and New', *Chronicles*, Vol. 16, No. 6.

Francis, S. (1993) *Beautiful Losers: Essays on the Failure of American Conservatism* (Columbia: University of Missouri Press).

Frank, T. (2002) *One Market under God* (London: Vintage).

Freeden, M. (1996) *Ideologies and Political Theory* (Oxford: Clarendon Press).

Freedland, J. (2001) 'The Right Is Left Bereft', *Guardian*, 22 August.

Frohnen, B. (1993) *Virtue and the Promise of Conservatism* (Lawrence, KS: University of Kansas Press).

Frohnen, B. (1996) *The New Communitarians and the Crisis of Modern Liberalism* (Lawrence, KS: University of Kansas Press).

Frum, D. (1994) *Dead Right* (New York: Basic Books).

Frum, D. (1997a) *What's Right?* (New York: Basic Books).

Frum, D. (1997b) 'The Libertarian Temptation', *Weekly Standard*, 21 April.

Fukuyama, F. (1989) 'The End of History?', *National Interest*, No. 16.

Fukuyama, F. (1992) *The End of History and the Last Man* (New York: Free Press).

Fukuyama, F. (1995) *Trust* (New York: Free Press).

Fukuyama, F. (2002) 'Conservatism Matures: the Fall of the Libertarians', *Wall Street Journal*, 2 May.

Furedi, F. (1992) *Mythical Past, Elusive Future* (London: Pluto Press).

Furedi, F. (1997) *Culture of Fear* (London: Cassell).

Gamble, A. (1994) *The Free Economy and the Strong State* (2nd edn) (London: Macmillan).

Geisler, N. and Turek, F. (1998) *Legislating Morality* (Minneapolis: Bethany House).

Gerson, M. (1996) *The Neoconservative Vision: From the Cold War to the Culture Wars* (Lanham, MD: Madison Books).

Giddens, A. (1994) *Beyond Left and Right* (Cambridge: Polity Press).

Giddens, A. (1998) *The Third Way* (Cambridge: Polity Press).

Gilder, G. (1990) *Microcosm* (New York: Simon and Schuster).

Gilder, G. (2000) *Telecosm* (New York: Free Press).

Gill, R. T. (1992) 'For the Sake of the Children', *Public Interest*, No. 108.

Gill, S. (1995) 'Globalisation, Market Civilisation, and Disciplinary Neoliberalism', *Millenium*, Vol. 24, No. 3.

Gilmour, I. (1978) *Inside Right* (London: Quartet).

Gilmour, I. (1992) *Dancing with Dogma: Britain under Thatcherism* (London: Simon and Schuster).

Gingrich, N. (1995) *To Renew America* (New York: HarperCollins).

Glasner, D. (1992) 'Hayek and the Conservatives', *Commentary*, Vol. 94, No. 4.

Goldsmith, E. (1988) *The Great U-Turn* (Hartland: Green Books).

Goldsmith, J. (1994) *The Trap* (London: Macmillan).

Goodin, R. (1992) *Green Political Theory* (Cambridge: Polity Press).

Gottfried, P. (1993) *The Conservative Movement* (2nd edn) (New York: Twayne Publishers).

Graham, G. (1986) *Politics in Its Place: a Study of Six Ideologies* (Oxford: Clarendon Press).

Gray, J. (1984) *Hayek on Liberty* (Oxford: Basil Blackwell).

Gray, J. (1993a) *Beyond the New Right: Markets, Government and the Common Environment* (London: Routledge).

Gray, J. (1993b) *Post-Liberalism: Studies in Political Thought* (London: Routledge).

Gray, J. (1995) *Enlightenment's Wake: Politics and Culture at the Close of the Modern Age* (London: Routledge).

Gray, J. (1997) *Endgames: Questions in Late Modern Political Thought* (Cambridge: Polity Press).

Gray, J. (1998) *False Dawn: the Delusions of Global Capitalism* (London: Granta Books).

Green, D. G. (1993) *Reinventing Civil Society: the Rediscovery of Welfare without Politics* (London: IEA Health and Welfare Unit).

Green, D. G. (1996) *Community without Politics: a Market Approach to Welfare Reform* (London: IEA Health and Welfare Unit).

Greenleaf, W. H. (1973) 'The Character of Modern British Conservatism', in R. Benewick, R. N. Berki and B. Parekh (eds) *Knowledge and Belief in Politics* (London: George Allen and Unwin Ltd.).

Greenleaf, W. H. (1983) *The British Political Tradition* Vol. 2 (London: Methuen).

Griffiths, B. (2001) 'The Business Corporation as a Moral Community', in B. Griffiths, R. A. Sirico, N. Barry and F. Field, *Capitalism, Morality and Markets* (London: Institute of Economic Affairs).

Habermas, J. (1985) 'Modernity – an Incomplete Project', in H. Foster (ed.) *Postmodern Culture* (London: Pluto Press).

Harries, O. (1992/93) 'Fourteen Points for Realists', *National Interest*, No. 30.

Harries, O. (1996) 'Does Realism Have a Future?', in K. Minogue (ed.) *Conservative Realism* (London: HarperCollins).

Hartz, L. (1955) *The Liberal Tradition in America* (New York: Harcourt Bruce Jovanovich).

Hayek, F. A. (1944) *The Road to Serfdom* (London: Routledge).

Hayek, F. A. (1960) *The Constitution of Liberty* (London: Routledge and Kegan Paul).

Hayek, F. A. (1973) *Law, Legislation and Liberty* Vol. 1 (London: Routledge and Kegan Paul).

Hayek, F. A. (1976) *Law, Legislation and Liberty* Vol. 2 (London: Routledge and Kegan Paul).

Heilbroner, R. (1974) *An Inquiry into the Human Prospect* (New York: Norton).

Heilbrunn, J. (1996) 'Neocon v. Theocon', *New Republic*, 30 December.

Henderson, D. (2000) *Anti-Liberalism 2000* (London: Institute of Economic Affairs).

Himmelfarb, G. (1989a) *Marriage and Morals among the Victorians and Other Essays* (London: I. B. Taurus and Co. Ltd.).

Himmelfarb, G. (1989b) in 'Symposium: Responses to Fukuyama', *National Interest*, No. 16.

Himmelfarb, G. (1991) *Poverty and Compassion: the Moral Imagination of the Late Victorians* (New York: Knopf).

Himmelfarb, G. (1995a) 'The Moral Crisis of Our Welfare State', *Rising Tide*, Vol. 2, No. 6.

Himmelfarb, G. (1995b) 'Preface', in D. Anderson (ed.) *This Will Hurt: the Restoration of Virtue and Civic Order* (London: Social Affairs Unit).

Himmelfarb, G. (1996a) *The De-Moralization of Society: From Victorian Virtues to Modern Values* (New York: Vintage Books).

Himmelfarb, G. (1996b) 'Second Thoughts on Civil Society', *Weekly Standard*, 9 September.

Himmelfarb, G. (1996c) 'Welfare as a Moral Problem', *Harvard Journal of Law and Public Policy*, Vol. 19, No. 3.

Himmelfarb, G. (2001) 'The Idea of Compassion: the British vs. the French Enlightenment', *Public Interest*, No. 145.

Hirsch, Jr., E. D. (1997) 'Why Traditional Education Is More Progressive', *American Enterprise*, Vol. 8, No. 2.

Hirsch, H. N. (1986) 'The Threnody of Liberalism: Constitutional Liberty and the Renewal of Community', *Political Theory*, Vol. 14, No. 3.

Hirst, P. and Thompson, G. (1996) *Globalization in Question* (Cambridge: Polity Press).

Hitchens, P. (1999) *The Abolition of Britain* (London: Quartet Books).

Hobsbawm, E. (1990) *Nations and Nationalism since 1870* (Cambridge: Cambridge University Press).

Hobsbawm, E. (1994) *The Age of Extremes* (London: Penguin Books).

Hogg, Q. (1959) *The Conservative Case* (Harmondsworth: Penguin).

Holbrook, D. (1994) 'The Virus of Evil in Culture', *Salisbury Review*, Vol. 13, No. 1.

Honderich, T. (1990) *Conservatism* (Harmondsworth: Penguin).

Hood, J. (1996) 'Regulation: Reich and Responsibility', *Reason*, Vol. 28, No. 3.

Hoover, K. and Plant, R. (1989) *Conservative Capitalism in Britain and the United States* (London: Routledge).

Horowitz, C. F. (1997) 'The Shaming Sham', *American Prospect*, No. 31.

Howell, D. (1995) *Easternisation: Asian Power and Its Impact on the West* (London: Demos).

Howell, D. (2000) *The Edge of Now* (London: Macmillan).

Hunt, D. (1994) *Right Ahead: Conservatism and the Social Market* (London: Conservative Political Centre).

Huntington, S. P. (1957) 'Conservatism as an Ideology', *American Political Science Review*, Vol. 51, No. 2.

Hutton, W. (1996) *The State We're In* (London: Vintage).

Ireland, P. (1995) 'Reflections on a Rampage through the Barriers of Shame: Law, Community and the New Conservatism', *Journal of Law and Society*, Vol. 22, No. 2.

Jenkins, S. (1995) *Accountable to None: the Tory Nationalization of Britain* (London: Hamish Hamilton).

Jewett, J. (2001) 'Enviro-Skepticism', *Policy Review*, No. 110.

Johnson, P. (1992) 'Review of Francis Fukuyama's *The End of History*', *Commentary*, Vol. 93, No. 3.

Johnson, P. (1996a) 'It Is Not True That There Are No Good Causes – Ending Abortion Is One', *Spectator*, 17 August.

Johnson, P. (1996b) 'When the Honourable Estate of Marriage Is Underestimated by Dishonourable Men', *Spectator*, 29 June.

Johnston, J. F. (1998) *No Man Can Serve Two Masters: Shareholders Versus Stakeholders in the Governance of Companies* (London: Social Affairs Unit).

Joseph, K. (1991) *The Importance of Parenting* (London: Centre for Policy Studies).

Joseph, K. (1996) 'Why the Tories Are the Real Party of the Stakeholder', *Economic Affairs*, Vol. 16, No. 2.

Josephson, J. L. and Burack, C. (1998) 'The Political Ideology of the Neo-Traditional Family', *Journal of Political Ideologies*, Vol. 3, No. 2.

Joyce, M. (1994) 'Citizenship in the 21st Century', in D. Eberly (ed.) *Building a Community of Citizens: Civil Society in the 21st Century* (Lanham, MD: University Press of America).

Joyce, M. (1998) 'On Self-Government', *Policy Review*, No. 90.

Judis, J. B. (1990) 'The Conservative Crackup', *American Prospect*, No. 3.

Kedourie, E. (1966) *Nationalism* (3rd edn) (London: Hutchinson).

Kekes, J. (1997) 'What Is Conservatism?', *Philosophy*, No. 72.

Kenny, M. (1996) 'After the Deluge: Politics and Civil Society in the Wake of the New Right', *Soundings*, No. 4.

Kesler, C. (1998) 'Statesmanship for America's Future: the Value of Conservatism', *Vital Speeches of the Day*, Vol. 64, No. 20.

Kesler, C. (2002) 'Big Government Conservatism?', *Claremont Review of Books*, Vol. 2, No. 3.

Kimball, R. (1990) *Tenured Radicals: How Politics Has Corrupted Higher Education* (New York: Harper and Row).

Kimball, R. (1996) 'Whose Enlightenment Is It? Review of Todd Gitlin's *The Twilight of Common Dreams*', *New Criterion*, Vol. 14, No. 8.

Kirk, R. (1953) *The Conservative Mind* (Chicago: H. Regnery Co.).

Kirk, R. (1962) *A Program for Conservatives* (Chicago: H. Regnery Co.).

Kirk, R. (1993) *America's British Culture* (London: Transaction Publishers).

Klein, D. (1994) 'Libertarianism as Communitarianism', *Freeman*, Vol. 44, No. 12.

Klein, N. (2000) *No Logo* (London: Flamingo).

Kopff, E. (1996) 'Postmodernism, Theory, and the End of the Humanities', *Chronicles*, Vol. 20, No. 1.

Kramer, H. (1999) in 'Symposium: What Can We Reasonably Hope For?', *First Things*, No. 99.

Krauthammer, C. (1993) 'Defining Deviancy Up', *New Republic*, 22 November.

Kristol, I. (1978) *Two Cheers for Capitalism* (New York: Basic Books).

Kristol, I. (1983) *Reflections of a Neoconservative* (New York: Basic Books).

Kristol, I. (1989) in 'Symposium: Responses to Fukuyama', *National Interest*, No. 16.

Kristol, I. (1991) 'The Good Life and the New Class', in P. Berger and I. Kristol (eds) *Health, Life-Style and Environment: Countering the Panic* (London: Social Affairs Unit).

Kristol, I. (1993) 'My Cold War', *National Interest*, No. 31.

Kristol, I. (1994) 'Countercultures', *Commentary*, Vol. 98, No. 6.

Kristol, I. (1995) *Neoconservatism: the Autobiography of an Idea* (New York: Free Press).

Kumar, K. (1993) 'Civil Society: an Inquiry into the Usefulness of an Historical Term', *British Journal of Sociology*, Vol. 44, No. 3.

Laclau, E. (1994) 'Introduction', in E. Laclau (ed.) *The Making of Political Identities* (London: Verso).

Lansley, A. and Wilson, R. (1997) *Conservatives and the Constitution* (London: Conservative 2000 Foundation).

Lanz, T. (2001) 'Capitalism – the Conservative Ideology', *Salisbury Review*, Vol. 19, No. 4.

Lapin, D. (1995) 'Ostracism and Disgrace in the Maintenance of a Precarious Moral Order', in D. Anderson (ed.) *This Will Hurt: the Restoration of Virtue and Civic Order* (London: Social Affairs Unit).

Lasch, C. (1991) *The True and Only Heaven: Progress and Its Critics* (New York: W. W. Norton).

Lawlor, S. (1990) *Teachers Mistaught: Training in Theories or Education in Subjects?* (London: Centre for Policy Studies).

Lawlor, S. (1992) 'Education: Working with the Grain', in D. Anderson and G. Frost (eds) *Hubris: the Tempting of Modern Conservatives* (London: Centre for Policy Studies).

Lawlor, S. (ed.) (1993) *The Dearing Debate: Assessment and the National Curriculum* (London: Centre for Policy Studies).

Leadbeater, C. (1991) 'Whose Line Is It Anyway?', *Marxism Today*, Vol. 35, No. 7.

Leadbeater, C. (1996) 'Seven Blue Moods', *New Statesman*, 4 October.

Le Fanu, J. (1994) *Environmental Alarums* (London: Social Affairs Unit).

Letwin, O. (1990) 'Three Myths of Government', in J. C. D. Clark (ed.) *Ideas and Politics in Modern Britain* (London: Macmillan).

Letwin, S. (1992) *The Anatomy of Thatcherism* (London: Fontana).

Letwin, S. (1996) 'British Conservatism in the 1990s', in K. Minogue (ed.) *Conservative Realism* (London: HarperCollins).

Levitas, R. (ed.) (1986) *The Ideology of the New Right* (Cambridge: Polity Press).

Lind, M. (1995) *The Next American Nation* (New York: Free Press).

Lind, M. (1996) *Up from Conservatism* (New York: Free Press).

Lind, W. S. (1991) 'Defending Western Culture', *Foreign Policy*, No. 84.

Lindberg, T. (1999) 'Conservatism at Century's End', *Policy Review*, No. 94.

Lingis, A. (1994) 'Some Questions about Lyotard's Postmodern Legitimation Narrative', *Philosophy and Criticism*, Vol. 20, Nos 1/2.

Lomborg, B. (2001) *The Skeptical Environmentalist* (Cambridge: Cambridge University Press).

Lovelock, J. (1979) *Gaia: a New Look at Life on Earth* (Oxford: Oxford University Press).

Ludlam, S. and Smith, M. J. (1996) 'Introduction', in S. Ludlam and M. J. Smith (eds) *Contemporary British Conservatism* (London: Macmillan).

Luttwak, E. (1998) *Turbo-Capitalism: Winners and Losers in the Global Economy* (London: Weidenfeld and Nicolson).

Lyotard, J. (1984) *The Postmodern Condition* (Manchester: Manchester University Press).

Machan, T. R. (1998) *Generosity: Virtue in Civil Society* (Washington, DC: Cato Institute).

MacIntyre, A. (1985) *After Virtue* (2nd edn) (London: Duckworth).

MacIntyre, A. (1988) *Whose Justice? Whose Rationality?* (London: Duckworth).

Malcolm, N. (1991) 'In Defence of Nationalism', *Spectator*, 20 July.

Mannheim, K. (1986) *Conservatism: a Contribution to the Sociology of Knowledge* (London: Routledge and Kegan Paul).

Mansfield, Jr., H. (1988) 'Democracy and the Great Books', *New Republic*, 4 April.

Mansfield, Jr., H. (1991) *America's Constitutional Soul* (Baltimore: Johns Hopkins University Press).

Mattox, Jr., W. R. (1995) 'Why Aren't Conservatives Talking about Divorce?', *Policy Review*, No. 73.

Mawhinney, B. (1996) *Safeguarding Our Constitution* (London: Conservative Political Centre).

McClay, W. (2001) 'America – Idea or Nation?', *Public Interest*, No. 145.

McCormick, J. (1991) *British Politics and the Environment* (London: Earthscan Publications Ltd.).

McElwee, M. (2000) *The Great and the Good: the Rise of the New Class* (London: Centre for Policy Studies).

McElwee, M. and Tyrie, A. (2000) *Leviathan at Large* (London: Centre for Policy Studies).

Mead, L. M. (1992) *The New Politics of the New Poverty* (New York: Basic Books).

Mészáros, I. (1989) *Power and Ideology* (London: Harvester Wheatsheaf).

Meyerson, A. (1990) 'The Vision Thing, Continued', *Policy Review*, No. 53.

Meyerson, A. (1996) 'Welcome to *Policy Review: The Journal of American Citizenship*', *Policy Review*, No. 75.

Miller, H. and Conko, G. (2001) 'The Perils of Precaution', *Policy Review*, No. 107.

Milne, K. (1994) 'Community: the Tories Fight Back', *New Statesman*, 22 July.

Miner, B. (1996) *The Concise Conservative Encyclopaedia* (New York: Free Press).

Minogue, K. (1967) *Nationalism* (London: Batsford).

Minogue, K. (1991/92) 'Review of Francis Fukuyama's *The End of History*', *National Interest*, No. 26.

Minogue, K. (1992/93) 'Uneasy Triumph', *National Interest*, No. 30.

Minogue, K. (1993a) *The Constitutional Mania* (London: Centre for Policy Studies).

Minogue, K. (1993b) 'The Law Is a Chatterbox', *Spectator*, 17 July.

Minogue, K. (1994/95) 'Necessary Imperfections', *National Interest*, No. 38.

Minogue, K. (1996) 'Does National Sovereignty Have a Future?', *National Review*, 23 December.

Minogue, K. (1997) *The Silencing of Society: the True Cost of the Lust for News* (London: Social Affairs Unit).

Moore, C. (1992a) 'What Has the Earth Done to Deserve a Summit?', *Spectator*, 23 May.

Moore, C. (1992b) 'The Womb of Time Will Bring Its Revenge', *Spectator*, 20 June.

Moore, C. (1995) *How to Be British* (London: Centre for Policy Studies).

Moore, S. (1995) 'The Unconstitutional Congress', *Policy Review*, No. 72.

Moore, T. G. (1995) 'Why Global Warming Would Be Good for You', *Public Interest*, No. 118.

Morgan, P. (1992) 'The Family: No Possibility of Ethical Neutrality', in D. Anderson and G. Frost (eds) *Hubris: the Tempting of Modern Conservatives* (London: Centre for Policy Studies).

Morone, J. A. (1996) 'The Corrosive Politics of Virtue', *American Prospect*, No. 26.

Morris, J. (ed.) (1997) *Climate Change: Challenging the Conventional Wisdom* (London: IEA Environment Unit).

Mount, F. (1992) *The British Constitution Now: Recovery or Decline?* (London: Heinemann).

Moynihan, D. P. (1993) 'Defining Deviancy Down', *American Scholar*, Vol. 62, No. 1.

Murray, C. (1984) *Losing Ground: American Social Policy 1950–1980* (New York: Basic Books).

Murray, C. (1990) *The Emerging British Underclass* (London: IEA Health and Welfare Unit).

Murray, C. (1992a) 'The LA Riots', *Commentary*, Vol. 94, No. 5.

Murray, C. (1992b) 'The Legacy of the 60s', *Commentary*, Vol. 94, No. 1.

Murray, C. (1994a) *Underclass: the Crisis Deepens* (London: IEA Health and Welfare Unit).

Murray, C. (1994b) 'What to Do about Welfare', *Commentary*, Vol. 98, No. 6.

Murray, C. (1995) 'The Partial Restoration of Traditional Society', *Public Interest*, No. 121.

Murray, C. (1996) 'The Coming White Underclass', in D. Brooks (ed.) *Backward and Upward: the New Conservative Writing* (New York: Vintage Books).

Murray, C. (1997) *What It Means to Be a Libertarian: a Personal Interpretation* (New York: Broadway Books).

Murray, C. and Herrnstein, R. J. (1994a) *The Bell Curve: Intelligence and Class Structure in American Life* (New York: Free Press).

Murray, C. and Herrnstein, R. J. (1994b) 'Race, Genes and IQ – an Apologia', *New Republic*, 31 October.

Nash, G. (1996) *The Conservative Intellectual Movement in America since 1945* (2nd edn) (Wilmington, DE: Intercollegiate Studies Institute).

Neal, M. and Davies, C. (1998) *The Corporation under Siege: Exposing the Devices Used by Activists and Regulators in the Non-Risk Society* (London: Social Affairs Unit).

Neuhaus, R. (1992) *America against Itself* (Notre Dame: University of Notre Dame Press).

Neuhaus, R. (1994) 'Combat Ready', *National Review*, 2 May.

Neuhaus, R. (1996a) 'The Internet Produces a Global Village of Village Idiots', *Forbes*, 2 December.

Neuhaus, R. (1996b) 'The Public Square: the Coming Age of the Spirit', *First Things*, No. 62.

Nisbet, R. (1953) *The Quest for Community* (New York: Oxford University Press).

Nisbet, R. (1974) *The Social Philosophers* (London: Heinemann).

Nisbet, R. (1976) *The Twilight of Authority* (London: Heinemann).

Nisbet, R. (1986) *Conservatism* (Milton Keynes: Open University Press).

Norton, P. and Aughey, A. (1981) *Conservatives and Conservatism* (London: Temple Smith).

Novak, M. (1989) *Free Persons and the Common Good* (Lanham, MD: Madison Books).

Novak, M. (1990) *Morality, Capitalism and Democracy* (London: IEA Health and Welfare Unit).

Novak, M. (1994) 'The Conservative Mood', *Society*, Vol. 31, No. 2.

Novak, M. (1995) *Awaking from Nihilism* (London: IEA Health and Welfare Unit).

Novak, M. (1996) 'Culture Wars, Moral Wars', in T. Boxx and G. Quinlivan (eds) *Culture in Crisis and the Renewal of Civil Life* (Lanham, MD: Rowman and Littlefield Publishers).

Novak, M. (1997) *The Fire of Invention* (Lanham, MD: Rowman and Littlefield Publishers).

Oakeshott, M. (1962) *Rationalism in Politics* (London: Methuen).

Oakeshott, M. (1975a) *Hobbes on Civil Association* (Oxford: Basil Blackwell).

Oakeshott, M. (1975b) *On Human Conduct* (Oxford: Oxford University Press).

O'Hear, A. (1991a) *Education and Democracy: Against the Educational Establishment* (London: The Claridge Press).

O'Hear, A. (1991b) *Father of Child-Centredness: John Dewey and the Ideology of Modern Education* (London: Centre for Policy Studies).

O'Hear, A. (1997) *Nonsense about Nature* (London: Social Affairs Unit).

O'Hear, A. (1998) 'Diana, Queen of Hearts', in D. Anderson and P. Mullen (eds) *Faking It: the Sentimentalisation of Modern Society* (London: Social Affairs Unit).

Ohmae, K. (1990) *The Borderless World* (London: HarperCollins).

Olasky, M. (2000) *Compassionate Conservatism* (New York: Free Press).

Olson, W. (1997) 'Judge Dread', *Reason*, Vol. 28, No. 11.

Ophuls, W. (1977) *Ecology and the Politics of Scarcity* (San Francisco: Freeman).

O'Riordan, T. and Cameron, J. (1994) *Interpreting the Precautionary Principle* (London: Earthscan).

Orwin, C. (1996) 'All Quiet on the (Post) Western Front?', *Public Interest*, No. 123.

O'Shaughnessy, T. (1994) 'Economic Policy', in A. Adonis and T. Hames (eds) *A Conservative Revolution? The Thatcher–Reagan Decade in Perspective* (Manchester: Manchester University Press).

O'Sullivan, J. (1996) 'Conservatism and Cultural Identity', in K. Minogue (ed.) *Conservative Realism* (London: HarperCollins).

O'Sullivan, J. (1997a) 'A Principality in Utopia: After Reaganism', *National Review*, 21 April.

O'Sullivan, J. (1997b) 'Blair's New Class', *Prospect*, No. 19.

O'Sullivan, J. (1998) 'American Nationalism and Western Civilization', *Chronicles*, Vol. 22, No. 7.

O'Sullivan, J. (2001) 'Not Vengeance, But a Meaningful Victory', *Chicago Sun-Times*, 18 September.

O'Sullivan, N. (1976) *Conservatism* (London: J. M. Dent).

O'Sullivan, N. (1986) 'Conservatism, the New Right and the Limited State', in J. Hayward and P. Norton (eds) *The Political Science of British Politics* (Brighton: Wheatsheaf Books).

O'Sullivan, N. (1989) 'The New Right: the Quest for a Civil Philosophy in Europe and America', in R. Eatwell and N. O'Sullivan (eds) *The Nature of the Right* (London: Pinter Publishers).

O'Sullivan, N. (1993) 'Political Integration, the Limited State and the Philosophy of Postmodernism', *Political Studies*, Vol. 41, Special Issue.

Pangle, T. L. (1988) *The Spirit of Modern Republicanism* (Chicago: Chicago University Press).

Pangle, T. L. (1992) *The Ennobling of Democracy: the Challenge of the Postmodern Age* (Baltimore: Johns Hopkins University Press).

Paterson, T. (1989) *The Green Conservative* (London: Bow Group).

Patten, C. (1990) *The Conservative Party and the Environment* (London: Conservative Political Centre).

Patten, C. (1991) Interview, *Marxism Today*, Vol. 35, No. 2.

Patten, J. (1995) *Things to Come* (London: Sinclair-Stevenson).

Peele, G. (1984) *Revival and Reaction: the Right in Contemporary America* (Oxford: Clarendon Press).
Pepper, D. (1993) *Eco-Socialism* (London: Routledge).
Phillips, M. (1996) *All Must Have Prizes* (London: Little, Brown).
Podhoretz, N. (1990) 'Right about Everything, Wrong about Nothing?', *Encounter*, Vol. 75, No. 1.
Porritt, J. (1984) *Seeing Green* (Oxford: Basil Blackwell).
Portillo, M. (1997) *The Ghost of Toryism Past: the Spirit of Conservatism Future* (London: Centre for Policy Studies).
Postrel, V. (1997) 'Laissez Fear', *Reason*, Vol. 28, No. 11.
Postrel, V. (1998) *The Future and Its Enemies* (New York: Free Press).
Prowse, M. (1994) 'What Was Right with the 1980s', *Financial Times*, 5 April.
Putnam, R. (1995) 'Bowling Alone', *Journal of Democracy*, Vol. 6, No. 1.
Putnam, R. (2000) *Bowling Alone: the Collapse and Revival of American Community* (New York: Simon and Schuster).
Quest, C. (ed.) (1994) *Liberating Women – from Modern Feminism* (London: IEA Health and Welfare Unit).
Quinton, A. (1978) *The Politics of Imperfection* (London: Faber and Faber).
Rabkin, J. (1999) 'The Culture War That Isn't', *Policy Review*, No. 96.
Rabkin, J. and Sheehan, J. (1999) *Global Greens, Global Governance* (London: IEA Environment Unit).
Raison, T. (1990) 'Divorce a La Mode', *Spectator*, 10 February.
Rankin, A. (1998) 'We Are All "Indigenous Peoples" Now', *Salisbury Review*, Vol. 17, No. 1.
Redwood, J. (1993) *The Global Marketplace: Capitalism and Its Future* (London: HarperCollins).
Rees-Mogg, W. (1995) 'The End of Nations', *Times*, 31 August.
Ridley, M. (2002) 'The Profits of Doom', *Spectator*, 23 February.
Robinson, M. (1992) *The Greening of British Party Politics* (Manchester: Manchester University Press).
Rorty, R. (1980) *Philosophy and the Mirror of Nature* (Oxford: Basil Blackwell).
Rorty, R. (1987) 'Thugs and Theorists', *Political Theory*, Vol. 15, No. 4.
Rorty, R. (1988) 'That Old-Time Philosophy', *New Republic*, 4 April.
Rorty, R. (1989) *Contingency, Irony, and Solidarity* (Cambridge: Cambridge University Press).
Rosin, H. (1997) 'Promise Weepers', *New Republic*, 27 October.
Rossiter, C. (1962) *Conservatism in America* (2nd edn) (New York: Vintage Books).
Rothbard, M. (1994) 'Nations by Consent: Decomposing the Nation-State', *Journal of Libertarian Studies*, Vol. 11, No. 1.
Ryn, C. G. (1993) 'Cultural Diversity and Unity', *Chronicles*, Vol. 17, No. 6.
Ryn, C. G. (1996) 'How Conservatives Failed "The Culture"', *Modern Age*, Vol. 38, No. 2.
Safier, P. (1996) 'Animal House Meets Church Lady', *American Prospect*, No. 25.
Salamon, L. M. and Anheier, H. K. (1997) 'The Civil Society Sector', *Society*, Vol. 34, No. 2.
Schambra, W. (1994) 'By the People: the Old Values of the New Citizenship', *Policy Review*, No. 69.
Schambra, W. (1998) 'All Community Is Local', in E. J. Dionne (ed.) *Community Works* (Washington, DC: Brookings Institution Press).

218   *References*

Schwartz, J. (1990) 'Antihumanism in the Humanities', *Public Interest*, No. 99.
Schwarz, B. (1997) 'The Break-Up of the Conservative Nation', *Soundings*, No. 7.
Scruton, R. (1984) *The Meaning of Conservatism* (2nd edn) (London: Macmillan).
Scruton, R. (1990) 'In Defence of the Nation', in J. C. D. Clark (ed.) *Ideas and Politics in Modern Britain* (London: Macmillan).
Scruton, R. (1992) 'In Inverted Commas', *Times Literary Supplement*, 18 December.
Scruton, R. (1994) *Modern Philosophy* (London: Sinclair-Stevenson).
Scruton, R. (1996a) *The Conservative Idea of Community* (London: Conservative 2000 Foundation).
Scruton, R. (1996b) *A Dictionary of Political Thought* (2nd edn) (London: Macmillan).
Scruton, R. (1998) *An Intelligent Person's Guide to Modern Culture* (London: Duckworth).
Scruton, R. (2000a) *Animal Rights and Wrongs* (London: Metro).
Scruton, R. (2000b) *Who, What and Why? Trans-National Government, Legitimacy and the World Health Organisation* (London: Institute of Economic Affairs).
Scruton, R. (2000c) 'Bring Back Stigma', *City Journal*, Vol. 10, No. 4.
Scruton, R. (2001a) *England: an Elegy* (London: Pimlico).
Scruton, R. (2001b) *The Meaning of Conservatism* (3rd edn) (London: Palgrave – now Palgrave Macmillan).
Scully, M. (1997) 'The New Malaise?', *National Review*, 27 October.
Shenk, D. (1997) *Data Smog: Surviving the Information Glut* (New York: HarperCollins).
Sherman, A. (2000) 'A Coincidental Resemblance: Conservatism and the Conservative Party', *Salisbury Review*, Vol. 19, No. 2.
Shils, E. (1991) 'The Virtue of Civil Society', *Government and Opposition*, Vol. 26, No. 1.
Simon, J. (1990) *Population Matters* (New Brunswick, NJ: Transaction Publishers).
Skocpol, T. (1996) 'Unravelling from Above', in R. Kuttner (ed.) *Ticking Time Bombs* (New York: New Press).
Sommers, C. H. (1993) 'Teaching the Virtues', *Public Interest*, No. 111.
Soros, G. (1998) *The Crisis of Global Capitalism* (London: Little, Brown).
Spectator (1995) 'Editorial: De Tocqueville vs. Blair', 20 May.
Stanlis, P. (1958) *Edmund Burke and the Natural Law* (Ann Arbour: University of Michigan Press).
Starobin, P. (1995) 'Right Fight', *National Journal*, 9 December.
Starobin, P. (1997) 'Rethinking Capitalism', *National Journal*, 18 January.
Starr, P. (1996) 'Restoration Fever', *American Prospect*, No. 25.
Stelzer, I. M. (1997) 'A Conservative Case for Regulation', *Public Interest*, No. 128.
Sternberg, E. (1998a) *Corporate Governance: Accountability in the Marketplace* (London: Institute of Economic Affairs).
Sternberg, E. (1998b) *Stakeholding: Betraying the Corporation's Objectives* (London: Social Affairs Unit).
Steyn, M. (1997) 'With Newt and the Lady', *Spectator*, 4 October.
Strauss, L. (1953) *Natural Right and History* (Chicago: University of Chicago Press).
Sullivan, A. (1998) 'Going Down Screaming', *New York Times Magazine*, 11 October.
Tam, H. (1998) *Communitarianism: a New Agenda for Politics and Citizenship* (London: Macmillan).

Taylor, R. (1992) 'Economics, Ecology, and Exchange: Free Market Environmentalism', *Humane Studies Review*, Vol. 8, No. 1.

Teachout, T. (1990) 'A Farewell to Politics', in T. Teachout (ed.) *Beyond the Boom* (New York: Poseidon Press).

Thatcher, M. (1990) *Our Threatened Environment* (London: Conservative Political Centre).

Thatcher, M. (1993) *The Downing Street Years* (New York: HarperCollins).

Thatcher, M. (1997a) 'Spreading the Word', *National Review*, 22 December.

Thatcher, M. (1997b) 'The Value of American Studies', *Society*, Vol. 34, No. 6.

Thomas, C. and Dobson, E. (1999) *Blinded by Might: Can the Religious Right Save America?* (Grand Rapids, MI: Zondervan Publishing House).

Turner, B. (1990) 'Introduction', in B. Turner (ed.) *Theories of Modernity and Postmodernity* (London: Sage).

Tyrrell, R. E. (1992) *The Conservative Crack-Up* (New York: Simon and Schuster).

Vincent, A. (1994) 'British Conservatism and the Problem of Ideology', *Political Studies*, Vol. 42, No. 2.

Vinson, Jr., J. C. (1996) 'Conservatives and Environmentalists', *Chronicles*, Vol. 20, No. 6.

Wagner, D. (1997) *The New Temperance* (Boulder, CO: Westview Press).

Walzer, M. (1991) 'The Idea of Civil Society', *Dissent*, Vol. 38, No. 2.

Weaver, R. (1948) *Ideas Have Consequences* (Chicago: University of Chicago Press).

Weekly Standard (1997) 'Symposium: Is There a Worldwide Conservative Crack-Up?', 1 September.

Weigel, G. (1995) 'Capitalism for Humans', *Commentary*, Vol. 100, No. 4.

Weston, J. (1986) 'The Greens, "Nature" and the Social Environment', in J. Weston (ed.) *Red and Green* (London: Pluto Press).

Weyrich, P. (1999) 'A Moral Minority', http://www.freecongress.org/Libaward/minority.htm (16 February).

Whelan, R. (ed.) (1995) *Just a Piece of Paper? Divorce Reform and the Undermining of Marriage* (London: IEA Health and Welfare Unit).

Whelan, R. (1999) *Wild in Woods: the Myth of the Noble Eco-Savage* (London: IEA Environment Unit).

Will, G. F. (1992) *Restoration: Congress, Term Limits and the Recovery of Deliberative Democracy* (New York: Free Press).

Will, G. F. (1994) *The Leveling Wind* (New York: Viking).

Will, G. F. (1996) 'The Cultural Contradictions of Conservatism', *Public Interest*, No. 123.

Will, G. F. (2002) 'Cranky Conservatives', *Washington Post*, 25 April.

Willetts, D. (1992a) *Modern Conservatism* (Harmondsworth: Penguin).

Willetts, D. (1992b) 'Theories and Explanations of the Underclass', in D. J. Smith (ed.) *Understanding the Underclass* (London: Policy Studies Institute).

Willetts, D. (1994) *Civic Conservatism* (London: Social Market Foundation).

Willetts, D. (1996a) *Blair's Gurus: an Examination of Labour's Rhetoric* (London: Centre for Policy Studies).

Willetts, D. (1996b) 'The Free Market and Civic Conservatism', in K. Minogue (ed.) *Conservative Realism* (London: HarperCollins).

Willetts, D. (1997) *Why Vote Conservative?* (London: Penguin).

Willis, E. (1997) 'Their Libertarianism – and Ours', *Dissent*, Vol. 44, No. 4.

Wilson, C. (1990) 'The Future of American Nationalism', *Chronicles*, Vol. 14, No. 11.

Wilson, J. K. (1995) *The Myth of Political Correctness: the Conservative Attack on Higher Education* (Durham: Duke University Press).

Wilson, J. Q. (1991) *On Character* (Washington, DC: American Enterprise Institute).

Wilson, J. Q. (1993) *The Moral Sense* (New York: Free Press).

Wilson, J. Q. (1995) 'Capitalism and Morality', *Public Interest*, No. 121.

Windschuttle, K. (1997) 'Absolutely Relative', *National Review*, 15 September.

Wolfe, A. (1989) *Whose Keeper?* (Berkeley: University of California Press).

Worsthorne, P. (1978) 'Too Much Freedom', in M. Cowling (ed.) *Conservative Essays* (London: Cassell).

Worsthorne, P. (1997) 'New Labour, New Tone – But New Nothing Else. I Approve', *Spectator*, 17 May.

Wright, R. (1989) 'Tao Jones: Review of George Gilder's *Microcosm*', *New Republic*, 20 November.

Young, J. (1990) *Post Environmentalism* (London: Belhaven Press).

Zakaria, F. (1995) 'Bigger Than the Family: Smaller Than the State', *New York Times Book Review*, 13 August.

Zinmeister, K. (1996) 'Coming Home to Community Life', *American Enterprise*, Vol. 7, No. 6.

Index

Oakeshottian perspective, 15, 156–8, 161
Ohmae, Kenichi, 119–20
Olasky, Marvin, 72, 75
Old Right (US), 4, 19
one-nation conservatism/conservatives, 15, 34, 74
Ophuls, William, 182–3
organicism, 13, 180, 185
O'Rourke, P. J., 110
Orwin, Clifford, 129
O'Sullivan, John, 12, 25, 42, 45, 47, 91–2, 96, 118, 139–40, 147
O'Sullivan, Noël, 9–10, 12, 67–8, 156–8, 161, 162

paleoconservatism/paleoconservatives, 13, 30, 57, 118, 130–1, 181
Pangle, Thomas L., 16, 48, 145
particularism, 60, 66, 84, 91–2, 117, 129, 152, 155, 157, 162–3, 192, 201
past, the, 8, 43, 44, 67, 94, 104, 110, 115, 126–30, 138, 164, 180, 190–1
see also history
paternalism, 15, 34, 56, 74, 130
Paterson, Tony, 172
patriotism, 89, 103, 117–18, 138–40
see also nationalism/national identity
Patten, Chris, 52, 172
Patten, John, 25, 45, 47, 56, 122, 137–8
Peel, Robert, 122
Peele, Gillian, 13, 19
Pepper, David, 175
Phillips, Melanie, 89, 90
Pirie, Madsen, 12, 16, 38
Plato, 167
pluralism, 67–70, 78, 93, 104, 109, 157–8
Podhoretz, Norman, 1, 2, 14, 15, 30, 86
Policy Review, 14, 61
political correctness, 2, 45, 83, 87, 89, 96–7, 101, 110–13, 142, 196, 197, 202
Popper, Karl, 20

Porritt, Jonathan, 172, 174–8, 180, 182, 184
Portillo, Michael, 72, 95
post-Cold War era/paradigm, 1–4, 7, 10, 12, 23–31, 32, 36–8, 47, 53–4, 57, 58–9, 71, 74, 82, 83, 84–8, 91, 110, 129, 136, 185, 196–204
postindustrialism, 122, 137, 153–4
postmaterialism, 153
postmodern conservatism/conservatives, 114, 142–68 *passim*, 184, 200
postmodernism/postmodernists (non-conservative), 10, 41, 48, 91–3, 142–68 *passim*, 172, 184, 197, 200, 202
Postrel, Virginia, 40, 135
post-socialism, 32, 40, 41, 46, 52, 198
post-traditionalism, 29, 44, 98
Powell, Enoch, 17, 21–2
precautionary principle, 173–4, 187
progress, 11, 20, 26, 29, 78, 119–26, 132, 134, 138, 150, 155, 174–5, 200, 202, 203
see also economic growth; science and technology
Promise Keepers, 99
Prowse, Michael, 52
Public Interest, 14, 60
'puritanism', 109–13
Putnam, Robert, 59, 62

Quinton, Anthony, 180

Rabkin, Jeremy, 85, 114, 192
race, 31, 42, 89, 91–3, 99, 109, 139, 154–5
Raison, Timothy, 96
Rankin, Aidan, 154
rationalism/rationalists, 10, 13, 15, 17, 20, 25, 34–6, 43, 44, 57, 67, 73, 117, 119, 125, 131, 142–68 *passim*, 175, 184, 195, 200, 202, 203
Reagan, Ronald, 5, 12, 22, 26, 28, 37, 50–1, 110, 136
'Reaganism'/Reagan administration, 5, 12, 22, 28, 37, 50–1, 110